Women Reaching Women

BEGINNING AND BUILDING A GROWING WOMEN'S MINISTRY

FOREWORD BY

ANNE GRAHAM LOTZ

COMPILED BY CHRIS ADAMS

LIFEWAY PRESS®
NASHVILLE, TENNESSEE

© 1997 • LifeWay Press®

Revised 2005
Third printing January 2007

ISBN 1-4158-2590-4

This book is the text for course LS-0034 in the Adult Leadership and Skill Development diploma plan in the Christian Growth Study Plan.

Dewey Decimal Classification: 248.843
Subject Heading: CHURCH WORK WITH WOMEN \ WOMEN--RELIGIOUS LIFE

Unless otherwise indicated, Scripture quotations are from the Holy Bible, New International Version, copyright ©1973, 1978, 1984 by International Bible Society.

Scripture quotations marked NASB are from the NEW AMERICAN STANDARD BIBLE. © Copyright The Lockman Foundation, 1960, 1962, 1963, 1968, 1971, 1972, 1973, 1975, 1977, 1995. Used by permission.

Scripture quotations marked NKJV are from The Experiencing God Bible copyright © 1994 by Broadman & Holman Publishers from the New King James Version. Copyright © 1979, 1980, 1982, Thomas Nelson, Inc., Publishers.

Scripture quotations marked HCSB® are taken from the Holman Christian Standard Bible®, copyright © 1999, 2000, 2001, 2002 by Holman Bible Publishers. Used by permission.

To order additional copies of this resource: write LifeWay Church Resources Customer Service, One LifeWay Plaza, Nashville, TN 37234-0113; FAX order to (615) 251-5933; e-mail your order to *orderentry@lifeway.com;* phone (800) 458-2772; order online at *www.lifeway.com*; or visit the LifeWay Christian Store serving you.

Printed in the United States of America

Leadership and Adult Publishing
LifeWay Church Resources
One LifeWay Plaza
Nashville, Tennessee 37234-0175

DEDICATED TO
MONTE CLENDINNING
1922–2005

When Monte Clendinning coordinated the first Women's Leadership Consultation at Southwestern Baptist Theological Seminary in Fort Worth in 1990, many women's leaders experienced their first opportunity to publicly and freely discuss the topic of women's ministry. Finally, leaders felt it was "OK" to do it differently from what we had always done if it would reach and disciple women and pass the heritage of faith to the next generation.

Women's leaders had struggled with how to effectively minister to and with women in the local church so that they would grow and serve in God's kingdom. Monte provided one of the first platforms for those discussions to take place openly among peers. We discovered we leaders were not alone in struggling with the issue of effectively ministering with women.

I had the privilege of serving with Monte on the steering committee for the following two consultations at Southwestern. After that, consultations took place annually at different Southern Baptist Seminaries. In 2005, we participated in the 13th leadership consultation, a testimony to Monte's continuing legacy.

Monte had a heart for missions and ministry, for her family, and, most importantly, for the Lord. I, for one (and I believe I represent hundreds more women like me), will be forever indebted to and grateful for the contribution Monte made to women in the local churches all over the country and to the entire kingdom. She took a risk, and women everywhere now reap the benefits of Monte's leadership and boldness.

In Him,

Chris Adams

Note: Monte wrote the chapter "Balanced Ministry" in this book.

CONTENTS

Meet the Writers

Anne Graham Lotz

Anne, founder of AnGeL Ministries, travels across the world as a featured speaker at conferences, seminaries, churches, and universities. She also serves on the Board of Directors for the Billy Graham Evangelistic Association. She makes her home in Raleigh, North Carolina.

Chris Adams

Chris is the Women's Enrichment Ministry/Ministers' Wives Specialist for LifeWay Church Resources in Nashville, Tennessee.

Esther Burroughs

Esther directs Esther Burroughs Ministries in Birmingham, Alabama. Esther ministers to women through her writing and speaking. Prior to this, Esther served as the evangelism consultant with the North American Mission Board.

Monte McMahan Clendinning

Monte was a homemaker in Brandon, Mississippi. An author, speaker, and conference leader on various international fields, she retired from Southwestern Baptist Theological Seminary as Adjunct Professor and also Conference Coordinator for the seminary's World Missions Center.

Jimmie Davis

Jimmie attended Converse College and has an Advanced Certificate in Women's Ministry from the New Orleans Theological Seminary. She is the Director of Girls' Ministries at First Baptist Church, Spartanburg, South Carolina, and is the author of *Virtual You!* and *Girls' Enrichment Ministry, Raising A New Generation of Women.* Jimmie served alongside her husband, Sam, in Youth Ministry for 25 years. They have two grown children and three grandchildren.

Merci Dixon

Merci formerly served as Director of Women's Ministries at Moss Bluff First Baptist Church in Moss Bluff, Louisiana.

Karla Downing

Karla is a speaker, author, and counselor with a passion to help people understand and apply the Bible in practical and life-changing ways. Her books include *10 Lifesaving Principles for Women in Difficult Marriages* and *When Love Hurts: 10 Principles to Transform Difficult Relationships.*

Karen Finke

Karen is a member of the Women's Ministry team at Noland Road Baptist Church in Independence, Missouri, where she also teaches a ladies Sunday School class. She has received both the Basic and Advanced Certificates in Women's Ministry from New Orleans Baptist Seminary and is a women's event speaker.

Judi Hayes

Judi Hayes is a baby boomer who has been blessed by the influence of several generations of wonderful women who have taught, mentored, led by example, shared their faith, and paved the way. A member of First Baptist Church, Nashville, she lives in Mt. Juliet, Tennessee.

Valerie Howe

Valerie has served as a Family Ministry Special Worker for the Women's Ministry Division of the Missouri Baptist Convention. She resides in Lebanon, Missouri.

Rhonda H. Kelley

Rhonda is Associate Director, Innovative Evangelism; Adjunct Professor; and coordinator of the women's ministry certificate program at New Orleans Baptist Theological Seminary in New Orleans, Louisiana.

Martha Lawley

An author, speaker, and Bible study leader, Martha contributed to *Transformed Lives: Taking Women's Ministry to the Next Level*, wrote articles for LifeWay's Women's Ministry web page, and wrote a new Bible study titled *Attending the Bride of Christ: Preparing for His Return*. She also serves on the Southern Baptist Convention's Executive Committee as the volunteer women's ministry consultant for the Wyoming Southern Baptist Convention.

Jaye Martin

Jaye is the Women's Evangelism Strategist in the area of Family Evangelism at the North American Mission Board. Her ministry, HeartCall, is designed to help women's ministries in the local church to be evangelistic.

Gerry Sisk

Gerry is Women's Ministry Director at First Baptist Church in Snellville, Georgia.

Janet Thompson

Janet started and leads the mentoring ministry at Saddleback Church in Lake Forest, California, and trains other churches to start Woman to Woman Mentoring. Author of *Woman to Woman Mentoring and Mentoring God's Way Bible Study Series*, Janet conducts mentoring leadership training events, is founder and director of About His Work Ministries/Woman To Woman Mentoring, and serves as a LifeWay Ministry Multiplier.

FOREWORD

ANNE GRAHAM LOTZ

One of the most thrilling stories in all of Scripture is recorded in the book of Exodus when God saw the misery of His people enslaved in Egypt, heard their cries, and raised up Moses to liberate them from bondage and lead them to the promised land (see Ex. 1–14). God confirmed Moses as His liberator by demonstrating His power again and again through the plagues and the parting of the Red Sea. However, the Apostle Paul tells us that two men, Jannes and Jambres, actually defied God by opposing Moses (see 2 Tim. 3:8). While we are not given the specifics, Jannes and Jambres must have opposed Moses by confronting the people with the choice of an alternative to God's prescribed way of liberation. And because God's way of liberation was the true way out of bondage, any alternative would lead not to liberation, but to destruction.

This is of special interest to those of us involved in ministering to women today, many of whom live in various types of bondage. God has seen the misery of their lives, He has heard their cries of emptiness,
>   of loneliness,
>   of meaninglessness,
>   of fearfulness,
>   of hopelessness.

And God has raised up His own Son, Jesus Christ, to liberate them from bondage and lead them to an abundant life of satisfaction,
>   joy,
>   purpose,
>   fulfillment,
>   peace,
>   and hope.

But the Apostle Paul indicates that in the last days there will be a unique attack on women similar to Jannes and Jambres' attack on Moses (see 2 Tim. 3:6-9). The implication is that in the last days women will be confronted with an offer of liberation that opposes God's chosen Liberator, Jesus Christ (see John 14:6).

Even though God has demonstrated His power again and again in the life of Christ, confirming once and for all through His death and resurrection that He is indeed God's prescribed way of liberation, women today are being deceived by alternatives. They are constantly bombarded by voices that promise to lead them out of bondage and misery. But the promised liberator is not Jesus Christ; it is a professional career,

> or an educational degree,
>> or financial prosperity,
>>> or material accumulation,
>>>> or a marital relationship,
>>> or maternal fulfillment,
>> or sexual pleasure,
> or physical beauty,
> or a famous reputation,

—the list of alternatives is almost endless.

While the choices confronting women today seem modern, the enemy behind them is ancient. He is trying to lure them away from God's Liberator with a destructive alternative. Tragically, the statistics on ...

>>>> abortion,
>>>> child abuse,
>>> adultery,
>>> abandonment,
>> alcoholism,
>> drug addiction,
> depression,
> and divorce

give silent witness to the effectiveness of the enemy's tactics.

My prayer is that God will use this book and the women's ministries established, equipped, encouraged, and enabled by it, to help women resist the enemy's attack. I pray God will open the eyes of women everywhere to the Liberator who has given His life to set them free from spiritual, emotional, social, and psychological bondage. May they choose the only way to true liberation by placing their faith in Jesus Christ as their own personal Savior, surrendering to Him as Lord and serving Him as King.

INTRODUCTION

*W*hat makes a swan beautiful? The color of its feathers? Its beautiful long neck? The graceful way it glides across the lake? Perhaps.

What makes a woman beautiful? Is it the color of her hair, the shape of her eyes, or the complexion of her skin? No. These things are only temporary. What truly makes a woman beautiful is who she is in Christ. As Christ enters a woman's life, something lovely is created within her that cannot be changed by earthly things. As a woman grows to become a disciple, she finds an assurance, hope, and a peace that only comes from the Lord. These are the elements of true beauty—inner beauty.

Women Reaching Women was written in response to what is happening today across the country among women in churches. Perhaps you, too, have sensed that God is at work in a mighty way among women. Maybe that is why you are reading this book.

In *Experiencing God,* Henry Blackaby writes: "We tried to find out what God already was doing around us. We believed that He would show us where He was at work, and the revelation would be our invitation to join Him. We began praying and watching to see what God would do next in answer to our prayers."[1]

Women's leaders have prayed, watched, and seen God at work in hundreds of grass roots women's ministries across the United States. Over the last several years, scores of ladies have asked for help and resources. Their requests have all been the same: "We are hungry for information and direction. Can you help us?"

God has definitely been at work among women of all denominations for many years. In fact, this revelation became the invitation to join Him in the important work reflected in this book. Thus, Women's Ministry was born.

Women's Ministry has sought to help churches begin and build women's ministries by providing resources, training, events, consultation, and a supportive network. Responding not only to the needs of Christian women but desiring also to utilize their spiritual gifts, Women's Ministry encourages women in spiritual growth, discipleship, ministry, and evangelism. This ministry continues the historical involvement of women in the church, builds on the biblical principles of women as gifted for ministry, and expands the philosophical perspective of women ministering uniquely to women.

*W*omen's leaders have prayed, watched, and seen God at work in hundreds of grass roots women's ministries across the United States.

Throughout history, women have played an important role in the work of the Lord. For instance, the Bible records Sarah's commitment to the Lord (Gen. 11:29–23:20). The distinguished judge, Deborah, exercised uncommon leadership over the people of Israel (Judg. 4:4–5:31). God provided the great King David through Ruth, a faithful Gentile woman who was devoted to her mother-in-law Naomi's God (Ruth 1–4). Hannah's faith in God gave her a much desired son, Samuel, whom she dedicated to the Lord's service (1 Sam. 1:8-28), and her godly life influenced Samuel as he grew to become a spiritual leader.

Scripture records that women were prominent in the New Testament as well, especially in the ministry of Jesus. In contrast to the society of His day, Jesus recognized the value of women and often chose to minister to them. For example, He touched the lives of Peter's mother-in-law (Mark 1:30-31); the widow of Nain (Luke 7:11-15); and the crippled woman (Luke 13:10-17). Jesus included women in His miracles and often referred to them in His parables or teachings about spiritual truths (Matt. 25:1-13; Luke 18:1-8). Several women ministered to Jesus (the woman in Bethany, Matt. 26:6-13; Mary, Luke 10:38-42; Joanna and Susanna, Luke 8:1-3), while others witnessed His resurrection (Matt. 28:1-8; Mark 16:1-8; Luke 24:1-12; John 20:1-9).

Women were also influential in the early church. First century women were active in public worship and in many aspects of church ministry. The Apostle Paul ministered with Euodia and Syntyche (Phil. 4:2-3); Persis (Rom. 16:12); and Tryphena and Tryphosa (Rom. 16:12). In addition, women hosted church meetings (Lydia, Acts 16:14-15; Priscilla, Rom. 16:3-5), taught the faith (Lois and Eunice, 2 Tim. 1:5), provided support (Phoebe, Rom. 16:1-2), and colabored in ministry (Mary ministered with Paul, Rom. 16:6; also Junias, Rom. 16:7). The role of women in the local church has maintained its importance through the centuries. While society has changed its view of women over time, Christian women have always provided significant ministry in the body of Christ.

For many years, women have been involved in missions education. For example, the Woman's Missionary Union of the Southern Baptist Convention began in 1888 with a three-fold purpose: to learn about missions, to do missions, and to support missions. The original purpose of WMU was reaffirmed in recent years in a mission statement: "To provide missions-related programs, information, resources, and training to motivate and enable churches and believers to meet spiritual, physical, and social needs, locally and globally." Today, many churches include this missions organization in their total church program.

Other Southern Baptist agencies have seen the importance of encouraging women in their spiritual lives. The North American Mission Board has a women's evangelism leader and the International Mission Board has a women's mobilization consultant. These are in addition to the LifeWay initiative in the area of women's ministry which began in 1993.

During the 20th century, women in many local churches recognized the need to branch out beyond missions and began to include other ministries. Several Protestant denominations, especially churches on the West Coast, began formal work with women. In the late 1970s and early 1980s, women's ministry groups emerged in churches because of women's spiritual hunger for in-depth Bible study

While society has changed its view of women over time, Christian women have always provided significant ministry in the body of Christ.

and personal prayer. This grass roots movement primarily focused on Bible study and special events. Presently many churches have organized women's ministry groups, developed budgets, planned programs, and hired staff. Women today are involved in all aspects of the church through staff positions, key leadership roles, and specific committees.

In the ministry of Jesus and the early church, Christian women performed vital ministry. In the contemporary congregations of today, women do the same. Therefore, we must provide training and resources for women in today's local church if we want to join God in His movement among them. This handbook is one such resource.

Women reaching women for Christ and discipling women in Christ: these are the basis upon which this book was compiled.

You obviously have a heart for ministry to and with women. Our hope is that through the contents of each chapter you will see God's hand at work in the women in your church. As you study, dream God's dream for the ladies in your church family. Let the Holy Spirit guide as you seek to follow where He leads.

WOMEN'S MINISTRY WHEEL

All ministry must be centered on God's Word and our relationship to the God of the Word. The following chart illustrates that spiritual growth must be the ultimate goal of each of the spokes: relational (social, family, communication, witnessing, service, fellowship), physical (health, nutrition, addictions), emotional (self-esteem, depression, crises counseling), and mental (decision-making, time management, finances, leadership skills).

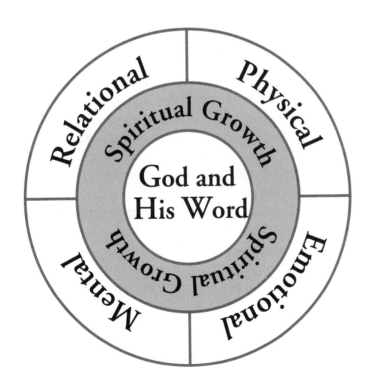

---

[1]Henry Blackaby and Claude King, *Experiencing God: Knowing and Doing the Will of God* (Nashville: LifeWay Press, 1990), 66.

LEADING WELL: LIFE LESSONS FOR LEADERS

CHRIS ADAMS

Who is the women's ministry leader? You are if you are reading this book. Or if you are simply a woman who is interested in finding out about building a women's ministry, you may be a potential leader. Before we talk specifically about the whys and hows of women's ministry, let's talk about you.

THE SPIRITUAL LIFE OF THE LEADER

We sometimes rush to books to help us learn skills for building ministry or to help us become more effective leaders. Leadership skill development is beneficial and necessary to do ministry. However, our own spiritual walks—our development as disciples of Christ—are more important than any skill we learn or idea we might hear from others. To be good leaders, you and I must want a growing relationship with Christ more than we want any ministry position, answer to a need, or relationship with any other person.

Growing more like Christ leads to passion and purpose in ministry. As you become more like Christ, you will lead with confidence and authenticity, and you will help create a safe environment for spiritual transformation to take place in women's lives. True leadership of Christians is a result of a leader's spiritual life. In *Breaking Free* Beth Moore says, "Our motivations for reaching out and serving others aren't always pure. My dear friend Kathy Troccoli, who ministers full-time, asked a critical question: 'Am I ministering out of my need or out of the overflow of my own relationship with God?' We would be wise to ask ourselves the same question. Do we crave the affirmation of those we serve and do they help us feel important? Or do we serve because Jesus has so filled our hearts that we must find a place to pour the overflow?"[1]

Ask the Right Questions

So, then, the first step in building a women's ministry is assessing our own spiritual development. Here are some questions we must ask ourselves:

Are we spending time in the Word daily? Why is this so important? Hebrews 4: 12 tells us, "The word of God is living and effective and sharper

Growing more like Christ leads to passion and purpose in ministry.

12

than any two-edged sword, penetrating as far as to divide soul, spirit, joints, and marrow; it is a judge of the ideas and thoughts of the heart" (HCSB). We see further reason in 2 Timothy 3:16-17: "All Scripture is inspired by God and is profitable for teaching, for rebuking, for correcting, for training in righteousness, so that the man of God may be complete, equipped for every good work" (HCSB). If we are not living our lives and leading ministry according to God's Word, then we are probably following the world's standards.

Are we daily submitting to God's authority? Do we trust Him for daily guidance in every detail of our lives? Psalm 143:8 became very special to me a few years back when I was not sure which direction my life should take regarding ministry. Daily I had to quote this verse to remind myself I must allow Him full access to all of my life and trust Him fully with it. "Let the morning bring me word of your unfailing love for I have put my trust in you. Show me the way that I should go, for to you I lift up my soul" (NIV).

Are we bathing everything in prayer?
> our lives?
>> our families?
>>> our churches?
>>>> our women's ministries?
>>>>> or at least the dream of beginning a women's ministry?

After telling us to put on the armor of God, the Bible tells us to pray: With every prayer and request, pray at all times in the Spirit, and stay alert in this, with all perseverance and intercession for all the saints (Eph. 6:18, HCSB).

Are we becoming more like Him daily? Can we look back and see progress in our walk with Him? First Peter 2:2-3 says, "Like newborn infants, desire the unadulterated spiritual milk, so that you may grow by it in your salvation, since 'you have tasted that the Lord is good.' " Daily feeding on God's Word will help our faith to flourish and our love for others increase (see 2 Thess. 1:3).

Prepared for Battle

What makes Christian leadership different or harder than other types of leadership? Let's face it, Christian leaders are under attack. The enemy will do all he can to discredit us, to tempt us, to cause us to lose integrity, or at least to bring our integrity into question.

When Godly People Do Ungodly Things by Beth Moore should be a required study for every woman in ministry. If we think we cannot be deceived by the enemy's tactics, then we are in a position to fall. Leaders today must be prepared and armored (Eph. 6) so we will be able to flee when God tells us to flee (1 Cor. 6:18; 1 Tim. 6:11; 2 Tim. 2:22) and stand firm when He tells us to stand firm in the face of the enemy (Eph. 6:11,14). Leaders we least expect to fall—those who seem to be strong and close to the Lord—are falling. Why? They were either not prepared, did not flee, or did not stand firm in their faith.

Falls can happen to any of us if we are not prepared and aware of Satan's deceptive ways. Galatians 6:1 tells us, "Brothers, if someone is caught in any wrongdoing, you who are spiritual should restore such a person with a gentle

Leaders must be prepared and armored.

spirit, watching out for yourselves so you won't be tempted also." As leaders, we are not immune.

Satan continually tempts us to sin, but we shouldn't confuse temptation with sin. Temptation is not all bad. Rick Warren says "every temptation is an opportunity to do good. On the path to spiritual maturity, even temptation becomes a stepping stone rather than a stumbling block when you realize it's just as much an occasion to do the right thing as to do the wrong thing. God develops the fruit of the Spirit in your life by allowing circumstances in which you are tempted to express the exact opposite quality. Character development always involves a choice. And temptation provides that opportunity."[2]

Temptation begins in the mind, so guard your mind. Guard your eyes and ears so impure thoughts do not hang on and invade the heart, becoming sin. Daily offer your life as a sacrifice to God and keep your heart and mind on what is honorable. (See Rom. 12:1-2 and Phil. 4:8-9.) Examine each thought, use your Sword, flee the enemy, and ask God's help as you put on His armor.

PURSUING HOLINESS

We must pursue holiness daily, but what does that mean? Does it mean that leaders must be perfect? We know that's not possible. But we must be set apart, becoming increasingly more like Jesus. We must be transparent with our own struggles and yet proclaim God's faithfulness. We must be consecrated, set apart, seeking to live out the holiness, purity, and morality of God's nature.

First Peter 1:13-16 clearly instructs us: "Therefore, get your minds ready for action, being self-disciplined, and set your hope completely on the grace to be brought to you at the revelation of Jesus Christ. As obedient children, do not be conformed to the desires of your former ignorance but, as the One who called you is holy, you also are to be holy in all your conduct; for it is written, *Be holy, because I am holy*" (HCSB, emphasis mine). We serve a holy God, so we are to be holy. As we walk in holiness, we are useful to the Master. "So if anyone purifies himself from these things, he will be a special instrument, set apart, useful to the Master, prepared for every good work" (2 Tim 2:21, HCSB).

I love Priscilla Shirer's quote of her mother in *He Speaks to Me*, "Do not go anywhere or do anything questionable where someone might mistake you for me."[3] As we walk in holiness, we establish credibility as leaders and become women of integrity. Integrity is essential—a non-negotiable in ministry. As women of integrity, we are trustworthy in our actions and consistent in our daily lives. Our yes means yes, and our no means no. We stand up for God's principles and do not consider compromise. Even in the arena of leadership, you may be alone in standing up for what you know is right in God's eyes. Ask God to help you stand true to Him—even if you're the only one.

We all face difficulty in ministry or our personal lives as we serve and lead. Do you hide those struggles? Do you put on your "I'm fine" face and keep going? Or are you transparent and open with others, seeking their support when you face challenges? We need each other as leaders in ministry and sisters in Christ.

Ask God to help you stand true to Him—even if you're the only one.

It's critical then that we prepare and continue to grow in Christlikeness so we can reflect Jesus in our daily walks and certainly in our leadership. May I share some "lessons" God has taught me over the years? I don't share these because I have mastered them but because I know they are important. God continues to work in these areas of my own life.

Lesson 1: "Marbleize" Women's Ministry

I first saw this phrase in an electronic newsletter from CrossWalk Women. Sharon Betters wrote that many women's leaders "see [women's ministry] as a program that is one layer of the church, rather than a vital ingredient that is marbleized into the whole community, an ingredient that is critical to the peace and prosperity of a local church and denomination."[4] We must make sure we see women's ministry as a part of the bigger picture of the church body and kingdom. If we create ministry that only focuses on itself, we miss the real reason God places unique ministries and individual passions into the church body. Women's ministry must interlock with and support the other ministries of the local body of believers.

Women's ministry must interlock with and support the other ministries of Christ's body.

Lesson 2: Train Someone To Take Your Place

As leaders, we do not know how long we will be in the positions we now hold. God may move us or take us home at any time, so we must make sure we leave the ministry in trained, capable hands when that time comes. Each of us should spend time mentoring at least one leader to step into our shoes of leadership. For each women's ministry position, a learner should be walking beside the leader and watching godly leadership in action. One of the first things Christ did in ministry was to train a team of 12 men to "follow" and then carry on the ministry when He would no longer be physically present.

As leaders we must model a servant's heart and train others to be servants. (See the chapter "Building Your Leadership Team" in this book for more.) We must also be teachable and enthusiastic about ongoing training. If we are not teachable, how can we continue to grow as followers of Christ and leaders of women's ministry?

Always keep in mind that the ministry you lead is not yours. It's not even the women's ministry. It's God's ministry. We are privileged stewards of God's kingdom work. Pass the vision on to the next generation, and model godly servant leadership for them.

Lesson 3: Stay Flexible

Just why is flexibility so important? It helps keep the ministry fresh, alive, and vibrant. We can stay flexible through ongoing evaluation of all we do. Through monitoring our own strengths and weaknesses, we'll see that some things need to continue as they are, others need to cease, and some need to be tweaked or changed to gain effectiveness.

Sometimes we have wonderful plans in place and have thought of all the details, but for some reason God chooses to change our plans mid-stream. Do you remember the Magi following God's leadership to "go home a different way" to avoid Herod (see Matt. 2:12)? Or Paul's change of direction for his missionary journey when he heard what we read in the Acts 16 Macedonian call? What if these men had not listened to the Holy Spirit?

We must be open to the Holy Spirit's leadership in every aspect of the ministry. His plan is always better than ours—even if it's very different. How we react to God's redirection will directly impact the leaders on our teams as well as the women we serve as they see how we allow the Holy Spirit to lead. We must handle sudden change in plans with grace.

Make your plans with God's direction, and change them with God's direction.

Lesson 4: Communicate with Staff

Never take for granted that you can just do ministry without the direction and sanction of the staff of your church. Hebrews 13:17 says: "Obey your leaders and submit to them, for they keep watch over your souls as those who will give an account, so that they can do this with joy and not with grief, for that would be unprofitable for you." The church staff is there to guide, support, and even provide protection for every area of ministry.

Also keep in mind that you will often provide the women's perspective with what might be a mostly or even completely male staff, and you represent over half the membership. Remember, male and female communication styles are different. Understand the most effective ways of communicating to your staff, speaking their language as you share the women's needs.(See more hints on pp. 58-59.)

Lesson 5: Be Personally Accountable to Someone

We need to be accountable to people who love us but are not impressed by us.

Romans 14:12 says, "So then, each of us will give an account of himself to God." We are ultimately accountable to God for our lives, but we all need to have earthly friends who will ask the hard questions and walk with us through the good times and bad. Accountability is a protective measure, as well. It makes us regard our own vulnerabilities and the need for those who will walk with us through spiritual warfare. We need to be accountable to people who love us but are not impressed by us. James 5:16 tells us, "Therefore, confess your sins to one another and pray for one another, so that you may be healed. The intense prayer of the righteous is very powerful." Admit when you are struggling, and accept help from your sisters in Christ. Remember, "if somebody over powers one person, two can resist him. A cord of three strands is not easily broken" (Ecc. 4:12).

Lesson 6: Take Retreats

For me a retreat is a week at the beach to listen to the waves, think, read, and enjoy God's presence. For you, it may be a morning at the park to enjoy God's creation and quiet. Whether your retreat is for five minutes or five days, find time to get away with God. Our world is too fast paced for us not to take the time to retreat occasionally.

Leaders must have time for rest, reflection, prayer, Scripture reading, and recreation—all without guilt. Jesus said, " 'Come away by yourselves to a remote place and rest a while.' For many people were coming and going, and they did not even have time to eat" (Mark 6:31, HCSB). Perhaps you feel like that. There's not even time for you to eat! A five minute break in a busy day to refocus or to reflect on God's control in your busyness can give you strength to continue what God has ordained for that day. Extended times of rest and what I call "vegging out" can also further restore and renew your heart and mind so you do not get "tired of doing good" (see Gal. 6:9).

Lesson 7: Don't Neglect Family

Family members and relationships are our primary ministry. God has given us husbands, children, parents, and others as gifts. If we neglect family to get on with "important ministry," we forfeit some of the greatest blessings we can experience through ministering to those closest to us.

Family members and relationships are your primary ministry.

Sometimes we fail to see family responsibilities as ministry, but Scripture tells us we are to do everything as unto the Lord. "Whatever you do, do it enthusiastically, as something done for the Lord and not for men, knowing that you will receive the reward of an inheritance from the Lord—you serve the Lord Christ" (Col. 3:23-24, HCSB). If we see our ministry to our families from God's perspective and do it for His glory, what seems mundane and routine can become ministry as unto the Lord.

Whenever possible, include your family in your ministry. Many activities can become teaching opportunities as they see you minister to others. Never push family to do ministry; instead, encourage their participation. Your family can become ministry partners as you seek their prayer and support as you serve.

Lesson 8: Step into the Water

Be bold and willing to move when God directs—even if the "water" (your different circumstance) has not parted yet. When the Israelites were told to cross over the Jordan, the water was flowing full force. It was not until the priests put their feet into it that it parted (see Josh. 3:15). Joshua told the Israelites to select representatives from each tribe to take memorial stones from middle of the river. This was the place where they stood on dry ground—a place of remembrance of God's faithfulness to protect and provide. These memorial stones represented God's provision when future generations asked about the stones' meaning. God's miracles would be repeated in the ages to come.

Is God asking you to do something beyond your abilities and comprehension? Maybe you see only the deep waters ahead. Step out in faith if He is leading you to move. He will part the waters to accomplish His assignments. Future generations will be blessed because of your faithfulness to trust in God's provision in your life and ministry.

Lesson 9: Surrender All to Him

In following Christ, we must die to ourselves and allow Jesus to live in and through us. We must lay down all we have and all we are. Luke 14:27 tells us, "Whoever does not bear his own cross and come after Me cannot be My disciple." Oswald Chambers deals with the issue of surrender many times in *My Utmost for His Highest:*

"True surrender will always go beyond natural devotion. If we will only give up, God will surrender Himself to embrace all those around us and will meet their needs, which were created by our surrender. Beware of stopping anywhere short of total surrender to God. Most of us have only a vision of what this really means, but have never truly experienced it."

"If we are truly surrendered, we will never be aware of our own efforts to remain surrendered. Our entire life will be consumed with the One to whom we surrender. Beware of talking about surrender if you know nothing about it. In fact, you will never know anything about it until you understand that John 3:16 means that God completely and absolutely gave Himself to us. In our surrender, we must give ourselves to God in the same way he gave Himself for us—totally, unconditionally, and without reservation. The consequences and circumstances resulting from our surrender will never even enter our mind, because our life will be totally consumed with Him."

"Most of us live only within the level of consciousness—consciously serving and consciously devoted to God. This shows immaturity and the fact that we're not yet living the real Christian life. Maturity is produced in the life of a child of God on the unconscious level, until we become so totally surrendered to God that we are not even aware of being used by Him. When we are consciously aware of being used as broken bread and poured-out wine, we have yet another level to reach—a level where all awareness of ourselves and of what God is doing through us is completely eliminated. A saint is never consciously a saint—a saint is consciously dependent on God."[5]

Lift up your soul daily to the One who can take it, protect it, and work all things for His good. Trust Him not only with the big needs and issues in your life. Trust Him with all the little things as well.

Lesson 10: Give God the Glory

Persist in God's calling in your life, even if you face obstacles.

All glory belongs to God—we are never to claim glory for ourselves or give it to others for what God has done in and through our ministries. To minister in service to Christ is an incredible privilege. Beth Moore says: "I am absolutely convinced that seeking God's glory rather than our own incredibly enhances life on a purely human level. The trouble is it can't be done on a human level. Few things are more contrary to our human natures than desiring anyone's fame above our own. ... To fulfill our God-given destinies—to allow the King of all creation to show Himself through us—we must overcome the temptation to seek our own glory by desiring His instead."[6]

Remember, the ministry in which you serve is not yours! The psalmist said: "Come and listen, all who fear God, and I will tell what He has done for me" (Ps. 66:16, HCSB). And he also wrote, "Not to us, Lord, not to us, but to Your name give glory" (Ps. 115:1, HCSB).

Lesson 11: Never Give Up

Galatians 6:7-10 says, "Don't be deceived: God is not mocked. For whatever a man sows he will also reap, because the one who sows to his flesh will reap corruption from the flesh, but the one who sows to the Spirit will reap eternal life from the Spirit. So we must not get tired of doing good, for we will reap at the proper time if we don't give up. Therefore, as we have opportunity, we must work for the good of all, especially for those who belong to the household of faith" (HCSB). Keep following God's call while you have the opportunity.

Take time to read about William Carey. What he faced as he served as a missionary in India would make most people give up and go home, but not him. Because he refused to disbelieve God's call in his life, an entire nation was changed. Persist in God's calling in your life, even if you face obstacles. The eternal rewards will be well worth the sacrifice.

LEAVING A HERITAGE

Keep in mind what you do today in ministry with women is laying groundwork for future generations. As we serve, we not only meet current needs, but we also build a future. Scripture tells us again and again we must pass our faith to the younger generations.

What you do in ministry today lays groundwork for future generations.

> My people, hear my instruction; listen to what I say. I will declare wise sayings; I will speak mysteries from the past—things we have heard and known and that our fathers have passed down to us. We must not hide them from their children, but must tell a future generation the praises of the LORD, His might, and the wonderful works He has performed. He established a testimony in Jacob and set up a law in Israel, which He commanded our fathers to teach to their children so that a future generation—children yet to be born—might know. They were to rise and tell their children so that they might put their confidence in God and not forget God's works, but keep His commandments (Ps. 78:1-7, HCSB).

> This will be written for a later generation, and a newly created people will praise the Lord (Ps. 102:18, HCSB).

We must also pass along the baton of leadership. As you model godly leadership and train up others to lead, you will continue the legacy of faith and even make a difference in those who have yet to be born. What a responsibility, but what an incredible privilege!

¹Beth Moore, *Breaking Free* (Nashville: LifeWay Press®, 1999), 216.
²Rick Warren, *The Purpose Driven Life*, (Grand Rapids: Zondervan, 2002), 201.
³Priscilla Shirer, *He Speaks to Me* (Nashville: LifeWay Press®, 2005), 47.
⁴Sharon Betters, "Marbleizing Women's Ministry," *Crosswalk Womens_Newsletter*, <http://link.crosswalk.com/UM/T.asp?A1.29.25743.1.1481163> (1 September 2004)
⁵Oswald Chambers, *My Utmost for His Highest* (Grand Rapids: Discovery House Publishers, 1992), n.pag.
⁶Beth Moore, *Living Free* (Nashville: LifeWay Press®, 2001), 51.

WHY HAVE A WOMEN'S MINISTRY?

CHRIS ADAMS

Several years ago God began stirring my heart in the area of reaching and discipling women. At the time, the only things we had specifically for women in my church were a weekly Bible study and a missions group. While these effectively met the needs of the small numbers of women who attended, the majority of ladies in our congregation were not involved. God increased the burden within me with this question: "How can we reach all our women and encourage them to grow and follow Christ daily?"

Three other ladies and I began praying, asking God what He would do to expand the ministry our church offered women. Because not much was available to help us develop a new and different ministry, much of what we did was through continual prayer and trial and error. We looked to see what other churches were doing to reach women. We visited and spent time with women's ministry leaders, picking their brains and learning from their experiences.

After many months and years of hard work, some mistakes, much prayer, and a willingness to "color outside the lines," we watched God develop a multifaceted women's ministry. We saw women who never thought of themselves as leaders begin to boldly take responsibilities and positions to serve the Lord. We also saw women come to know Christ, and immature Christians base their entire lives on God's Word.

What a privilege to be a part of the Lord's work, to minister to and alongside women, to share what God has done in my life as He uses it to touch and change someone else! Women today need to know faith truly works, no matter what the world tells them. They need to know how to stay faithful in a world that has forsaken Christ.

For believers, ministry is not an option. Ministry is our responsibility. God calls each of us to serve Him. He empowers and gifts us to accomplish what He calls us to do.

For believers, ministry is not an option.

Women are qualified to minister to others for a variety of reasons. Both the Old and New Testaments provide examples of women who were a part of God's ministry. In the Old Testament Ruth chose to follow and minister to her distraught mother-in-law, Naomi, as they grieved the loss of husband and son. In 2 Timothy Lois and Eunice, Timothy's mother and grandmother, actively passed along their heritage of faith. Dorcas (see Acts 9) served both in her church and community, ministering to the less fortunate. The example of Jesus also qualifies women to minister. He ministered to and with women throughout His earthly ministry.

Redemption and giftedness are additional qualifications that should inspire women to be busy about the Lord's work. Because of our salvation, we have the gift of life to share with the world. Because of our personal giftedness (see 1 Pet. 4:10), we are equipped to serve Christ as He leads. It is both a privilege and responsibility to use the gifts God has given us. Since Jesus has commanded that we "go and make disciples" (Matt. 28:19), how can women *not* minister? The only prerequisite is that we experience life's joys, trials, victories, and sorrows and share transparently what God has done through each experience.

Leadership skills develop as women boldly step out in faith to attempt the great tasks God assigns to them.

Leadership skills develop as women boldly step out in faith to attempt the great tasks God assigns to them. For example, a woman I know had never felt qualified to accept a leadership position in her church. After attending a women's Bible study, she realized God had given her gifts to use for Him, despite the fact that she felt inadequate. When a leader invited her to take part in planning a women's retreat, she accepted. Through that experience she learned the importance of serving and giving others the opportunity to serve. Eventually she became a ministry leader in her church. When God moved her family to a new city, she was prepared to share her gifts and experiences to help develop a women's ministry there.

REASONS FOR HAVING A WOMEN'S MINISTRY

Do you have a vision for reaching women and discipling them for life change? Is God stirring the hearts of the women in your church, creating within them a hunger for serving Christ? Are they seeking to know Christ more intimately, to serve Him more faithfully, and to share their faith with those who need a Savior? Are you prepared to lead them as they seek to grow spiritually?

An exciting thing is happening in many of our churches. I continually receive calls from pastors and women's ministry leaders who say, "There seems to be a movement of God among our women. God is at work in their lives, and we want to be ready to respond."

Women desire to reach out to hurting women as well as disciple them. They have a deep spiritual hunger to know Christ and experience Him personally. They want to know how to survive in a world that has forgotten God. They want to know how to balance responsibilities and live a full and meaningful life. They need leaders who will reach out and disciple them.

Many church leaders have attempted to develop women's ministries. They ask, "What can we do to help? How can we reach women whose needs are not already being met by other ministries in our church? How can we minister to these women and disciple them so that they become all God desires them to be—serving Him faithfully in their families, professions, churches, and communities?" These leaders seek to reach women for Christ, to disciple them, and to equip them to reach others. Women's ministry was born on the grass-roots level to meet these needs.

No man can meet all the needs of a woman; women need relationships with other women. They need godly role models; wiser, more spiritually mature women after whom to pattern their lives. The Bible says in Titus 2:3-5, "Likewise, teach the older women to be reverent in the way they live, not to be slanderers or addicted to much wine, but to teach what is good. Then they can train the younger women to love their husbands and children, to be self-controlled and pure, to be busy at home, to be kind, and to be subject to their husbands, so that no one will malign the word of God."

Because they no longer live close to their families, many younger women need mentors who will encourage and teach them. They need someone who has been there to say "I understand, and I'll pray with you through this," or "Here is how God spoke to me as I was experiencing the same thing." Brenda Hunter quotes her friend Ree, "A mentor comes alongside, puts her arm around you, and says, 'You can do it.' "[1] A mentor does what Paul asked Timothy to do, "And the things you have heard me say … entrust to reliable men (and women) who will also be qualified to teach others" (2 Tim. 2:2).

An effective women's ministry is not a stand-alone program in the local church, but actually a piece of the puzzle that makes up a body of believers. In carrying out their purpose, women support the purpose of the entire church. A women's ministry can create synergy that comes from the unique ministry to and with women as it addresses their unique needs. Because of the diversity of women, a ministry to women must be diverse in content, options of activities offered, time of day conducted, and day of week held. The individual needs of both professional women and full-time homemakers must be addressed. We must consider the unique needs of empty nesters, singles, senior adults, and single mothers. As we do, we can develop ministry to help each woman accept and love who God created her to be, providing encouragement for her to grow in her relationship to Christ, fellow believers, and a lost world.

As we began to develop our women's ministry, we considered women in our church, their lifestyles and life phases, their needs, and their gifts and talents. We offered large-group Bible study and worship one morning a week to draw them together for fellowship and discipleship. We also provided an evening Bible study geared to women employed outside the home. These included elective courses as part of each semester's studies and included discipleship studies such as *Experiencing God, The Mind of Christ,* and *WiseCounsel*; marriage, homemaking, and parenting studies; crafts and aerobics classes; community ministries such as a soup kitchen and clothes closet; mission studies and participation; and prayer groups. Special events were planned each quarter and monthly noon luncheons were offered for all women. This diversity enabled us

Women's enrichment ministry is not a stand-alone program but a piece of the puzzle that makes up the body of believers.

to reach a larger number of women. Even in a small church, variety is important to reach a variety of women.

Today's woman lives in a world that tells her she can have it all, do it all, and be "super woman" through it all. Many women feel guilty because they cannot accomplish this in their personal, professional, and spiritual lives.

If today's woman reads secular publications and watches television, she is bombarded by humanistic answers to her needs. When those do not work, where will she turn? Will this woman, desperate for relationships and attention, find a support group of like women to help her walk with Christ daily? Will she be challenged in her spiritual life to spend time with God in prayer and to dig deep into His Word to find answers? What a challenge for us as women's ministry leaders! What a responsibility! What an opportunity!

Why have a women's ministry? For the same reasons we have single adult, senior adult, children's, youth, or men's ministry. First, we want to meet the unique needs of the target audience. In this case, the target audience is women of all ages and all walks of life. And second, to encourage ministry as a way of life. All believers are called to minister and serve. In *Experiencing God: Knowing and Doing the Will of God,* Henry Blackaby says you cannot be in relationship with Christ and not be on mission. Ministry emerges from our relationship with Him.

CONCERNS ABOUT WOMEN'S MINISTRY

Some people have the idea that women's ministry is only concerned with personal growth; learning but not applying knowledge. This is not the case if the ministry is conducted appropriately. Effective ministries will lead women to seek God's Word, to apply it, and to share it throughout their daily lives. As that happens, they are unable to contain their joy in the Lord, and it spills over to all with whom they come in contact. Sharing their faith verbally as well as by lifestyle becomes a way of life.

Effective ministry leads women to seek, apply, and share God's Word.

A second common concern about women's ministry is that women participating in it will become a detached group, functioning on their own without the knowledge or support of the church staff. As leaders are trained to effectively relate to staff (see "Building Your Leadership Team," p. 106), they share their burden and vision for reaching women and seek the staff's support and direction. They support the purpose of the church as a whole, not just women's ministry.

BENEFITS OF A WOMEN'S MINISTRY

There are a number of benefits that result from providing and supporting a women's ministry in the church.

1. WOMEN GROW IN THEIR RELATIONSHIP WITH THE LORD.
It was through a young women's Bible study that I was first challenged to get up in the morning before my children woke to spend time in prayer and Scripture reading. It was truly a challenge. Not only was I tired most of the time (I don't even like

to get up early when I am rested!), but I found it made a huge difference in my attitude and focus for the day as I reflected on the Lord's constant presence in my life.

Women grow in their relationship with the Lord as they participate in study, prayer, and ministry to others. As women grow spiritually and learn how to minister, their families, churches, and communities benefit.

2. THE CHURCH GROWS NUMERICALLY.

The church grows as participants in women's ministries seek out and meet the needs of women in their community with the message of Christ.

For example, Janet lived in our city for only a few months while her husband was on a job site. She knew they would relocate within a few months. Janet joined our church because our women's ministry offered her a place to study God's Word during the week and make friends quickly during the fellowship time before and after our study.

As women invite neighbors and coworkers to participate in women's studies and activities, prospects are discovered and encouraged to become a part of the church. Members bring lost friends to our women's ministry activities where they find Christ—and thus encourage the body of Christ to grow.

3. NEW MEMBERS FIND THEIR NICHE.

A women's ministry draws in women who have recently joined the church to help them become familiar with and find their "niche" (area of ministry). In the church where I served, we began a New Member Shepherding Ministry that reached out to each woman who joined the church. Leaders of this ministry committed to having at least five "touches" with each woman to make sure she didn't slip through the cracks or leave through the back door of the church because she did not find her area of service or the place where her needs could be met. "Touches" included a visit to share information about the church and its ministry opportunities, an invitation and a free ticket to the next women's event, a follow-up phone call to see if she had any questions regarding the church, or an invitation for coffee or lunch. We also made sure she knew where to find Sunday morning Bible study classes both for herself and for her family members.

4. MEANINGFUL RELATIONSHIPS FORM.

A women's ministry opens the door for relationships between women from different backgrounds, ages, and life stages. Fellowship is one activity that seems to take place spontaneously when women get together. As the women's ministry of your church offers activities for all women, fellowship takes place automatically. As ladies study, pray, and worship together, lasting and meaningful relationships develop.

5. WOMEN ARE ENCOURAGED TO DISCOVER, DEVELOP, AND USE SPIRITUAL GIFTS.

Scripture teaches, "Based on the gift they have received, everyone should use it to serve others,a as good managers of the varied grace of God" (1 Pet. 4:10, HCSB). Although each woman is gifted, she may not realize it, or may not know what her gifts are. Others know their gifts but do not understand how to use them to serve God.

Women's enrichment ministry opens the door for relationships between women from different backgrounds, ages, and life stages.

For years after I became a Christian, I didn't realize God had gifted me to serve Him. I thought God skipped me when He handed out the gifts. But as I began to study about how each believer is gifted (1 Pet. 4:10), I realized that included me. Organization has always been fairly easy for me. I thought everyone had a calendar, marked important items on it, and looked at it periodically so nothing would be missed. I discovered that is not necessarily true. Maybe the gift of administration was the gift I was to use in ministry. As I began to let God develop that strength in me, He opened doors and called me to serve. As I looked at the women in our church, I realized I was not the only one who did not understand what God's Word says about spiritual gifts. Through women's ministry, women can discern their gifts and find opportunities to use those gifts in service for the Lord.

6. EACH WOMAN IS IMPORTANT TO GOD, AND WE MUST MINISTER TO HER.

Women today have almost no spare time and will only spend what little time they have on things worth the sacrifice they must make to be involved. The busy woman today must feel the activity is something she needs to make a difference in her own life or in someone else's. We must offer study and ministry opportunities at various times throughout the week to accommodate women with different schedules, lifestyles, and family responsibilities. If we only offer a Tuesday morning discipleship study, what does that say to the woman who works Monday through Friday from 8:00 to 5:00? She may feel as though she is not important to you and your women's ministry. Where will she find a group of women with whom she can share, pray, and study? By providing a diverse schedule and diverse options for study, we let each woman know she is important to us and to God.

Busy women today will give of their time and energy if the activity makes a difference in their lives or in the lives of others.

7. COORDINATION AND ORGANIZATION ARE PROVIDED FOR INREACH AND OUTREACH TO WOMEN.

Often churches provide various studies and activities but no central source of information. A structure of organization will provide a network of information. Each woman should know that studies to help her grow in her relationship with Christ, ministries to meet her needs, service opportunities in the church, and community outreach ministries are available.

When we began to organize our women's ministry, there were several groups already established, but no one person really knew the details of each. There were many ministries (both within the church and in the community) where a woman could serve, but no place to find out all that was available. As we set up our structure, we listed all the opportunities a woman had for fellowship, study, and service—even if these were not just for women. We wanted to serve as a central source of information so each woman could discover ways she could participate throughout the church. This was especially helpful to new church members who were inquiring about opportunities for women.

8. WOMEN RECEIVE WOMAN-TO-WOMAN UNDERSTANDING AND LAY COUNSELING.

Women need women who can share emotions and experiences and help round out life's experiences. In her newsletter, *Just Between Us*, Jill Briscoe writes,

"After all, who but a mother can fully empathize with a young woman who has suffered a miscarriage or struggled with being shut up with small children all day long? Who but a woman can sympathize with mercurial monthly emotions or PMS or the changes that come unbidden when we hit 50! What a wide open door our very sex affords us. We can walk right into the hearts and lives of half the human race and present Christ, all because we are female."[2]

I have a dear friend and mentor who shared her walk with the Lord with me in a way that greatly influenced my life. I saw her struggle with a difficult family issue and yet exhibit peace, joy, and incredible faith through it. Little did I know one day my family would experience the same type of struggle. What I had seen in her life and in her walk with the Lord encouraged me to trust God. Often I would call her just to say, "Tell me again how you made it." What a comfort when she and other Christian friends called to say, "Our family has experienced what you are going through, and we are praying for you." Only someone who has been there can truly say "I understand." A woman dealing with crisis needs to know she is not the only woman to go through the same type of situation.

After praying and waiting for God's timing, our church established a lay counseling ministry for women. Counselors first trained by studying *Wise-Counsel: Skills for Lay Counseling* (see "Tapping Resources for Women's Ministry," p. 222). This study prepares women to listen, to ask appropriate questions, and to know when to refer others for professional counseling. The name chosen for this ministry was "Heartstrings: Confidential Conversation for Women."

The group is led by women who experienced difficult life situations and with the Lord's help "made it." They are willing to listen and encourage women who are dealing with similar issues. Local ministries can provide a list of women who are "on call" if someone needs to talk to a woman who has been through what she is now experiencing. Names used for this ministry in other churches are "Care and Share," "Encouragement Network," "Called to Encourage," and "YokeFellow Ministry." The participation is temporary, not long-term, and each one ministered to is encouraged to use her experience to minister to another woman. This aspect of women's ministry will lighten the staff ministers' load at times when a woman really only needs someone to listen and share with, rather than a professional counselor.

9. OLDER WOMEN MENTOR YOUNGER WOMEN.

Throughout a woman's life, she should continually look for someone to mentor—someone spiritually younger with whom she can share insights the Lord has given her. At the same time, each woman should be looking for someone to mentor her—a woman from whom she can learn about life and relationships. No matter where we are in age or our spiritual walks, mentoring and being mentored should be a pattern we follow.

I have already told about some friends in my life who have mentored me spiritually. Another friend that God sent my way early in my marriage was Anne. She was an older lady who was a widow and had no children. She "adopted" my husband and me when we moved to her neighborhood in East Texas. My mother lived several hours away, and I could not pick up the phone and call her every time I had a domestic crisis in my kitchen. Anne filled the gap. She was the one I called almost daily with questions about homemaking. She taught me much about managing a home, loving my husband, and the importance of joining a local church. Anne knew it would impact our marriage, our children, and our lives. She is with the Lord now, but I still thank God for her friendship and her love for Him and for us.

10. ENTIRE FAMILIES ARE AFFECTED AS WOMEN ARE DRAWN CLOSER TO THE LORD.
When a woman is reached through women's ministry, her family is also touched. I have seen marriages transformed when wives began to put Christ first in their lives. I have seen mothers become more at peace with themselves and their children as they discovered they are not alone in dealing with the daily work of preschool children or the difficulties of the teenage years. I have also seen single women begin to trust God with their "singleness" as they learned from other singles that they are essential to the effective functioning of the church body. When you influence a woman's life for Christ, you touch all those in her sphere of influence as she lives out her faith.

11. WOMEN GET HELP TO FIGHT SPIRITUAL BATTLES.
All of us face spiritual warfare. It goes with living for Christ in this world. It would be all too easy to hide in our homes and avoid the world entirely, but as women of God we must reach out and help restore lives. More than likely, each of us will need a hand at some point in our journey. We need to be willing to give and accept help to face the enemy whose goal is to destroy our Christian witness to the world.

Women need to stand alongside one another as they daily walk in a world that is in bondage to sin. When one woman is weak, she needs others to stand with her, encouraging her to be strong and pointing her to God and His Word.

When a woman is reached through women's ministry, her family is also touched.

THE TASKS OF WOMEN'S MINISTRY

What are the tasks of every women's ministry? Women's ministry exists to:
- *equip* local church women to enrich the lives of other women through Christ;
- *help* women discover their God-given gifts for ministry, determine needs in their communities, and match those needs with their gifts of service; and
- *lead* women to accept Christ as Lord, become women of deep prayer, and become women who study the Bible and base their lives on the Word of God.

The remainder of this book is devoted to achieving the tasks of women's ministry.

---

[1]Brenda Hunter, Ph.D., *In the Company of Women* (Sisters, Ore.: Multnomah Books, 1994), 182.

[2]Jill Briscoe, "A Letter from Jill," *Just Between Us: Jill Briscoe's Newsletter for Ministry Wives* (Jacksonville, FL.: Preaching Resources, 1990), n pag. (This resource is now a magazine published by Telling the Truth Media, Brookfield, WI, 1-800-260-3342).

THE GENERATIONS OF A POSTMODERN WORLD

JUDI SLAYDEN HAYES

From my 105-year-old grandmother Faye, to my 4-year-old great-niece Mykayla, the women in my family span five generations. Faye was born into a horse-and-buggy world. Mykayla takes air travel for granted. Faye was born into a world just beginning to know the benefits of electricity. Mykayla is on her second computer system. Faye was born long before the First World War. Mykayla was born after September 11, 2001; she's never known a time without war and terrorism. Faye was born in the modern world. Mykayla was born in the postmodern world.

Between Faye and Mykayla are three generations of wonderful women, each shaped by our experiences in an ever-changing world. The women of our family are members of churches in three states where we minister alongside others in the body of Christ. We minister to others at home and around the world, and we receive ministry from our brothers and sisters in Christ. Along with our husbands, fathers, brothers, and sons, we are an American family.

GENERATIONS OF AMERICANS

Two recent family events remind me of how we are shaped by our experiences and the world around us.

On their 63rd anniversary, I took my parents to dinner. I asked them to tell me about their dating and pre-children years of marriage. They talked about train travel, rationing during World War II, Daddy's wartime military service, and going on a date in a borrowed car to watch airplanes land at the airport. Hearing their old stories was fun, but as a relatively early baby boomer, I realize that I've experienced most of the events of their lives. They have lived through all the world events of my life, and I have lived through nearly three-fourths of theirs. I am intimately connected to the generation before me.

Jessica, the daughter of my first cousin, graduated from high school this week. I listened to the speaker remind us these graduates were born during

Generations overlap and are influenced by the world into which they are born.

Ronald Reagan's presidency. While I continue to marvel every time I look something up on the Internet, send an e-mail, watch satellite TV, answer the cell phone, get directions on the GPS, and use the microwave, Jessica's never known a world without all the good and bad technology has to offer. I've lived through all the years of her life, but she's lived through only a third of mine. Still, our generations are interconnected.

Generations are not distinct entities that stand alone. They overlap. Older generations have lived through all the years the younger generations have, but they have been shaped by events and world changes that the younger generation has not. For example, I took my parents to Glorieta one year. While I was in a meeting, they bought groceries. Within two days the bread they bought had molded, and we had to throw it away. They talked about the shame of wasting that loaf all week. I just wanted to get a new one. Their childhood was shaped by the depression, while my generation never experienced widespread economic hardship. Even though the generations overlap, our responses to life are shaped by the world into which we are born.

Each woman is a unique person created in God's image. We don't want to separate women into generations to label their behavior or to stereotype them. However, stopping to take a look at the generations of women in our churches today can help us meet the needs of women of all ages. Instead of shaking our heads and wondering why women in other age groups act the way they do, we can listen with informed understanding and seek to meet their needs. Those of each generation can learn from and contribute to the understanding of others.

Louis Hanks offers this valuable information about generations:

GENERATIONAL ASSUMPTIONS

Several assumptions must be understood to allow teachers and leaders to accept the value of generational perspectives.

1. Generational theory as a tool to understand people is a valid approach in discovering the cultural currents of broad groups of people.
2. A generation, as a social category, is distinct from other social categories like gender, race, region, and age, and probably offers a more reliable basis for generalization of people than the other social categories.
3. Generational characteristics relate to the population of the United States and reflect cross-cultural application.
4. Generational descriptions of peer personalities—those signature traits of each generation—are intended to paint a broad profile of the generation.
5. All generations reflect social, emotional, psychological, intellectual, and spiritual dimensions. The difference between the generations is typically a matter of varying degrees of emphasis along a continuum.
6. Generational unity and diversity co-exist. Overall, a generation has a core of common attitudes, values, and behaviors; but first and second age waves within the generation can create distinctives. These attitudes, values, and behaviors never show up uniformly across all of its members.
7. Each generation experiences "defining moments" that create a common bond of shared experiences. People in one generational group are basically

Stopping to take a look at the generations of women in our churches can help us meet the needs of women of all ages.

illiterate regarding the "defining moment" experiences and cultures of other generations, thus, creating a "generation gap."

8. Each generation redefines and/or interacts with each phase of life according to the peer personality of the cohort-group. Characteristics identified in one phase of life may significantly shift or change during next phases.

9. Generational points of view—consciously or unconsciously—help to shape an individual's worldview. Members of a generation "look through their generation lens" in responding to life's events and in relating to other generations.

10. A generation's future pattern of attitudes, beliefs, and behavior is somewhat predictable and can be cyclical in nature like the seasons.[1]

THE BUILDER GENERATION

Builders were influenced by the Great Depression, rationing, World Wars I and II, Pearl Harbor, cars, radio, and big band music. Born before 1946, this generation of Americans built the country as we know it today—economically, morally, and religiously. They have produced more U.S. presidents than any other generation. Many continue to hold powerful positions with both wealth and influence. The older women of this generation even built airplanes and other products during World War II while the men were fighting.

Both physically and organizationally, this generation has shaped the church. They are known for their faithful stewardship, loyalty, and encouragement. They are loyal to the institutions they built and served.

The older half of this group, those born between 1900 and 1924, are often known as the GI Generation. They may be builders because of what they overcame—primarily the depression and World War II. They took charge and built homes, businesses, schools, civic organizations, and churches.

The younger part of this group is called the Silent Generation. They were too young to serve in World War II, too old to serve in Vietnam. They are known for their stability and dependability. They have faithfully served and supported the institutions the GI Generation worked so hard to establish.

The family life of the Builder Generation meant loyalty. Divorce rates, though higher for the Silent Generation than the GI Generation, are lower than subsequent generations. They lived on one income. The father often stayed with one company all of his life. Hierarchy was accepted and expected in all organizations; bureaucracy gave order and stability. Many saw the beginning of change at the end of their careers, when loyalty between a company and employees became less valued than the bottom line, and seniority was often seen as a liability instead of an asset.

Gender roles were clearly distinguished, and the family had the stability of hierarchical leadership. They had children and supported schools and bettered communities through civic organizations. This is the family that stayed and prayed together.

The members of this generation supported the church and were loyal to their denominations. They believed in organization and playing by the rules. This group faithfully used eight- and six-point record systems and gave regularly and systematically to the church and through the church to the Cooperative Program.

The builder generation has shaped the church physically and organizationally.

They believed in and supported missions and evangelism. More Builders call themselves Christians than any other generational group. They continue to lead—and even control—the way some churches are organized, the style of worship, and how money is spent. In other churches they are largely ignored.

Some Builders are frustrated in churches today. They don't see younger adults supporting the church with the same determination and loyalty they had. Many are overwhelmed by change. With all the changes they have experienced in their lifetime, more of that change has come in the past 10 years than in all the years prior. They see that same change going on in the church, and many times they don't understand the reason for it. They don't necessarily want everything to be the way it once was, but they do long for stability.

Today members of this generation are or soon will be retired. They have financial concerns, living on Social Security and a pension. They need affordable housing and dependable transportation. They are focused on their health and medical care. Many continue to serve in the church. Others face spiritual concerns as they prepare for death.

Louis Hanks has provided a summary of this generation's strengths, weaknesses, opportunities in the church, and threats. This list focuses on the GI Generation:

The builder generation longs for stability.

Strengths

An attitude of friendliness.
An optimistic outlook on life.
Strong community spirit.
Champion of the "nuclear" family.
Outer-directed and selfless toward others.
Patriotic warriors conquering world evil.
Intensely left-brained—analytical achievers.
Rational problem-solvers and Nobel Prize winners.
Competent superpower builders.
Builders of rockets, suburbs, and interstates.
Technological innovators.
Wide, distinctive gender roles between men and women.
Concern for the well-being of their peers.
World-class leaders, "the establishment."
Gigantic political power, pro-government.
Passionate work ethic.
Achieved affluent standard of living and the "American Dream."

Weaknesses

Focus on science, technology, and humanism over spirituality.
Tend to be overachievers.
Short on ability to frame vision.
Low introspection and personal reflection.
Insensitivity toward others beyond peer group.
Parental nurturing style of own children relaxes protection and structure.
Tends to provide economic rather than emotional support for grown children.

Authoritarian disciplining style.
Overemphasis on masculinity typified by "Father Knows Best."
Diversity devalued.
Overfocus on materialism and consumerism.
Use of nuclear weapons and the cold war.
Sanctioned the outlawing of prayers in the public school.
Massive federal debt.
Strong sense of public economic entitlements.
Environmental abuse.
Demonstrate "we-first" attitude as first "senior citizens."
Prefer to live among like-minded peers away from families.

Opportunities in the Church

Demonstrate a positive and optimistic outlook in elderhood.
Model for stable marriage and family for younger generations.
Strongest mission-minded generation in the 20th century.
Value the Cooperative Program concept of missions teamwork.
Champion the church as a bedrock institution.
Committed and loyal "citizens" of the local church.
Value the church organized for ministry.
Continue to preside as the stewards of financial issues.
Leading tithers and build financially sound congregations.
Positive spirit and contagious energy in the church community.
Good health, longer life, and desire to participate in purposeful activity;
    10 percent of the total population is over 70.
Wealth of experience and know-how can be tapped and shared.
Value the role of the deacon as administrator with the pastor.
Rich source to lead outreach efforts in retirement communities.

Threats

Fear being cast aside and not valued or appreciated.
Physical decline will be hard to face, leading to depression.
Increasingly lonely senior adults may be inclined to try suicide.
Of all adults, 6 percent of women and 1 percent of men are widowed and
    may require special attention.

As this generation ages and dies, churches will lose their strongest tithers, most loyal participants, and the original builders of successful church programs.[2]

This list focuses on the younger half of the Builder generation, the years of the Silent Generation:

Strengths

Strong sense of "other-directedness."
Champions of a pluralistic, inclusive, multicultural society.
Outstanding human relational skills.
Generally compassionate, sensitive, empathetic, polite.
Nonjudgmental fairness and openness.

Strong social consciousness.

Raised to be survivors and savers.

Advocates of racial harmony and peace.

Driving force of the special education movement.

Value structure and organization.

Process, planning, policy, and systems oriented.

Compliant with and protective of institutional order.

High educational achievement—especially for men.

Prefer helping careers like teaching, public service, medicine.

Competent experts, managers, bureaucrats, administrators.

Excellent facilitators, negotiators, therapists.

Creative, poetic, artistic, musical.

Advantaged, low competition due to small generation.

Financially prosperous due to rise in income and wealth.

Strongest generation of caring grandparents.

Weaknesses

Raised in the most overprotected environment of the century, became low riskers and conformists.

"Be seen and not heard" attitude from parents created early attitudes of insecurity and passivity.

As youth, tended to be withdrawn, unimaginative, unadventurous, no burning causes.

Raised their own children with the most underprotected, hands-off nurturing style of the century.

Pluralistic attitudes of many create tolerance for all lifestyles and worldviews.

Many express a value-neutral view of life, "I'm OK, You're OK."

Emphasize process over principles.

Compelled to compromise to reach consensus to make decisions, easily swayed, can't wrap things up.

Overkill in use of focus groups, meetings, and analysis resulting often in little getting done.

High rate of abortions.

High rate of divorce and stepchildren.

Advocates of "no fault" divorce laws.

High rate of mothers working outside the home out of choice rather than economic necessity.

High rate of latchkey children with little supervision.

Sense of fairness drove the liberation movements too far—undermining authority and glorifying individual achievement over family obligations.

Most prominent feminist leaders of the women's liberation movement are from this generation.

Rigid commitment to established structure and organization, rules and regulations.

Overemphasis on therapy and psychoanalysis as cures for human problems.

First generation to identify the midlife crisis.

Leading directors, producers, writers, and advocates of X-rated and sexually explicit films and TV.

Political views considered ambivalent and fuzzy.

Opportunities in the Church

Sense of outer-directedness cause them to be leaders in evangelistic outreach.

Spirit of inclusion encourages reaching all groups of people.

Most likely generation to promote racial harmony.

Enjoy and promote intergenerational ministries.

Excellent tithers and advisers on financial issues.

Rich corps of volunteers who give time, talent, and money.

Superb preschool and children's workers.

Sense of adventure as older adults cause them to enjoy working with youth.

Leaders of well-organized and functioning Sunday Schools.

Lead out in special education ministry efforts in the church.

"Seniors-only" activities will not be attractive to this generation, unlike the prior generation; prefer broad groups of interaction.

View deacons' role as servant and minister, not church administrators.

Able administrators; advocates of church constitution and bylaws, policy and procedures, and job descriptions for church staff.

Threats

Security, as a major life goal, can be easily threatened.

Caught financially and emotionally between aging parents and many young adult children still living at home.

Being "brand loyal" to traditional church structure, order, and practices will create significant friction with younger generations.

Openness to varying points of view can weaken biblical doctrine and authority of the Bible.

Secular entertainment leaders continue to drive the values-neutral, sexually explicit film and television industry.[3]

THE BOOMER GENERATION

Baby boomers—a lot of them—were born after World War II. Children of the Builders, they were born between 1946 and 1964. Among the influences that shaped this generation are television; the Cold War; assassinations; civil rights; Vietnam; Kent State; rock and roll; the sexual revolution, including the birth control pill, legalized abortion, and illegal drugs; Kennedy's "new frontier," the peace corps, and the space race; Water Gate and the resignation of President Nixon. Is it any wonder this generation mistrusts authority and government?

Besides upheaval on a national scale, they began to see parents who had been loyal to a company for a lifetime lose their jobs. They were drafted to serve in a war many didn't believe in and came home to disrespect for their efforts. Disillusioned by the very institutions their parents honored and served, Boomers quickly became known as the "me" generation. They were no longer willing to sacrifice for the good of the community.

Their relationship with the church became more personal than institutional. They would rather go to China on a mission trip than give to Lottie Moon. They want relationships, so the church has to provide fellowship and community. They are supportive of individuals but not institutions. They are more tolerant than their parents of differences among people. And while their parents lived to work, this generation works hard and plays hard.

In the family, both spouses work. This generation is the first where more than 50 percent of marriages end in divorce. While both men and women are equally college educated, gender differences are evident in the workplace and home.

Boomers have thrived on technology and snatched on to the latest gadgets. Their motto is, "Buy now, pay later," sending consumer debt soaring. Self-focused, they have responded to marketing slogans that proclaim, "Get it now. You deserve it." They are a generation that has been wealthy but also a generation known more for their spending than for their saving.

At this point in their lives, Boomers are concerned about traditional values, a second career and looming retirement, spiritual search, health and fitness, leisure activities, and trying to slow the pace of their hectic lifestyles. Dealing with midlife transitions, many are experiencing the death of the American dream. Many hit mid-career thinking they were going to soar, only to face lay-offs, downsizing, and starting over again. Now, instead of having money set aside for retirement, many are in debt, struggling to put kids through college, taking care of aging parents, and wondering what to do with adult kids who just won't leave home.

Boomers have radically changed the world. As they've aged, they've become more conservative but remain unpredictable. According to the Barna Report:

> Once viewed as spiritual antagonists, political activists, and non-traditionalists, Boomers have retained their penchant for confounding the experts. Though they were the first generation raised with omnipresent television and were instrumental in introducing computers to the world, they are more likely to read for pleasure than any other generational group in the nation. The generation that made "sex, drugs and rock-and-roll" its theme, Boomers are now only one-third as likely to have extramarital sex as are Busters; are the generation least likely to get drunk; and are no more likely to illegally download music from the Internet than are the Net-impaired Seniors. Despite their early flirtation with eastern religions and philosophy, only 3 percent of Boomers engage in yoga in a typical week (compared to 10 percent of Busters).[4]

Made to go to church as children, many Boomers abandoned it at the first opportunity but returned when their children were born. Today they control many churches. Barna writes: "Even within the local church, Boomers rule the roost. Today, 61 percent of Protestant senior pastors are from our generation. Among the current lay leaders, 58 percent are Boomers. And if money talks, then we have the floor: 50 percent of the money given to churches last year came out of the pockets of Boomers. (That's more than double the amount given by any other generation.)"[5]

Many boomers who left the church returned when their children were born.

A big issue in the church today is becoming who will succeed this generation in leadership roles. Expressing his concern about this, George Barna writes:

Hey, fellow Baby Boomers. Can we talk?

For many years, we have sweated, argued, fought, manipulated, analyzed, partnered, prayed and strategized to get our own way. We wanted the nation's values to reflect our own. We wanted to have our fair share (or more) of the decision-making authority. We wiggled our way into key positions as soon as possible. After a period in which we said the system was the problem, we took over the system. Today, we are the system, and there are two generations following us who see that as a serious issue. …

Unfortunately, we are not good at sharing. If we are the richest generation the world has ever encountered, we are also its most selfish. And we are driven by the one value that defines us and on which we are willing to squander our money: power. We believe so deeply in our decision-making capacity, and we enjoy the control and perks of calling the shots so much, that we have no intention of relinquishing that power, regardless of traditions, expectations, reason or future interests. …

Here's the bottom line: our generation's time on the throne is quickly coming to an end. In 2011 the first Boomer will reach age 65. By 2015, 15 million of us will be 65-plus; by 2020, 31 million; by 2025, the U.S. will harbor a mid-sized nation within its borders of 65-plus Boomers (an estimated 48 million).

If all went according to plan, we'd be hard at work implementing the world's most sophisticated and superbly executed transition plan to install the new strata of leaders. We are brilliant strategists and tacticians—just ask us. No generation has ever risen to the heights of excellence that we have, when we put our minds to it. The Builders were a can-do, get-it-done generation. But the Boomers are the ultimate take-no-prisoners generation when it comes to shaping society—and, in some cases, the world.

But where is that transition plan? … When are we planning to hand over the keys to the kingdoms we have built these last several decades? Who are the successors we are preparing to stand on our shoulders and build on the foundations we have laid—as our fathers did with us?

You'd think that since we are the richest generation in world history, and we have acquired more toys, amenities, comforts, security mechanism and pleasure options than we can even quantify, we'd be excited about helping our children to follow in our footsteps.

It makes sense. But it's not happening.

The sticking point is our core value: power. We love power. We live for power. Power lunches, power ties, power suits, power offices, power titles, power cars, power networks. Whether it is because of an unhealthy desire for control, a reasonable concern about maintaining quality, a sense of exhilaration received from making pressure-packed, life-changing decisions or due to other motivations, Boomers revel in power. The sad result is that most Boomers—even those in the pastorate or in voluntary, lay-leadership positions in churches—have no intention of lovingly handing the baton to Baby Busters.[6]

Transitioning leadership is a big issue in many churches. In others Boomers are leaving the church as quickly as they returned to it when their children were born. With their children grown, many decide that the church is no longer interested in them. Everything is changing beyond their control. Many are slipping away, perhaps even more quietly than the first time. Sometimes the only one to note their disappearance is the church treasurer.

Louis Hanks provides the strengths, weaknesses, opportunities in the church, and threats for this generation:

Strengths

View themselves as a generation of destiny.

Idealism-focused on the inner world of ideas and values.

Passion for finding and knowing truth and principles.

God as Truth is emphasized.

High spiritual sensitivity and desire for spiritual awakening.

High intensity to shape cultural and moral issues and the direction of civilization.

Achieved the most advanced level of education in the century.

View their mission as the new Puritans, purifying society.

Compelled to champion vision, principles, and moral rightness.

Created the most active era of church formation in the 20th century.

Weaknesses

Highest emphasis on individuality among the generations.

For the most part, spoiled and indulged as children and youth.

Most self-absorbed generation when coming of age in the 20th Century.

First wave demonstrated low marital stability and high divorce rates.

First wave were the major contributors to skyrocketing abortions.

Tend to be workaholics due to intensity of focus on careers; view work as self-fulfillment.

Strong-willed, unyielding opinions on most issues

High level of personal perfectionism.

Tend to spend rather than save money, building significant debt.

Many need assistance in carrying out the practical "how to" dimensions of a major cause.

Tend to have difficulty achieving consensus and mobilizing as a unit.

First wave had to catch up training for the computer revolution.

Tend to be judgmental.

Actions can be ruthless, selfish, and arrogant.

Generally, a low interest in personal evangelism.

Opportunities in the Church

Desire and expect authenticity from their spiritual leaders.

Their style of leadership takes a righteous, moral point of view.

They will tend to want to influence the culture and values of the church.

Most respond negatively to high levels of organization, process, and hierarchy and prefer simple models of structure in the church and small groups.

Their incredible spiritual thirst opens the door to reaching the generation with the message of the gospel.

Their belief in absolute principles of right and wrong tend to make them practice deductive logic over inductive experimentation, but many like to discover biblical truth for themselves.

Prayer, fellowship, and support groups are valued.

Both men's and women's ministries will flourish even though opportunities for couples to study and minister together are valued.

They prefer the informal over the formal.

Men and women look for ways to be a better spouse and parent.

Creative approaches to worker enlistment often are necessary to fill teacher positions.

They will expect careful attention to their children from quality religious education to protection at youth retreats.

While most desire to grow in biblical knowledge and doctrine, many prefer personal choice and flexibility in the selection of topics of study.

Many actively participate in meaningful moral and ministry causes in the community.

Threats

A great demarcation line exists between persons born before and after 1945 or World War II, and the potential for conflict exists.

Power displayed by big institutions including the church turn them off.

Many prefer to support local missions and ministries rather than national or worldwide, cooperative ministries.

Compared to previous generations, they are not strong tithers.

They tend to focus on imposing principles over the church's financial security.

A tension exists between advocates of marketing the church to the unchurched through low-key techniques and those who feel this approach softens the confrontational message of the gospel.

A tension exists between those who remained loyal to the church and those who left but came back to the church.

Many prefer contemporary styles of music and worship that often cause tensions with members who prefer traditional approaches.

The overuse of choruses preferred by some of the generation will prevent younger generations from learning the rich heritage of Christian hymns through corporate worship services.

Many prefer to participate in an adult class rather than teach.

With the focus on choice and topical studies in Bible study, churches will need to ensure a balanced, comprehensive, and relevant curriculum plan for Christian growth in all areas of life.

Because they prefer to spend time at home with their families, they will need to recognize the value of participating in quality church ministries that are worth their time.[7]

Busters were born between 1965 and 1981. The Boomer Generation exploded in numbers of births. In 1965, the birth rate in the United States dropped from 3.8 million in 1965 to 3.1 million, a real bust in numbers.[8] They are also called Generation X or Gen X, a generic generation that remains largely unknown and not understood. The X seems to indicate that the world is waiting to see what will be the distinguishing characteristics of this generation.

Busters have been shaped by the AIDS epidemic, legalized abortion (Roe v. Wade), technology, a varying economy, video games and television, the *Challenger* disaster, the fall of the Berlin wall and the end of the Communist threat, the Persian Gulf war, the Clinton administration, and music. Events of this generation have led them to accept situational ethics, truth that is in the eyes of the beholder, and living in shades of gray instead of black-and-white. They are well aware that absolute truth and morality no longer exist in the United States. One Buster said it this way, "No rules, no boundaries, no wacko religious morality."[9]

Not only were Busters the end of the boom of births in the United States, but this generation has also delayed marriage. Disillusioned by their parents' divorce and not wanting to bring children into the world to live as latch-key children, Busters have sometimes had an attitude of "what's the use?" This attitude is reflected in the workplace as well as the home. They are turned off by their parents' work ethic and the lack of resulting rewards. Many move from job to job, changing jobs if they don't feel good about what they are doing or in order to move ahead. They didn't see companies honoring their parents, so they see no reason to stay with an employer when they decide it's time to move on.

Some have said this generation has a short attention span based on their television viewing habits. They quickly tire of one electronic gadget and want the next. Their generation is not known for one type of music. They like different kinds and move from one to another. They are tolerant of diversity, partly because they can't decide what is true. Relationships are important, but they often discard them at the first sign of conflict.

Many Busters see the empty values of their parents' generation and the lack of ethical values exhibited by leaders. They seek truth but don't know where to find it. Since they've experienced that one truth is as good as another, many bounce from one religion to another or begin to incorporate a little of each into their lives.

Many Busters seek truth but don't know where to find it.

If they go to church, they prefer one that has definite beliefs, "clear and convictional doctrine."[10] But most Busters don't go to church. Rainer estimates that only one out of seven go to church.[11]

Louis Hanks summarizes this generation's strengths, weaknesses, opportunities in the church, and threats:

Strengths

Hold a realistic rather than an idealistic view of life.
Demonstrate a streetwise, practical approach to problems.
As a problem is solved, they want to move on to the next one.
Achieved a high level of education.

Prefer practical fields of study and careers.

Perceive themselves to be survivors and resilient.

Accept personal evaluation and critique.

Savvy and literate with multimedia and computer technology.

Demonstrate courage and bravery on the battlefield and in at-risk occupations.

Express high interest in relevant spiritual issues.

Slowed the pattern of divorce and abortions.

Highly value relationships with close friends and family.

Believe in marriage.

Potential to become very creative writers and artists.

Desire clear, step-by-step procedures.

Adventurous.

Practice parallel thinking—read, listen to music, talk at the same time without losing their train of thought.

Willing to experiment with entrepreneurial opportunities.

Independent thinkers.

Will follow an assignment through to completion.

While individualistic, value of community will increase.

Deeply care for and tightly protect their own children.

Urgent but optimistic view of their future in spite of their past.

Weaknesses

Perceived as bad, many came of age emotionally weakened with low self-esteem.

Can be cautious, skeptical, and cynical.

Many have practiced an amoral lifestyle.

Initially perceived by older adults to be slackers and whiners.

Initially low level of economic security, then fueled by 1990's economic expansion, then at-risk unemployment in 2002.

High level of sexual activity and other at-risk behaviors.

Unrealistic expectations desiring to match their parents' level of achievement at an early age.

With the overall divorce rate for all new marriages in 2000 at about 43 percent—down from 50 percent—a major concern about marriage is the threat of divorce; therefore, many believe living together before marriage is a behavior to prevent divorce.

Ravenous consumers and technology junkies.

Many are pleasure seekers.

Many prefer an "edutainment" approach to learning.

Many lack an anchor to a strong set of morals and values.

View whatever works best as their philosophy of life.

View truth as relative rather than absolute

Many have short attention spans and often are passive learners.

Corporations have had to reinvest skill training to overcome deficiencies, and managers often act in the role of parent to them.

Opportunities in the Church

Typically the least likely to attend church, especially since marriage and family have been delayed.

Between 1997 and 2000, the number of adults aged 25 to 34 declined by 6 percent, since there are fewer young adults overall.

The church can reach this generation with relevant, useful biblical messages.

Attracted to nontraditional schedules and spiritual growth options.

The generation will be more responsive to Christianity through a study of apologetics rather than through comparative religions.

Fellowship and relationships draw them to the church and Bible study groups.

Attracted to alternative Christian music bands like Jars of Clay and dc Talk.

A church that cares for and protects their children will more likely reach them.

They want to know that they are loved and the church cares for them.

They desire leaders who are transparent, vulnerable, and most of all real.

The generation will be more responsive to meeting the practical needs of the community rather than the church.

They become involved when the activity is personal and local.

Generally, as international missionaries, are willing to go to the "hard places" like the Last Frontier.

Potentially excellent volunteers and leaders in the church.

The church can increasingly reach and teach them through low-hype but high-tech multimedia strategies.

They desire concrete examples and illustrations.

A common denominator in the church for all generations will be the protection and growth of their children.

Potential to emerge as champions of personal evangelism.

Busters desire leaders who are transparent, vulnerable, and most of all real.

Threats

A rivalry with the previous generation could emerge in society and perhaps in the church—particularly as Boomers rail about the amorality of Busters.

Sustained economic insecurity could hamper their sense of well-being.

Many have a cynical attitude toward some public religious leaders as a result of hypocritical actions.

Not emerging as strong tithers.

Seven out of 10 women work in the labor force and do not have the time and energy to participate in events at the church.

Overhyping reaching strategies and overstating the ministries and opportunities in the church will turn them away.

Their penchant for relativism over absolute truth will require a clear approach to teaching biblical truth.

Delayed marriages will increase the demands on single adult ministries.

The generation—especially males—will take longer to assimilate into the life of the church due to their prolonged reliance on their parents.

With the highest incarceration rate, this generation continues to demonstrate destructive behavior.[12]

Bridgers were born between 1982 and 1994. Some researchers combine this generation with the last. And some combine it with the next, calling the group Millennials. Bridgers have been shaped by live reporting on television, even from war zones; the World Wide Web; the loss of integrity, and therefore respect, for authority figures, government officials, sports heroes, and even clergy, with sex scandals rocking the Catholic Church as well as some local churches; a multiethnic, multicultural world; and violence and terrorism. The issues that have formed Bridgers have led to their being known as the most serious, stressed, and worried generation.

They worry about everything—grades, getting into the right college, finding the right spouse, choosing the right career, finding the best job, staying fit and taking care of their health, the economy, the environment, and terrorism. To deal with their stress they often turn to drugs—both legal and illegal—and alcohol.

This group is spiritual but not very religious. They are truth seekers, but they generally want to determine for themselves what is true, accepting all religions as valid ways to salvation.

This generation is seeing the family redefined. Our country no longer has only families where a child grows up in a home with his or her birth mother and father, blended families, and families led by a single mother. Now there are single-dad families, children being raised by grandparents, children of multiethnicity, children from test tubes and in vitro fertilization, and even homes with two mommies or two daddies.

They are materialistic and want the best of everything. As complicated new items come on the market and they don't have time to determine by a product's attributes which one they want, they determine just to buy "the best," which is usually defined as the most expensive with the most options. Many no longer are content with one home and one car; they aspire to have two or more cars and a vacation home.

Bridgers need unconditional love, a safe place for building relationships, and leaders who won't abandon them. They need to hear the good news of Jesus Christ, and they need a place where they can get involved in ministry to others.

Bridgers are truth seekers, but they generally want to determine for themselves what is true.

VALUES OF GENERATIONAL UNDERSTANDINGS

These brief summaries of American generations show some distinct differences among the generations. Keeping such information in mind is beneficial for a number of reasons. Here is Louis Hanks' list:

Why study the movements, cultures, and influences of each generation? Primarily because the membership roles of most churches are made up every generation. An understanding of the generations:

1. Opens a rich dimension into the core makeup of individuals. It is the peering into the "why" behind the "what." The generational worldview is like DNA—the building block of attitudes, beliefs, and values—that acts or reacts to the Christian and biblical worldview. Generations create broad, structural changes in society.

2. Provides a framework for churches and leaders to understand the context and cultural perspectives of the generations in order to reach secular people.

3. Provides the opportunity for a church to maximize the potential contributions and talents each generation "brings to the church table."

4. Creates an awareness of the strengths, weaknesses, opportunities, and threats involved in building generational relationships and fellowship in the church.

5. Encourages leaders to think with a new mind-set—beyond the typical age segments and life stages that are no longer predictable—to a new level of empathy that allows leaders to resonate with the issues and struggles of the generations.

6. Causes the professional church staff to recognize that all leaders in the church approach their roles and use their gifts from distinctive points of view.

7. Assists Bible study teachers in being relevant with organizational options, issues, teaching methods, and Bible application customized to the generation—and in broad groupings of people—intergenerational application.

8. Assists the church in developing effective leadership training models and leadership tracks, tailored for "generational fit."

9. Creates an opportunity to bridge differences in negotiable church practices including worship styles, church administrative approaches, music preferences, use of materials, and place and time preferences for the structured ministry programs of the church.

10. Compels churches "to look down the road" to anticipate probable trends and to plan accordingly. Churches can more adequately identify needs, issues, and attitudes that will drive far-reaching changes in the future of the church.[13]

How can a church, specifically women's ministry, respond to the differences in generations? First, we must realize that each needs the good news of Jesus Christ, and every generation has many people who do not yet know Him. Second, women in all generations need relationships. They need Christian friends, and their lives are enriched by knowing women of all ages. Third, women need opportunities to serve. All Christian women have gifts, strengths, skills, and talents. Many are just waiting to be asked to put their unique set of abilities to work.

Based on our differences—both personally and generationally—here are a few other things to keep in mind.

- Some women prefer long-term commitments, perhaps a year-long assignment. Others want only a short-term commitment of a week or two.
- Some will want one woman to be in charge; others will respond better to a team approach.
- Some women enjoy Bible study with an "expert" teacher. Others prefer to discuss the topic with their peers, even if they have to search for answers.
- Some will accept anything leaders say, plan, or suggest. Others will challenge everything until they understand it thoroughly.
- As members of the family of God, united in love and service to Him, we can work together and serve side by side with women from all generations.

We live in a postmodern world. It is not generational, though it is often identified more with younger people. It is not something that affects only cutting-edge congregations; it affects everyone. Although many of us may feel more comfortable in a modern rather than a postmodern world, the choice is not ours to make. Postmodernism is a reality in all of Western society. Because change of epochs is gradual, the grand scale of change is harder to see.

To understand postmodernism, let's begin with a little history.[14]

Western civilization can be divided into three epochs: premodernism, modernism, and postmodernism. Premodernism lasted from the beginning of Western civilization until approximately 1500, during which time the worldview was universally God-centered and the church was the most powerful institution. Communication was largely oral. Most people did not read and write. Written language was limited to hand-written documents, and all books were reproduced by scribes. Depictions of biblical stories in cathedral stained-glass windows were not there for beauty alone. They told the stories of the Bible and reminded worshippers of the words of the sermons. The Bible was the authoritative source for all truth; yet few owned, had access to, or could read a Bible. The preindustrial economy was based on agriculture, trade, and craftsmen.

The modern world was industrial and eventually became technological. Although modernism is often equated with the Enlightenment, the age of reason, the Enlightenment is associated particularly with the 18th century, while the modern world is generally much longer, from about 1500 to about 2000. The Enlightenment was a time of progress and optimism because of all humans were accomplishing. It was the end of the age of superstition and myth. With the invention of the printing press, people could more easily learn to read. They were no longer dependent on the church's interpretation of the Bible. Knowledge became power. People began to search for the truth rather than to accept what they were told. Scientific discoveries were being made. Inventions were changing the world. The progress of science and technology led people to believe the world was becoming increasingly better and they had the capacity to solve all problems.

Human reasoning, logic, and science were the basis of understanding—even in helping to explain and interpret God. For many the certainty of science began to replace religion as the source of truth. Reason was more important than faith. It was the beginning of secular humanism.

Knowledge was empirical, certain, powerful, based on science, factual, objective, not based on values, and discernable. Truth was knowledge. It was not subjective but could be verified by science, by cause and effect.

Personal beliefs and conviction were at a subjective level. People dealt with issues of faith and spirituality, ethics, and morals.[15]

The dates for the modern and premodern eras differ somewhat among writers. The date often used, 1500, closely parallels the advent of the printing press, invented by Johann Gutenburg in 1450. Others date the modern era from Descartes' famous 1641 statement, "I think, therefore I am." It certainly represents and defines this age well.

Likewise, dates for ending the modern era and beginning the postmodern age vary. Some date the change in 1969 with Woodstock. Others equate the transition with the fall of the Berlin wall in 1989. Many use the date 2000, the beginning of a new millennium, a new age, and a new way of seeing the world.

The postmodern era marks the end of absolute truth from either the Bible or science. The Enlightenment, the age of reason, has ended. People are not inherently good. They are not becoming increasingly better, nor are they consistently solving problems and making the world a better place.

Each individual chooses what is truth at any particular time and place. Many of those "truths" may contradict and conflict with one another. Everything is based on personal experience rather than belief in any system outside oneself.

Communication is no longer limited to print or even television or radio. The Internet has made information, both good and bad, readily available around the world at the same time. It is up to the reader to determine information's usefulness and accuracy.

Many people see the Bible as only one of many religious books and and consider it, like everything else, subject to interpretation. They perceive all paths to truth as being valid and equal and are suspicious of those who speak with authority.

Reason, which dominated the modern age, is rejected in the postmodern era as the only path to discover truth. Experience and intuition are equally valid. This is much of the basis for subjective truth. Truth discerned by experience or intuition comes from within rather than from an objective search based on scientific processes.

As is evident, postmodernism grew out of modernism. In many ways the new age is a reaction to the failures—or perceived failures—of the modern age. If the modern age claimed to have all the answers, the postmodern world has none. Note the contrast in the following list of parallel descriptors from author Graham Johnston:[16]

Postmodernism allows everything to be based on personal experience.

Modern	Postmodern
romantic view of life	absurd view of life
purpose	play
design	chance
hierarchy	anarchy
word	silence
a completed work	a process
analysis from a distance	analysis through participation
creation/synthesis	deconstruction/antithesis
present	absence
centering	dispersal
semantics/words	rhetoric/presentation
depth	surface
narrative/*grande histoire*	antinarrative/*petite histoire*
metaphysics	irony
transcendence	immanence

Let's try another approach to understand the difference between the modern age and the postmodern. Modern-age television shows focused on the ultimate good of people and their ability to reason and solve problems. Some of those shows include "Father Knows Best," "Ozzie and Harriet," "The Dick Van Dyke Show," and "The Brady Bunch." Postmodern shows make losers the stars. The plot often seems to go nowhere and has no respect for truth and authority. An adult with a modern mind-set may wonder what the point is. Examples include "The Simpsons," "Married with Children," "Seinfeld," and "South Park."

Another example of postmodern television is the "X-files." Supernatural elements took place without scientific or rational explanation. The show revealed our society's underlying suspicion of insiders (those who really know what's going on), perpetually deceiving the public with elaborate conspiracies. ... "X-files" contends life's mysteries are beyond reach, laden in conspiracies too elaborate to unravel. The different perspectives speak to the complexity of life as we enter the new millennium. The truth may be out there, but we will never know it. ... The average Joe is forced to live as an agnostic, muddling through life with unresolved issues. Ambiguity remains constant to postmodernity.[17]

A review of the generational descriptions made clear the number of Christians in each generation who support the church is declining. Chris Altrock notes: "The postmodern era could also be called post-Christian or anti-Christian. The Boomers ... , Busters ... , and Net-Gens [Bridgers] ... are the transitional generations within this cultural shift. The highly publicized differences between these generations can thus be attributed to factors beyond simply generational differences. Their differences are largely the result of the varying degrees to which they have been raised in postmodernism."[18] Altrock lists seven "faces" of postmodernism, saying that postmoderns are uninformed about the basics of Christianity, interested in spiritual matters, anti-institutional, pluralistic, pragmatic, relational, and experimental. He points out that these characteristics may not be unique to postmoderns, but postmoderns display them altogether and with more intensity than people of the modern age.[19]

In *Postmodern Pilgrims,* Leonard Sweet provides an acronym for remembering the primary characteristics of postmoderns: EPIC—experiential, participatory, image-driven, connected.[20] The church must keep these characteristics in mind as its leaders seek to reach those born into and influenced by the postmodern world. Understanding postmodernism is critical to reaching persons in this generation.

Hebrews assures us, "Jesus Christ is the same yesterday, today, and forever" (13:8, HCSB). The gospel message is the same, but we need to communicate it in ways for all generations to hear and respond. "For the Lord is good, and His love is eternal; His faithfulness endures through all generations" (Ps. 100:5, HCSB).

My mother has a little plaque on her kitchen wall with these words, "Home is where we live for one another and all live for God." All five generations of women in my family take those words to heart. Those same words seem fitting for those in the community of faith as well. As we live in relationship with one another and together for God, we will find ways to communicate the good news and work to further His kingdom.

The gospel message is the same, but we need to communicate it in ways for all generations to hear and respond.

[1] Adapted from Louis B. Hanks, *GenScapes: The Cultural Worldviews and Signature Traits of American Generations* (Nashville: LifeWay Christian Resources of the Southern Baptist Convention, 2002), 13.

[2] Ibid., 18-19.

[3] Ibid., 24-25.

[4] "Fragmented Populations Require Diverse Means of Connection," 23 June 2003. http://www.barna.org/FlexPage.aspx?Page=BarnaUpdate&BarnaUpdateID=142. Accessed 28 May 2005.

[5] George Barna, "Gracefully Passing the Baton," 26 April 2004. *http://www.barna.org/FlexPage.aspx?Page=Perspective&PerspectiveID=1*. Accessed 28 May 2005.

[6] Ibid.

[7] Adapted from Hanks, *GenScapes*, 32-33.

[8] Thom S. Rainer, "The Buster Generation," *Leading Adults*, Winter 2003–2004, 26-27.

[9] Ibid., 26.

[10] Ibid., 27.

[11] Ibid.

[12] Adapted from Hanks, *GenScapes*, 38-39.

[13] Ibid., 8.

[14] The historical overview depends heavily on Dan Kimball, *The Emerging Church* (Grand Rapids: Zondervan, 2003).

[15] Graham Johnston, *Preaching to a Postmodern World* (Grand Rapids: Baker, 2001), 25.

[16] Ibid., 27-28. Johnson also cites David Harvey, *The Condition of Postmodernity: An Enquiry into the Origins of Cultural Change* (Cambridge: MIT Press, 1987), 43.

[17] Ibid., 28.

[18] Chris Altrock, *Preaching to Pluralists: How to Proclaim Christ in a Postmodern Age* (St. Louis: Chalice Press, 2004), 8.

[19] Ibid., 9-10.

[20] Leonard Sweet, *Postmodern Pilgrims* (Nashville: Broadman & Holman, 2000), xxi.

Resources

Rainer, Thom S. "The Bridger Generation, the Family, and the Church." *http://www.rainergroup.com/rainergroup/bridger_generation.asp*. Accessed May 28, 2005.

Rainer, Thom S. "The Builder Generation," *Leading Adults*. Summer 2004, 26-27.

Stiller, Brian C. *Preaching Parables to Postmoderns*. Minneapolis: Augsburg, 2005.

Strauss, William and Neil Howe. *Generations: The History of America's Future, 1584 to 2069*. New York: William Morrow, 1991.

Women Using Their Gifts...to Share The Gift

ESTHER BURROUGHS

Growing up with five brothers and sisters, I found that my home was certainly a place where lessons were taught and learned. Once my mother gave my older sister a handful of candies, telling her to divide them with her brothers and sisters. Carefully, my sister carefully counted them out, but the numbers did not come out evenly. Mother watched as my sister pondered the dilemma and decided on a solution. My sister promptly ate enough candy to make the number come out evenly—and then she shared what was left! Her actions were not exactly fair and certainly do not reflect how our Heavenly Father gives gifts to His children.

God's gift-giving is more like my uncle's. I once stayed with my maternal grandmother as we waited for her son, my uncle, to come home from the Navy. Each day I swung on the fence gate, hoping he would come. When the day finally came, he picked me up and carried me down the sidewalk to my grandmother's house. "I have a gift for you," he said. He put his hands behind his back and asked me to choose. I knew that no matter which hand I chose, he would give me the gift anyway.

Perhaps this looks more like God's gift giving; the gift is always there because God does not trick us. James 1:17 says, "Every good and perfect gift is from above, coming down from the Father of the heavenly lights, who does not change like shifting shadows." This is great news in our changing times. No matter how we respond, the Giver of the gift never changes.

Kingdom citizens live with this radical truth! God's gift of salvation and subsequent spiritual gifts are not based on our acceptance or rejection, our worthiness or unworthiness, our temperament, or our personality types—all of which the culture deems important. God's gifts are based solely on His unchanging,

We benefit from relationships with women both in the generations before and after our own.

gift-giving love. Our culture bases much of its behavioral values upon the gifts people receive and the gifts they are able to give. We, as the body of Christ, have the gift our culture truly needs, and it is our challenge to accept and share the gift of Christ through our spiritual gifts. As leaders, we must challenge the women we lead to do the same.

GOD IS CREATOR

First, we must first embrace the truth that we are made in the image of God and are created with a purpose. Paul's words in Ephesians 1 tell us how blessed we are. We have our inheritance in Christ Jesus. We are chosen, holy, blameless, adopted, redeemed, and forgiven according to the riches of His grace. We are blessed with every spiritual blessing in Christ Jesus. What is His is ours, because we are His. God's words to us are like the Father's words to the elder brother, "My son, you are always with me, and everything I have is yours" (Luke 15:31).

Women of each generation can help women of other generations realize that acceptance depends not upon the world's standard, but on Christ's. "God created man in His own image, in the image of God he created him; male and female he created them" (Gen. 1:27). Verse 31 says, "God saw all that he had made, and it was very good." We are "very good" in the estimation of God.

Jesus claimed His birthright and His position as the Son of God. His mission was to die on the cross, taking our place, and giving us new birth. Jesus came to show us what God, His Father, looks like. Jesus asks us to claim our birthright in Him and to live in such a way that others know we are His.

Jesus said to His *earthly parents*, "I must be about My Father's business" (Luke 2:49, NKJV).

Jesus said to *His disciples,* "Don't you believe that I am in the Father, and that the Father is in me? The words I say to you are not just my own. Rather, it is the Father, living in me, who is doing his work" (John 14:10).

Jesus says to *us,* "[You] will do even greater things than these" (John 14:12).

During Jesus' earthly ministry, He showed the world what God is like in human flesh. Several years ago, singer Amy Grant sang a tune titled, "My Father's Eyes." The words challenged: "as the world looks at me, let them see My Father's eyes." Just as Jesus did His Father's work and modeled for the disciples what that looked like, He calls us to imitate God the Father today. We can do that by keeping our eyes on Jesus.

At family reunions we hear remarks like, "She has her mother's eyes" or, "He is just like his grandfather."

While visiting my oldest granddaughter, she said, "Nana, just look! My mother's hands are just like yours." Then she looked at her own hands and said, "And my hands look just like my mother's. Wow, Nana!" She was correct. My daughter has my hands and eyes. Her three daughters have her hands and eyes. One of the miracles and joys of grandparenting is seeing the grandchildren and recognizing the family likeness. That is both frightening and exciting!

We are children of the Heavenly Father, and we share a family resemblance. Does our Heavenly Father delight in our likeness to Him? To be made in His image is an awesome privilege and responsibility. Perhaps heaven will be like a family reunion where everyone notices how much each of us resembles our

We must embrace the truth that we are made in the image of God.

Heavenly Father. I believe we best reflect our Father when we accept our position in Christ, claiming our kinship and remembering whose we are. We should give thanks to our Creator Father and ask Him to help us grow to be more like Him. In Ephesians 5:1 Paul says, "Be imitators of God, therefore, as dearly loved children."

GOD IS GIFT GIVER

Psalm 139 identifies God's uniqueness. He is omnipresent and omniscient.
>   Oh Lord, Thou hast searched me and known me.
>   Thou dost know when I sit down and when I rise up …
>   Even before there is a word on my tongue,
>   Behold, O Lord, Thou dost know it all.
>   Thou hast enclosed me beyond and before,
>   And laid Thy hand upon me.
>   Such knowledge is too wonderful for me (Ps. 139:1-2,4-6, NASB).

Romans 11:33 tells us what Paul believed about this creator God.
>   Oh, the depth of the riches of the wisdom and knowledge of God!
>   How unsearchable his judgments,
>   and his paths are beyond tracing out!

We reflect our Father when we accept our position in Christ, claiming our kinship, and remembering Whose we are.

Even in our computer world, and even with word search, nothing can compare to the ways of God.

The psalmist also says there is no place we can go to escape God. I love the line, "Darkness is as light to you [God]" (Ps. 139:12). When women go through dark times or situations in their lives, they can cling to the fact that nothing has changed with God. He is light and in Him is no darkness. The psalmist continues,

>   I praise you because I am fearfully and wonderfully made;
>   your works are wonderful,
>   I know that full well (Ps. 139:14).

With the psalmist we must declare, "How precious to me are your thoughts, O God! How vast is the sum of them!" (Ps. 139:17). Imagine a God whose thoughts about us outnumber the very sand of the sea. That is a thought worthy of our praise and adoration.

We accept that the God of creation is our Creator, and He intimately knows us and calls us into a personal relationship with Himself. From that intimacy, we share the gifts He has given us with the body of Christ, which will impact our world and the kingdom of God.

GOD'S SPIRIT EMPOWERS THE GIFT

In his book *Mirror, Mirror on the Wall,* Ken Hemphill says, "Spiritual gifts are individualized endowments of grace from the Father, equipping you to play a vital role in His plan for the redemption of the world."[1] Consider characteristics of gifts that need to be shared with the women under your leadership.

The Holy Spirit Reveals the Gifts

At the very moment we accept Jesus Christ as our personal Savior, the Holy Spirit enters our lives, giving us gifts. That is referred to as the baptism of the Holy Spirit. The baptism of the Holy Spirit is a one-time experience. But the filling and empowering of the Holy Spirit is a continual process. Without this continual filling, our gifts would be powerless. The Holy Spirit gives specific gifts to every believer (see Eph. 4:1-16). No one is left out.

Prayer Is the Key in Discovering Gifts

Each of us should ask God to reveal our special areas of giftedness. We can ask others in the church body to pray with us to help us discern our personal gifts. As we pray, we shouldn't be afraid to try different things in the body of Christ which will help us discover our gifts. We can teach preschoolers, work with teenagers, or share in a Meals-on-Wheels program. Through prayer and the use of our talents, the Holy Spirit not only helps us recognize our gifts, but also helps us develop them.

The Body of Christ Grows Stronger as Gifts Are Used

Each believer is to exercise her gifts in the body of Christ—for the body of Christ. As we share our gifts with others, we should each ask ourselves: *Am I making myself look better, or the body of Christ look better?* Our gifts are not regarded as spiritual awards but are God's means for service and ministry. We must give our gifts back through the body of Christ.

In 1 Corinthians 12, Paul paints an amusingly profound word picture of the body of Christ. He says the body has many members. Every member has a function and is a vital part. He reminds us that no part is better than any other. No part is greater than any other part. All parts of the body are needed for the body to be complete, to properly function, and to fulfill its purpose in the kingdom of God. The reason for our spiritual gifts is the building of the body of Christ through the ministry of those gifts, which brings glory to the Father in His plan of redemption.

Too many Christians today are working in the body of Christ without exercising their gifts. The body of Christ will be healthy only when each believer is fulfilling her purpose, exercising her individual gifts, and not just filling a position.

Nothing is more exciting than watching Christians use their gifts in the body of Christ and watching how that enhances and impacts the whole body and ultimately the kingdom. Spiritual gifts utilized energize the body of Christ. For instance, when I am the recipient of another's gift, I am drawn to Christ and encouraged in my faith. When I share my gift in the body, I sense the Spirit and the power of God working through me and find it humbling beyond explanation. I feel utter dependence upon the Gift Giver, and know that without His touch, I have nothing to share. My gift is God's gift; it is for His kingdom.

We should not waste a moment desiring another's gift. We should work hard to develop the gifts God has given us to make the body stronger. "You are exactly who God designed you to be. Your function is vital to the body because God made you just as He desired."[2]

Don't waste a moment desiring another's gift. Work hard to develop the gifts God has given you.

Gifts Are Given Out of God's Grace.

Paul points to the work of the Spirit by repeating phrases such as "same Spirit," and "one Spirit" (see 1 Cor. 12: 4,9). Verse 4 uses the term that comes from the Greek root word for *grace* and can be translated *manifestation of grace.* Our gifts are given because of God's grace, not for our boasting. When I think of the manifold grace of God, I think of a pleated skirt. It has pleat after pleat, as if there were no beginning or end. God's grace is like that: many-folded and unending.

The Scripture theme for Women's Ministry is taken from 1 Peter 4:10, "Based on the gift they have received, everyone should use it to serve others, as good managers of the varied grace of God" (HCSB). The Father would have us accept our gifts from Him, always aware that He is the Giver, we are the receivers, and in obedience, we share the gifts with the body of Christ. This brings glory to God through the body of Christ, His church.

Gifts Should Be Affirmed and Celebrated.

Recently, I prepared to speak to a very diverse group of women. In preparation, I looked at 1 Corinthians 12. I had read it many times, but on this day the Holy Spirit highlighted it for me. "There are different kinds of gifts, but the same Spirit. There are different kinds of service, but the same Lord. There are different kinds of working, but the same God works all of them in all men" (1 Cor. 12:4-6). Wow! As I read, I wondered, *How can I question or critique another's gift when the same Spirit gave gifts to all?* Believers must affirm and celebrate each other's part in the body. Every gift is special.

Gifts Should Be Accepted Among Believers.

Christians are dependent on each other. Women need to learn to accept each other's gifts, knowing each gift is placed in the body for the purpose of ministry. We will be more like Christ as we celebrate these gifts and our places in God's family, desiring the family portrait to better resemble Him.

Christians are dependent on each other.

When we understand different gifts in the body are given by the same Spirit—all for the purpose of sharing God's redeeming love with the world, we take the focus off ourselves and our gifts and place it properly at the feet of Christ. We recognize we are stewards of the gifts, not owners. We are parts of Christ's body. Only when we accept our gifts as part of that body do our gifts have meaning. If today's church is to make any difference in the world, the whole body of Christ must put aside labels, idioms, and programs, and join hands to imitate Christ to our culture.

Women are caregivers by nature, but we should go a step further. We must affirm, encourage, and help develop the spiritual gifts in others, empowering them to exercise their God-gifts in and through God's family, the church.

Take time to read 1 Corinthians 12. Then read just a bit more and see chapter 13 through the lens of chapter 12. You will have a better understanding of how God calls His body to live as you discover that we *never* look more like Him that when …

- we use the gifts He has given us.
- the gifts of the body bring glory to Christ.
- the body, the church, reaches out to become Christ in everyday living because we are *kingdom citizens.*

The goal in any women's ministry should be: *Women gifted by the Holy Spirit ... empowered by the Holy Spirit ... ministering to one another ... as good stewards of the manifold grace of God.*

GOD COMPELS US TO USE OUR GIFTS

Our spiritual gifts are to be used to minister to others in the name of Christ. The amazing thing about giving away our gifts is that both givers and receivers are blessed. The old saying *what goes around comes around* is true. Let me share some true-life stories that may trigger an idea or two for your women's ministry.

The Gift of Hospitality

A church in the western United States designed a dinner event to intentionally reach the unchurched in their community. In the beginning, two or three church couples planned to get together for dinner. Each shared in the preparation—from cleaning the house to preparing and serving the food. This way the work of hospitality was shared.

Hospitality is difficult today with the schedules we have to keep, but what a great idea! Planning an event with others is always more fun. As time passed, each couple began inviting unchurched neighborhood friends or coworkers to the special dinner. The conversation flowed easily among the couples.

Later in the year, they planned another dinner event. This time, the couples exchanged responsibilities and again invited their unchurched friends. By now, they knew each other's interests, and sharing about their relationships to Christ became easier.

Later in the year the church hosted a banquet, featuring quality entertainment and a special guest speaker. Once again, the unreached friends were invited as special guests. At the end of the message, an appeal was given to anyone who might be interested in finding out more about a relationship to Christ. In the first year of this event, 80 people came to know Christ. That, my friends, is kingdom living—sharing the gift of hospitality to share *The Gift*.

The Gift of Listening with the Heart

One dedicated pastor's wife makes her way to meet the neighbors each time her family moves into a new community. After introducing herself, she offers their children a Saturday morning play time with her children. She tells her neighbors she will tell the children Bible stories, help them do crafts, and play games with them. She shares her gift of love for children to impact God's kingdom.

When I heard this woman's story, I was stunned. My children are grown, but when they were little I often invited their friends over to play. To be honest, I never thought of it as a time to share Bible stories!

Think of the impact this kind of ministry could make in today's world with so many mothers working outside the home. Think of single mothers and fathers who need this gift. By exercising this ministry on a regular basis, women might develop neighborhood ministries. How wonderful for the children of single moms or dads who don't have time for such wonderful Saturday morning or after-school activities to experience God's love through a neighbor! It seems

In giving away your gift, you and the receiver are both blessed.

to me this kind of caring, nurturing gift could make the kingdom of God look more inviting.

I am convinced that if we would refine our gift of listening—listening with our hearts—we would have opportunity to share Christ more often. Each of us should look at the people in today's world. We'd see tired faces, stooped shoulders, tears, anger, and loneliness. But some of us have the spiritual gift of listening. We could change the kingdom of God with listening hearts.

The Gift of Being Yourself

Recently, I was headed for a weekend speaking engagement for high school girls. On the flight out, we experienced airplane trouble, and I knew I would not make it in time to speak. Forty-five minutes into the flight the pilot said, "Ladies and gentlemen, we have an indication that there is a problem with the left engine, so to make sure everything is all right, we are heading back to Atlanta. We're sorry for any inconvenience we've caused you."

As the passengers left the plane, many began attacking the ticket agent. A woman standing by me began literally eating cigarettes, not smoking them! She would put one in her mouth, bite it, and throw it down. Somewhat out of control, she began to rant and rave about not getting back on the plane. She grabbed me by the arm, asking me how to get to a bus station. (I was dressed in red and black that day, so I guess she thought I worked for the airline.) I looked up the phone number and gave it to her.

I sat down beside her and began trying to calm her. As we quietly talked, she said, "Well, what's wrong with you anyway?"

"Nothing," I responded.

"That's what I mean," she said. "Why are you so calm?"

I explained that I was on my way to speak to a group of teenage girls about the most important relationship in my life. I'm not sure if she was interested in what I was saying or if what I was saying took her mind off that plane! I continued to share with her my relationship to Jesus Christ and how that made a difference in my life. About that time, a man whom I had never seen before tapped me on the shoulder, saying we could get rebooked through Charlotte and I could go with him to the ticket counter. As I closed my conversation with the woman, I noticed she had calmed down. I wished her well.

As I walked away, I stopped to compliment the ticket agent on the way she had handled the crowd. I asked for her name and badge number so I could write the airline about her good work. Stunned by my remark, she said, "You just made my day! Thank you!"

Being gifted in the body of Christ simply means using our spiritual gifts in the most natural way. that may include being courteous, listening, looking up phone numbers, being calm in the chaos of life, or just giving the world a glimpse of part of the body of Christ. We can impact the kingdom of God with the secret weapon of spiritual giftedness!

Oh, by the way, the man I mentioned earlier said to me as we walked away, "I'm a deacon at a church here in this city. I prayed for you as I heard you share Christ with that woman." Yes!

The Gift of Grace

The CEO of a successful company recently discovered a huge mistake had been made by her employees. It would cost the company an enormous amount of money to fix. The CEO raised her voice, accusing the supervisor and the other people at fault. Then she walked back into her office and slammed the door, rattling the windows and pictures, and feeling a bit justified in her response. She later explained, "After settling in my office and reflecting on what had happened, I remembered that God is *my* CEO, and He would not have been pleased with my actions."

Feeling convicted, she went back to the workroom and apologized to the staff. Later, her office door opened; the supervisor peeked inside and said, "I guess this Christian thing does work after all."

In this scenario, the kingdom looked more like Christ because of the obedience of one part of His body that displayed the spiritual gift of grace.

As believers, we are part of something much bigger than ourselves. It takes every one of us giving everything we can to make the body look more like Christ. When one part (like that CEO) makes a positive difference, the whole body looks good. Likewise, when one part fails to use his or her gift, the whole body fails. What an awesome thought!

My prayer is that you will take the issue of your gift-part of the body of Christ seriously and challenge the women in your ministry to do the same. Waste no time or concern about another person's gifts, except, of course, to encourage them. Consider instead the heavy realization that without every part being its best, the whole cannot be complete. It will not bear the family resemblance of Christ as it should. We are kin by the blood of Christ, and our family must act like a family—knowing what it cost God to make us His children.

As believers, we are part of something much bigger than ourselves.

The Gift of Bible Teaching

During a recent visit to the doctor's office, I glanced at the calendar and said to the nurse, "That's the wrong date on your calendar. I only know because today is my 35th wedding anniversary."

"Wow," she replied. "How have you stayed married that long?"

I replied with a grin, "I'm sure it's because we have worked hard at it and had lots of help from Christian friends, family, and the church."

The nurse shared that she was a new Christian, and I enthusiastically asked for the details. Because of the recent events in the Middle East, she explained, many people on the hospital staff had been asking, "Who are the Jewish people?" As a result, a doctor began teaching a Bible class at noon on Thursdays to anyone on the staff who wanted to come. Not only did this nurse attend his class, but she asked Christ into her heart because of it. She went on to tell me that before the Bible study was over, 19 people in that hospital had accepted Christ. Because one part of the body exercised his spiritual gift of teaching, the kingdom of Christ grew.

The Gift of Witnessing

I have a dear and quite remarkable friend who has a talent for quilting. Her home is like a museum; her quilts enhance the warmth of her house. She also has the gift of evangelism. While living in Utah, she invited her Christian friends for coffee one day. She showed them the quilts she had designed based on hymns that told the story of her spiritual journey with Christ. Prior to her friends leaving, she told them, "I want you to pray for me next Friday because I am inviting my Mormon neighbors to my house, and I'm going to share my testimony with them. I was just practicing on you." She used her quilting gift and her own faith story to invest in growing God's kingdom.

The Gift of Sharing a Talent

My friend was a career model before she married and had a family. As her daughter entered the teen years, she and her daughter planned a sleep over. They sent invitations to the daughter's school and church friends, baked the refreshments, and prepared for guests. The mother gathered makeup, mirrors, and accessories.

The girls had a wonderful evening of fun, learning how to present themselves in the best possible way. They learned how to take care of their bodies, and my friend also shared about inner beauty and God's desire for our hearts to belong to Him. What a gift from mother to daughter. She gave them the gift of her time and experience, investing in their lives for the sake of the kingdom.

The Gift of Being Part of the Family of God

I got on the motorized cart in the Dallas/Fort Worth Airport to go from one side of the airport to the other. A priest got on at the next stop. Looking at me, he asked, "Is Dallas your home?" "No," I responded, thinking I would tell him where I lived. Before I could complete my sentence, he said, "It's not mine, either. Mine is Cloud 22." I then replied, "If yours is 22, then mine is 23." He reached out, gave me a high five, and said, "Then praise God! You must know Jesus." There we were, total strangers until that exchange of information, now celebrating the gift of the family of God while tooling through the Dallas airport in a motorized cart! Everyone on the cart heard our testimony.

THE RESULT OF "GIFT GIVING"

Often I say in my seminars, "We can live in the expectancy of what the Holy Spirit will do through gifts and obedience as we share Christ in the everydayness of living."

Several years ago, I came to know that Uncle Peter, the one who gave me gifts as a little girl, did not know Christ and was deathly ill. Mother told me that my father had shared Christ with my uncle many times, but he always responded that he was just not ready. My heart nearly broke.

I promised my mother I would join her and my aunt in praying for Uncle Peter's salvation. I learned from Oscar Thompson's book *Concentric Circles of Concern* to pray, " 'Lord, engineer circumstances in [Uncle Peter's] life to draw him to You.' "[3] And as I began to pray, "God, manage the circumstance in Uncle Peter's life to bring him to Yourself," I was led to write my uncle a personal letter, the first one in many years.

When we use our spiritual gifts, we show a life invested in kingdom authority.

I had just read a book about expressing yourself in word pictures to conjure up emotions and help the receiver accept the message. I did just that. I wrote all about being at my grandmother's home as a little girl. I reminded him of the old outhouse, complete with the Sears catalog; the crunching sound of the cinder sidewalk under our feet as we walked around; the gate upon which we used to swing and get in trouble; and the softness of my grandmother's comforting arms. I even reminded Uncle Peter about the times he brought me small and simple gifts and how they were so appreciated. Then I closed, "Please forgive me that I have never shared with you the most important gift in all my life," and I shared the Roman Road plan of salvation and the prayer to pray to receive Christ. "This is God's gift to you, Uncle Peter," I added, "and I will be praying that you will receive this gift."

Sometime later, my aunt visited Uncle Peter one last time to share the gift of Christ. After the nurse let her in., she told Uncle Peter why she'd come. He whispered with a slight smile, "That's all settled. I got a letter from Esther."

God took different gifts in the body to bring a child to Himself. He used my father's consistent testimony. He used prayers, concern, letters, and caring relationships with my mother, grandmother, Uncle Peter's sister, and his niece to love Uncle Peter into the kingdom. What a reunion we will have in heaven!

When people see you, do they see your Heavenly Father's eyes, hands, heart, and likeness? What imitation of our Heavenly Father are you currently living? Are you challenging the women in your women's ministry to do the same?

Please, with love and abandon, give the gift Christ has endowed to you to bring Him glory and to impact eternity. Spiritual gifts are about kingdom living, family reunions, and celebration. We are the family of Christ.

What imitation of our Heavenly Father are you currently living?

---

[1] Ken Hemphill, *Mirror, Mirror on the Wall* (Nashville: Broadman Press, 1992), 13.
[2] Ibid., 62.
[3] Oscar Thompson, *Concentric Circles of Concern* (Nashville: Broadman Press, 1981), 77.

Beginning a Women's Ministry

CHRIS ADAMS

We cannot stay where we are and go with God.

In *Experiencing God,* Henry Blackaby says we cannot stay where we are and go with God. In other words, our relationship with Him must constantly change, grow, and move forward. In women's ministry this means we must be willing to obey God's calling to develop opportunities for service and growth, even if "we have never done it that way before."

So, what things should we consider when God leads us to begin a women's ministry? Let me suggest the following process.

PRAY

The first thing you as a women's leader must do is pray. Your vision for women in your church and community must be God's vision, or it will be on a shaky foundation. Through prayer, allow the freedom for God's Holy Spirit to guide all you do. So pray with a group of ministry-minded women to see where God is at work and how He wants you to join Him in developing ministry to and with ladies in your church. Focus your prayer on changing lives rather than creating programs. Some items to include in your prayer are leadership, program options, moving the ministry from entertainment to discipleship, purpose, organizational structure, reaching more women for Christ through this ministry, and the staff person to whom you will relate. Effective preliminary prayer could take weeks, months, or even a year before you proceed to the next step. Even then, prayer must continue to be a thread woven into every area of this ministry if you are to stay in tune with God's leadership.

SHARE YOUR VISION WITH THE CHURCH STAFF

Share with your pastor or staff liaison your vision for women's ministry. Several pointers may help as you take this step.

1. Be specific. Consider presenting a one-page proposal that lists goals and objectives for consideration.
2. Remember that it is your responsibility to contribute a female point of view to what may be an all-male staff. Be respectful.

3. Let the staff know that women's ministry is available to assist and help in all programs of the church.

4. Know and obey church policies concerning facilities, childcare, and publicity.

5. Listen to the staff. Ask their perspectives and expectations of women's ministry and their advice as you begin planning. Take interest in their areas of ministry. Learn from them. Consider asking, "What can I do to undergird your area of ministry?"

6. If you attend a staff meeting, understand the rules. Ask questions ahead of time to understand what is expected during these meetings.

7. Choose the right time to address the pastor or staff. Ask for an appointment that allows the time you will need. Try giving back the last five minutes of that time. Your staff will appreciate that unexpected gift! You might even send a written list of questions ahead of time for their consideration.

8. Be specific and take a short list of issues to discuss. Remember to get to the bottom line quickly. A church staff's plate is full already. Try not to add more information than is necessary by giving details they do not need.

9. Turn in calendars early so the women's activities will not conflict with other church functions.

10. Ask the pastor's wife and/or other staff wife to serve as an advisor on your committee. She can contribute her unique perspective on various issues, but do not expect her to attend or be involved in everything your women's ministry is planning.

11. If whatever you desire to do will hinder the church in any way—drop your plan! Women's ministry exists to build up and enrich the church.

NETWORK

Look beyond the borders of your church to see what others are doing to reach and disciple women. Begin to network with others who are involved in women's ministry in your community and state, both within and outside your denomination (see information on groups you can network with on p. 225). Find out what is being done, what is working, and problems to avoid in beginning and growing a women's ministry. Look for churches that have a well-developed ministry with women, and spend the day with the leaders. Call, write, and get together with those in the network you develop. Ask how they got started. Remember, what works in one church will not necessarily work in another, but giving and receiving ideas, resources, and information stimulate thinking and guide prayer. Look together with other women's leaders for answers to common questions regarding women's ministry.

Networking with others will strengthen your ministry with women.

ASSESS NEEDS

Once you've covered your efforts in prayer and have gained staff approval, gather a group of women from all areas of your church to comprise a "survey study team." Team members should be of various ages and life phases. These women should believe that God desires women to know Christ personally and to mature as believers. The purpose of this group is to decide what type of survey (see Sample Questionnaire, p. 66) will best identify the needs, availability, time preference for studies and ministry activities, child care needs, and other important information of those in your church. No matter how meaningful the activities, if it is not what women want or need, they will not participate. Women today want choices, and they want to be asked, not told, what they need.

You must have a clear understanding of your church as well as the needs of the ladies in it to begin developing an effective women's ministry. Check to see what ministries are available through your church. Do not duplicate what is being offered. Instead, encourage women to participate in those ministries while offering new ones.

DEVELOP A PURPOSE STATEMENT

As you pray, meet together, and develop a survey, you and your team should also be forming your purpose statement. This could be one sentence or a short paragraph that can be shared whenever you are asked what your women's ministry is all about. The purpose statement of your group should support that of your church and should have a scriptural reference. All activities and plans should reflect this statement. If any plan does not support your purpose, you should question whether it is valid. You may choose to use words such as evangelize, encourage, fellowship, inform, teach, pray, worship, learn, glorify God, serve, minister, and involve in missions in your statement. The following examples will help you get started:

- The vision of women's ministry is to seek to fulfill Christ's mission by encouraging women with a sense of belonging to God and each other, enabling them to become all they are to be in Christ, and equipping them to bless others with the love, grace, and truth of Jesus Christ (Eph. 4:11-12).
- Women's Ministries Goals: Sharing Christ with those who do not know Him, strengthening Christians who do, and fervently praying for each ministry opportunity (Matt. 28:19-20).
- We purpose to keep balance between being ministered to and ministering to others, to confront women with the love of Jesus through outreach, to minister to the needs of our ladies, to help them develop their God-given potential as persons of value in their homes, church, and community, and to involve them in creative service under the Holy Spirit's leadership (1 Cor. 14:26).
- The Women's Ministry is designed to meet the complex needs of today's woman, providing encouragement, prayer, and guidance. Our goal is to bring together women of all ages and stages for edification and service opportunities. As women grow and mature in godliness, they are better equipped to nurture and serve in their families, to enrich the church, and to evangelize their communities (Titus 2:3-6, 2 Tim. 2:2).
- The goal of women's ministry is to grow in our relationship with the Lord, to serve Him with our Christian sisters, and to minister to the world around us (1 Pet. 4:10).

You must have a clear understanding of your church as well as the needs of the ladies in it to develop an effective women's ministry.

CONSIDER CHILDCARE

If you intend to reach young mothers, you will need to consider how best to provide for their children during your women's ministry activities. If your church cannot cover the expense, consider charging participants a small fee (perhaps $1 per child) or passing the plate so everyone can help.

To keep costs low, consider enlisting help from the church. For instance, several youth, supervised by an adult, may volunteer their time or accept donations toward a youth camp or missions trip. You can also ask those who are not attending the function to volunteer their time to take care of the children. Due to distance from their families, grandmothers often are not able to spend much time with their grandchildren. Childcare may be the perfect ministry for them. Perhaps their dads would volunteer for special events.

Remember, if you provide a Bible lesson for the children during your weekly activities, moms will be even more encouraged to leave their children in childcare, knowing that their children's spiritual lives are also important to women's ministry. Continually lift your childcare workers to the Father in prayer. They are a vital part of your ministry.

DETERMINE FINANCIAL NEEDS

Consider your financial resources for your women's ministry. Does your church have budget money available to support this ministry? If not, you must make each endeavor recover its costs by selling tickets, charging for Bible study materials and child care, or taking donations. Remember to also consider your human resources. Many people would be happy to donate time, talents, and materials to help promote women's ministry.

CONDUCT A SURVEY

Compile and print the survey your survey study team selected. The most successful way to receive feedback from the survey is to promote it through Sunday morning Bible study. With the approval of your minister of education, take a few minutes at the beginning of the class or department time to explain why you are requesting that the ladies complete the survey. Ask them to fill it out and hand it to you before their class begins. You may want to do this two Sundays in a row to allow greater participation.

If you choose not to conduct a survey, there are other options for discovering needs. You can go to an uninvolved person or group and ask them what it would take to get them involved in ministry with women. You could also target a particular group such as young mothers or professional women and spend time talking with them to discover their needs. The goal is to uncover unmet needs and begin finding ways to meet them.

ORGANIZE LEADERSHIP

Once the survey is taken and the information compiled, it is time to choose a team leader, director, chairperson, or coordinator, who will help you facilitate women's ministry. She must be an organizer, have great diplomatic skills, have a faithful daily walk with Christ, and have time to devote to the ministry. Decide with her ahead of time how many studies or ministries you will offer, and add leaders for each area (see Building Your Leadership Team, p. 106). Remember, you cannot do everything the first year. Use the results from the survey to determine what you will do first. Other opportunities may be added as needed to provide for growth of the ministry and the individuals within it.

Local churches use a number of organizational models. We have illustrated four at the end of this book (see pp. 226-227). No two women's ministries will look alike. Get ideas from a variety of sources, but let God design a ministry unique to your church.

COMMUNICATE WITH THE CHURCH

As you promote your women's ministry, use a variety of ways to communicate to your church. Bulletin boards, church newsletters and bulletins, pulpit announcements, and mailings are excellent ways of getting the word out. (See "Publicity and Promotion," p. 216.) Word of mouth may still be the most effective way of encouraging women to participate, grow, and minister. Challenge your women to invite at least two other women to your first event.

KICK OFF YOUR WOMEN'S MINISTRY

Make the kick-off for your new ministry special. You might plan a tea and time of fellowship and information to take place in a home. In each room you could station one ministry leader. As women visit that room, they could learn about a specific ministry being offered as a part of the new women's ministry program. Offering handouts or favors including pertinent information would be beneficial to this approach.

Allow leaders and participants time to enjoy and get to know one another. Make sure each woman understands how special she is and what a benefit she would receive by being a part of your women's ministry. Help her see that there will be opportunities for her to grow and develop her spiritual life, develop relationships, share her faith, and minister to others. Let her know that your ministry needs her gifts and talents.

STUDY GOD'S WORD

Just as prayer must undergird women's ministry and is essential to its effectiveness, studying God's Word is also essential. Women must diligently study the Bible as they seek God's will for every area of their lives.

Bible study needs to be at the heart of your women's ministry. Plan various opportunities for your women to learn God's Word. Several in-depth Bible studies for women are available from LifeWay Press. See "Tapping Resources for Women's Ministry" on page 222 for suggested studies, or visit www.lifeway.com for a growing list of options.

Bible study needs to be at the heart of your women's ministry.

In addition to the women's studies listed, in-depth courses such as *Experiencing God: Knowing and Doing the Will of God; The Mind of Christ; Life in the Spirit;* and *WiseCounsel: Skills for Lay Counseling* are excellent study options for women's ministry participants. Six-week courses available are *In God's Presence: Your Daily Guide to a Meaningful Prayer Life, When God Speaks: How to Recognize God's Voice and Respond in Obedience,* and *Living God's Word: Practical Lessons for Applying Scripture to Life.* Support-group resources such as *Making Peace with Your Past* and *The Search for Significance Workbook* are also excellent tools to use in your ministry.

EVALUATE

Continual evaluation will keep your ministry fresh. Evaluate the effectiveness of studies, groups, leaders, projects, special events, and mission and service opportunities. By updating the program from year to year, you stay abreast of current needs and how to meet them. (See sample evaluations on pp. 64 and 65.)

As you further develop your women's ministry, keep in mind that you must offer a diverse ministry to minister to women with various needs. As the needs of your women and their families change, your ministry options should adapt to meet them. Flexibility is key to providing meaningful, effective ministry to and with women in your church and community.

BALANCE

The key to an effective women's ministry is balance. Although the extent of ministries you can provide and the organizational structure may differ, the principles are the same no matter what size the church. In your own life you must balance what you take in spiritually with what you give back in service. Your women's ministry must maintain this balance also. One of my staff ministers once said, "Consumption without contribution makes for a stuffed Christian, and contribution without consumption makes for a shallow Christian." We must offer options that provide spiritual, mental, emotional, relational, and physical growth. At the same time, we must continually encourage women to take what they are learning, put it into practice in their lives, and serve the Lord by reaching women for Christ and leading them to become disciples.

The key to an effective women's ministry is balance.

Continue to pray and see where God is working. Then boldly follow where He leads you and your leadership team as you help pass the baton of faith from generation to generation.

Help your large-group leader and small-group facilitator prepare for future leadership roles by evaluating their effectiveness in the following leadership areas.

Large-group Leader

Rank the following by number: (1) Excellent; (2) Good; (3) Fair; or (4) Needs improvement.

_____ Promoted the study adequately

_____ Conducted registration smoothly

_____ Had sufficient supplies available, (member books, pencils, Bibles)

_____ Arranged for comfortable and adequate meeting facilities

_____ Provided administrative leadership and organizational direction in a caring, efficient manner

_____ Clearly communicated logistical details and course requirements

_____ Conducted meaningful large-group sessions

_____ Handled problems effectively

Additional comments:

_____

_____

Small-group Facilitator

Rank the following by number: (1) Excellent; (2) Good; (3) Fair; or (4) Needs improvement.

_____ Began and ended sessions on time

_____ Was prepared

_____ Encouraged participation

_____ Created an atmosphere of love, concern, support, and acceptance

_____ Demonstrated sensitivity to the Holy Spirit's leadership

_____ Exhibited enthusiasm for the course and for God's Word

_____ Kept the focus on God's Word and His work in our lives

_____ Directed the discussion appropriately and meaningfully

_____ Was flexible in adapting the discussion questions according to the group's needs and interests

_____ Encouraged prayer for one another

_____ Worked to build relationships

_____ Handled problems effectively

Additional comments:

_____

_____

Please help us continue to provide an effective women's enrichment ministry by completing the following questionnaire.

1. Which activities did you participate in this period?

_____

_____

_____

2. What is your overall evaluation of these activities?
   O What I expected
   O Better than what I expected
   O Less than what I expected

3. Which activities will you participate in next period?

_____

_____

4. What other topics or speakers would you like to have in our ministry?

_____

_____

5. Were there any problems we need to be aware of?   O yes   O no
   If yes, please explain.

_____

_____

6. How can we best help you through our women's ministry?

_____

_____

(This evaluation may be used at the end of each period of women's ministry activities to help plan for the next year.)

Please fill this out as completely as possible to help our church plan ministry to and with women. Your responses are not binding. Check all that apply.

1. Fellowship

I would participate in:

- ○ Women's retreat (Friday night/Saturday)
- ○ After-church fellowship
- ○ Women's conference at the church
- ○ Other:_____
- ○ Prayer/share partners
- ○ New member activities
- ○ Banquets and luncheons
- ○ Mentoring

2. Study Opportunities

I would participate in:

- ○ Discipleship studies
- ○ Identifying spiritual gifts for ministry
- ○ Women's Bible study
  - ○ Weekday
  - ○ Weekday evening
  - ○ Weekday noon
  - ○ Sunday evening
- ○ Book reviews (Type: _____)
- ○ Study of social and moral issues in our society
- ○ Study of how to help others with personal problems (lay counseling)
- ○ Study of prayer
- ○ Other:_____

3. Missions and Evangelism

I would participate in:

- ○ Witnessing training
- ○ Praying for missionaries
- ○ Short-term mission trip   ○ USA   ○ Overseas
- ○ Interaction with local missionaries
- ○ Other:_____

4. Community Ministries

If you speak a second language, please specify: _____
I would be willing to help our church expand its ministry in:

- ○ Literacy
- ○ Tutoring
- ○ Children's home
- ○ Prisons/jails/youth offenders
- ○ Campus ministry
- ○ Handicapped/disabled persons
- ○ Clothes closet
- ○ Soup kitchen/food closet
- ○ Other:_____
- ○ Medical/dentistry
- ○ Homebound
- ○ Hospital ministry
- ○ Internationals
- ○ Latch-key kids/hotline
- ○ Meals-on-Wheels
- ○ Nursing homes/adopted grandparents/aging members

5. Interests

I would participate in and/or teach:

PARTICIPATE		TEACH	PARTICIPATE		TEACH
○	Calligraphy	○	○	Cooking/nutrition	○
○	Marriage enrichment	○	○	Creative writing	○
○	Drama	○	○	Car repair	○
○	Exercise	○	○	Financial planning	○
○	Gardening	○	○	First aid (with CPR)	○
○	Home repair	○	○	Interior decorating	○
○	Needlework	○	○	Quilting	○
○	Painting	○	○	Sewing	○
○	Ceramics	○	○	Parenting/grandparenting	○
○	Personal grooming	○	○	Self defense	○
○	Time management	○	○	Single again	○
○	Divorce recovery	○	○	Other:_____	○

6. Talents

I would be willing to utilize my talents through:

- ○ Artwork
- ○ Distribution of information
- ○ Book reviews
- ○ Creative displays
- ○ Posters
- ○ Graphics
- ○ My speciality: _____
- ○ Nursery volunteers
- ○ Bulletin boards
- ○ Photography
- ○ Telephoning
- ○ Creative writing
- ○ Newsletters
- ○ Computer technology

7. Especially for Career Women

I would participate in and/or teach:

PARTICIPATE		TEACH
○	Witnessing at work	○
○	Midlife careers	○
○	Christian ethics on the job	○
○	Beginning a business at home	○
○	Time management at home/work	○
○	The working mother and her relationship to her children	○

8. Teaching/Leading

I am interested in teaching or leading:

- ○ Bible Study
- ○ Music
- ○ Vacation Bible School
- ○ Sunday School
- ○ Retreats/conferences
- ○ Preschoolers
- ○ Youth
- ○ Children
- ○ Short (4-6 weeks) discipleship studies
- ○ Longer (8-13 weeks) discipleship studies
- ○ Video studies
- ○ Non-video studies
- ○ Camps
- ○ *Experiencing God*
- ○ *WiseCounsel*
- ○ *Disciple's Prayer Life*

(List continues on next page)

○ Intercessory Prayer Ministry   ○ Young Adults
○ Median Adults   ○ Other:_____
○ Senior Adults

9. Speakers/Musicians

I would like to hear (insert person or group's name) ...
   ○ Within our church membership_____
   ○ Outside our church membership _____

Comments to improve or broaden women's ministry:

_____

_____

_____

10. Schedule

DAYTIME
   ○ I could attend a weekly program. Best day: _____
   ○ I could only attend a monthly meeting. Best time: _____
   ○ I could only attend special events and projects periodically.

NIGHTTIME
   ○ I could attend a weekly program. Best night: _____
   ○ I could only attend a monthly meeting. Best time: _____
   ○ I could only attend special events and projects periodically.

11. Personal Profile

AGE GROUP
   ○ 18-24   ○ 25-32   ○ 33-41   ○ 71+
   ○ 42-52   ○ 53-62   ○ 63-70

STATUS
   ○ Single   ○ Married   ○ Widowed   ○ Divorced

AGES OF CHILDREN AT HOME, IF ANY: _____

EMPLOYMENT
   ○ Full-time homemaker   ○ Employed outside the home part-time
   ○ Home based business   ○ Employed outside the home full-time

I CURRENTLY ATTEND ...
   ○ Sunday School   ○ Discipleship classes
   ○ Women's Bible study   ○ Women's retreats
   ○ Women's conferences   ○ Worship
   ○ Mission's meetings/events ○ Other:_____

Were you active in any women's ministries this past year?
○ Yes ○ No   Why or why not?

_____

_____

Have you ever been active in other women's groups? ○ Yes ○ No
Which groups?
  ○ Bible Study Fellowship
  ○ Precept Bible Study
  ○ Christian Women's Club
  ○ Other:_____

Name: _____

Address: _____

City/State/Zip: _____

Telephone: Home: _____

           Work: _____

           Cell: _____

E-mail: _____

Thank you for taking the time to complete this questionnaire.

BALANCED MINISTRY

MONTE McMAHAN CLENDINNING

Consider what the following have in common:

- a lovely flower arrangement;
- a lady's attractive outfit;
- an appealing living room;
- a well-proportioned, healthy body.

The word balance no doubt comes to mind. A lovely flower arrangement reveals symmetry and balance. Balance is achieved in a lady's attractively coordinated outfit through carefully selected color, texture, and style. An appealing room happens when all elements are in harmony. One primary factor necessary in producing a well-proportioned body is a well-balanced diet.

Balance can be defined as a steadiness resulting from all parts being properly adjusted to each other, with no one part outweighing or out of proportion to another.

In the same manner, an effective women's ministry is the result of balance. Such balance does not happen by chance or by wishing it to be so. Rather, it is the result of careful, prayerful planning. Women's leaders have the awesome responsibility of joining hands with God in helping women of their church become mature in Him. These leaders should never forget they are working with God's creation: "So God created man in His own image, in the image of God he created him; male and female he created them" (Gen. 1:27).

With a sense of awe, the psalmist joins other writers in the Old Testament in praising God:

For you created my inmost being;
   you knit me together in my mother's womb.
I praise you because I am fearfully and wonderfully made (Ps. 139:13-14).

Women are special because God created them! He made provision for their salvation through Jesus. Every woman in the church is special, whether she is the most inactive church member or the most prominent leader. Each is gifted by

God and has a special contribution to make in building up the body of Christ. Women's ministries should always seek to involve women in such a way that all might grow toward maturity in Christ and find their places in extending God's kingdom.

The leader of the women's ministry in the local church will find help in developing women by asking questions such as:

1. What is our purpose, or reason for being?
2. What are some general observations to be considered in developing a women's ministry?
3. What are the basic elements necessary to develop a well-balanced women's ministry?
4. How is balance maintained?

This chapter seeks to address each of these questions, and a significant component to remember is *time*. Flowers, bodies, and well-balanced women's ministries do not materialize overnight. Maturity and growth—both physical and spiritual—develop over a period of time. The final product is not completed all at once. The ultimate goal is balance for the total program. Leaders should keep this goal in mind as they give attention to a proper balance throughout the process of growth.

RELATING PURPOSE AND BALANCE

Examine the purpose statement of your women's ministry to discover its intent, its scope, and how it relates to your church's mission or vision statement. If your church has not recorded such a statement, encourage women's leaders representing all phases of church life to work along with a church staff member to write one. Ask that they spend time in God's Word and in prayer as they seek to develop a foundational statement which reflects the direction and spirit of the church's mission or vision. Also ask them to consider the functions of a church: evangelism, discipleship, ministry, fellowship, and worship.[1] In this particular grouping, missions is listed as a result of evangelism. Remember, women's ministry is not separate from the church; it helps the church accomplish its God-given mission.

The women of Travis Avenue Baptist Church in Fort Worth, Texas, penned this purpose statement to coincide with their church's: *Our purpose is to equip our women toward maturity in Christ; fellowship with one another; service through our church; sharing Jesus with family, friends and others; and involvement in missions locally and around the world.*

Five key ideas from their statement guide their choice of curriculum.

1. Maturity in Christ immediately brings to mind the need for Bible and discipleship studies that contribute to each woman's spiritual growth, which in turn touch her family.
2. Fellowship with one another calls for an understanding of how Christians should relate to each other.
3. Service through the church should give a woman the opportunity to identify and use her spiritual gift(s) to meet needs of individuals in her church and community.

Women's ministries help women grow toward maturity in Christ.

4. Sharing Christ grows out of a woman's personal experience with Jesus and being equipped to share her faith.

5. Involvement in missions through study, prayer, giving money, and short- or long-term missions reminds women that missions is not optional.

Purpose statements not only aid in developing a balanced ministry but serve as tools for evaluation. Giving proper attention to a purpose statement in light of the church's functions and mission/vision statement can contribute to a larger vision for women's ministries than if women develop their own activities without giving consideration to fitting into the church's mission. Women are wise to plan for the years—not just for the year. What an awesome responsibility leaders carry! They seek God's vision for what a woman should be in 10 or 20 years and are busily engaged in offering curriculum which can be used of God to help that woman mature in Him.

Michelangelo, the famous Italian sculptor, had a vision for each of his sculptures. Biographers report that he could look at a piece of marble and envision a form to be released from that block of marble. Similarly, women's leaders need God's vision of what women can become, and they need to be ready to create classes and activities in which they can help those ladies mature in Christ.

Women's ministries do not all have to look alike. Just as God made each woman different, the work accomplished among women will differ from church to church. Regardless of form, the elements should be the same to ensure a balanced ministry.

Women's ministries do not have to look alike.

DEVELOPING A BALANCED MINISTRY

Before addressing specific topics to be included in women's ministry, let me make three general observations.

General Context and Balance

Leaders should reflect on the context in which balance is to be achieved in their local church and denomination. A careful listing of what the local church offers women through different settings will help avoid duplications. Leaders should consider where women are involved in the life of the church and then create new classes and activities only where needed. If meaningful classes and experiences already exist, they should take advantage of networking with them.

For example, in Sunday night discipleship a church might offer the study *Experiencing God.* A group of women who wish to take a personal growth class cannot be present on Sunday night but could attend a weekday class. Instead of developing something different, the women's ministry could offer *Experiencing God* on a weekday when those women can attend. One of the teachers who has already prepared for the Sunday night sessions might be available to lead the group during the week.

Your denomination may strongly emphasize Bible study, evangelism, and missions. Leaders should ask, How is our women's ministry involving women in these areas?

While Bible study is basic throughout the Sunday School, women today seem to hunger for a deeper understanding of God's Word. Therefore, most women's ministries offer in-depth Bible studies for a large or small groups, either at the church or in different settings.

Leaders should also ask, Are my church's women equipped to share their faith? Do they know how to share Christ with others, beginning with their family members? Many women have taken advantage of special training such as FAITH. (For more information on witnessing resources, see p. 224.) However, large numbers of women have not developed a lifestyle of witnessing. This creates the need for women's ministries to seriously study the subject.

Missions is closely related to evangelism. If a women's organization such as Women on Mission is already in place in the church, a leader will find networking with that organization can take advantage of that expertise. If not, missions involvement for the women must be developed. Missions and evangelism both need to be incorporated into a woman's lifestyle. Neither is optional. Both are commanded by Jesus Himself, "But you will receive power when the Holy Spirit comes on you; and you will be my witnesses in Jerusalem, and in all Judea and Samaria, and to the ends of the earth" (Acts 1:8).

Leaders need to be open to God's work among women and draw ideas from all kinds of effective ministries. Their ultimate responsibility is to develop classes and programs to serve women in their church and denomination.

Women's Needs Versus Desires

A helpful guiding question throughout developing a women's ministry is "What does Jesus want the women of my church to become?" While most women's leaders would agree that this is significant, in practice the question is sometimes forgotten in the eagerness to offer growth opportunities suggested by the women themselves. Tension may develop in the minds of those who design women's ministries between what women say they want and what Jesus indicates they need. A balanced ministry will offer both the subjects women want to study and subjects necessary for Christian discipline and growth. Again, keeping a balance is important. Consider Jan's experience.

Jan was attracted to a church's women's ministry because of a craft class offered after the Bible study. Although she was a Christian, Jan had no interest in Bible study and came only in time for the craft class. A friend asked her to attend the Bible study with her. Finally Jan agreed to go, but only to please the friend and to be on time for craft class.

Little by little Jan became interested in the Bible study as she came to realize God's truths were relevant to her needs. Much to her surprise, she found herself looking forward to each week's Bible study as well as to the craft class.

Several years later, Jan moved to another state. She wrote a friend in the former church, "Can you believe it? The women in my church had no women's ministry, so I helped them pull one together. And, yes, we include both crafts and Bible study!"

Had that original women's ministry been organized only on what women like Jan desired, they would have missed the opportunity to help women become better grounded in God's Word. "Sanctified bait" is the label one woman placed on classes such as crafts. She believes God can use those kinds of personal interest groups to draw women toward a greater interest in spiritual matters.

A balanced ministry offers subjects women want and subjects necessary for Christian discipline and growth.

Balancing the New and the Old

Balance plays an important part in a well-dressed woman's wardrobe. A closer look at what she is wearing might reveal a stunning piece of jewelry that belonged to her grandmother. Rather than discarding the old piece, she had it mounted in a new setting—actually enhancing it.

And in a pleasantly decorated home a woman often points with pride to furniture passed down from her family. She knows that an old piece of furniture in the proper setting lends charm and a sense of stability to the room, providing a significant link to the past.

What do these ideas have to do with women's ministries? Many churches have an organization called Women on Mission. Women who have not been recently involved with this organization may be totally unaware of its significant changes. Today's woman would do well to become a part of the heartbeat of a movement which has helped women for over a century reach out and minister to peoples of the world—for Jesus' sake.

Women's leaders should try to balance the old and the new. When the old is discarded altogether, the new can never have the depth, beauty, and balance it could have when God's balance is achieved between the two. In the same manner, if the "old" maintains its original ways without sensitivity to needed changes, it can hinder a freshness of God's Spirit in permeating the group.

BASIC ELEMENTS FOR A BALANCED MINISTRY

The Person (Woman Learner)

Three factors are present in every woman: mind, heart, and will.

Women may differ in appearance, temperament, and spiritual growth; but three factors are present in every woman: mind, heart, and will. Women think; they are emotional; and they are doers. While some women have a tendency toward one more than another, all three are important and must be involved to complete the learning cycle. Christian educators quickly point out the significance of the Holy Spirit as the teacher (see John 14:26), but they are often unaware that these three elements could actually interfere with the balanced growth of women. For instance, a program that offers Bible-study opportunities alone cannot adequately complete the learning cycle. Balance is needed.

MIND

A woman's mind must be involved if she is to learn and grow. She needs to read, study, think, memorize, and reason. As significant as this is, learning is incomplete if the heart and will do not follow.

HEART

It seems God has given women an unusual capacity to feel. When a woman studies something, her heart needs to be involved. She should ask questions such as: "What does this truth mean to me?" "How do I feel about it?" "How does it touch me?" Without the heart, learning can be intellectual and cold. Incorporating the heart helps personalize and apply the truth. But again, if ministries are planned to reach the heart only—apart from the mind and will—imbalance will occur.

74

WILL

The third factor is the will. Each learner must know and feel the truth; but she must also ask: "What will I do with this truth?" Or, "Because I have read a certain truth and responded to it from my heart, what action will I pursue?" Perhaps an example will help explain.

Suppose a devastating tornado strikes the town where you live. A woman reads about it in the newspaper (mind). As she reflects on the destruction, she feels for the people involved who have lost their homes and all they have (heart) and begins to ponder what she could do to help. As she seeks God's guidance as to how she can help, she decides (will) to gather up extra clothing, bedding, and food for the victims. Thus, the woman's mind, heart, and will are all involved.

In developing a well-balanced women's ministry, pay careful attention to planning opportunities in which women can keep a balance between study and service. The woman who devotes her energies only to service without replenishing her spirit may face burnout. Likewise, the woman who only studies without serving will not grow as she could.

Jesus is our model for service.

Jesus provides the model. The Gospels record numerous accounts of His being about His Father's business and taking time to be alone with God. Others reveal His compassionate heart. And Mark 10:45 reveals His servant heart, "For even the Son of Man did not come to be served, but to serve, and to give his life as a ransom for many."

The Process (How Women Learn)

As we discussed the person, we introduced the learning process. We established the necessity for involving the mind, heart, and will in complete and balanced learning. the process of teaching learners deals with such questions as:

1. What courses and other learning experiences could I offer to involve the use of the minds, hearts, and wills of the women of our church?
2. What level of learning do I want the women to reach? Do I want them to learn statements and facts alone or to understand and be able to apply the truths they learn? What level of cognitive ability do I want them to reach?

Dr. William "Budd" Smith refers to Benjamin S. Bloom's definition of cognitive learning which deals "with the recall or recognition of knowledge and the development of intellectual abilities and skills."[2] In the same manner he recognizes affective (emotional) learning as "objectives which describe changes in interest, attitudes, and values, and the development of appreciations and adequate adjustment."[3] Those changes, of course, are to be voluntary.

Leaders should wish to involve learners in ways that enhance their value systems. In cooperation with the Holy Spirit, the activities in women's ministries should be designed to lead each woman to a total commitment to Jesus Christ which is consistently reflected in her lifestyle.

Women's leaders have the awesome responsibility of joining hands with God to select courses, teachers, and activities to lead women to that total commitment to the Christian lifestyle. Much prayer and thought must be invested in designing a women's ministry that ensures godly balance.

Probing how a person learns should not dishearten the leader but rather challenge her to offer the best opportunities to help women mature in Christ.

The Plan (Curriculum)

In one sense curriculum is the sum total of a person's life experiences, knowledge, intellect, emotions, and actions. However, Webster defines *curriculum* as "a set of courses constituting an area of specialization."

The Women's Ministry Wheel can give direction to the desired balanced development.

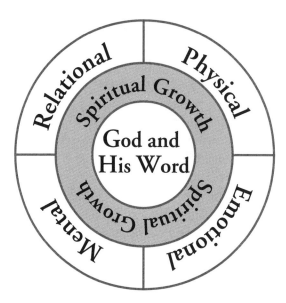

A look at the various components will give assistance in the search for balance in a women's ministry.

GOD AND HIS WORD

At the center of the wheel is God's Word. Notice the wording, "God and His Word." Not only does this suggest that Bible study is central and basic for women's ministries, but the emphasis is on the core message of Scripture: a personal relationship with God through Jesus. The goal is for every woman to know Jesus as personal Savior. Growth cannot occur until there is birth.

SPIRITUAL GROWTH

This concentric circle surrounds "God and His Word" and is an outgrowth of the center. After a woman becomes a Christian, she is nurtured through God's Word toward maturity in Christ. This includes application of God's Word, prayer, and discipleship. Four large areas of growth make up the next circle.

RELATIONAL GROWTH

Relational growth includes family issues, fellowship with Christians and others, effective communication, sharing one's faith in Jesus Christ, and being involved in ministry through the church.

A woman's spiritual growth should include a deep understanding of how to love unconditionally—like Jesus. This kind of revolutionary love is called *agape.* One of Jesus' last commands is "A new command I give you: Love one another. As I have loved you, so you must love one another" (John 13:34). Women who love as Jesus did—accepting, forgiving, building up, taking the initiative—are learning how to love unconditionally.

PHYSICAL GROWTH

Scripture says, "Do you not know that your body is a temple of the Holy Spirit, who is in you, whom you have received from God?" (1 Cor. 6:19). Such knowledge should prompt women to carefully consider taking good care of their bodies. Therefore, attention should be given to a woman's health, nutrition, and—where necessary—addictions. Some churches offer excellent programs in this area, so networking may be all that is necessary to meet the physical growth need. If these programs are not available, consider the human and financial resources in your church and provide classes for your women if possible.

EMOTIONAL GROWTH

Thought should be given to how to help women with self-esteem problems, depression, crises, and counseling needs. In New Testament times Jesus raised the status of women to unbelievable heights. As women grow in Christ, they should be learning who they are in Christ—valued, loved individuals.

MENTAL GROWTH

Women should be acquiring skills to help them toward maturity. Therefore, women's ministries should consider offering help in decision-making, time management, stress management, finances, and leadership. Women need to be open to acquiring an enlarged vision of the world and determined to find their places in God's purpose for it.

The Women's Ministry Wheel and a purpose statement can help develop a well-balanced women's ministry. If a leader haphazardly selects courses, more than likely haphazard growth will occur. She might plan electives and overlook basics for spiritual development. Or, she might plan only basics and hinder the growth of women by not including electives. Basics upon which electives might be built will lend themselves to balanced ministries.

The Power (Spiritual)

The spiritual element of a balanced ministry is God's work, and God has the power available to accomplish all He wants to do. Amazingly, God chooses to use human instruments through which His power and love can flow. God reminded King Jehoshaphat, "Do not be afraid or discouraged. … The battle is not yours, but God's" (2 Chron. 20:15).

While many churches provide a women's ministry, they often do not plan a strategy of prayer to undergird it. One of the best ways to ensure balance is through concerted prayer from such a strategy. One approach might be organizing a prayer network for the sole purpose of undergirding the ministries in which women are involved. Personal prayer requests, except in case of emergencies, should not be included. Rather, the chairperson or a designated woman could elicit priority prayer requests from each leader of women's work. Major events of the church could be included.

Consider including in the prayer group a representative from every phase of women's work in the church. An effective balance could be achieved when an attempt is made to include women of different ages—chronological and spiritual. The group should meet on a regular schedule, lifting to the Father requests from a previously prepared list. When appropriate, thanksgiving can be offered for answered prayers. Each group member should leave with at least one prayer request for which she will pray for a specified length of time.

A word of caution: a women's ministry cannot meet all women's needs. However, it can help identify needs and offer suggestions of where women might find help in meeting those needs. The women's ministry is one part of the entire church. Some of those needs may be met through participation in established programs outside the parameters of the women's ministry. Cooperation and networking need to be present as women's ministry leaders help women develop toward full maturity in Christ.

Remember that your women's ministry is one part of the entire church.

MAINTAINING A BALANCED MINISTRY

A balanced ministry can be maintained through regular evaluation, sensitive observation, and an outsider's perspective. Let's look at each of these.

Regular Evaluation

How can a leader know when she has an effective balance in her women's ministry? Leaders should evaluate their ministries on a regular basis. Every 12 months offers a good time for analyzing. A purpose statement created and adopted by the women can be a helpful tool. For example, one group identified fellowship as an important part of their ministry. Their format included a Bible study for all ages. In evaluating this particular phase of their ministry, leaders observed the interaction among the different ages and how they ministered to one another when special needs arose. They also took note of reactions from visitors in the meetings. One out-of-town visitor remarked, "I am amazed at the large number of women of different ages gathered together for Bible study—and they all seem to have a great time just being together!"

Each phase of women's ministry should be evaluated. The ministry should be checked against the purpose statement and/or elements in the Women's Ministry Wheel. Where there are successes, God should be thanked and celebrated. The area (or areas) where progress is needed should be identified, and leaders should try to determine why that particular area has not progressed.

Leaders should prayerfully seek God's direction for improving. They should always be alert to enlarging the women's ministry to include new church members or those who have recently had a major life change (for example, new retirees).

Sensitive Observation

Leaders should consider the spirit among the women. Do they have a spirit of anticipation, excitement, and joy? Leaders may find that observing statistics such as the number enrolled and attending in each group or activity can be helpful. Since women are "feelers," the level of enthusiasm with which they participate is often observable.

Leaders should also look for changes in the lives of women. Are the women achieving a better balance in their personal lives as they grow more like Jesus?

An Outsider's Perspective

An outsider's perspective offers an objective view of women's ministry. The church staff is a great resource for obtaining this. For example, a leader could ask the pastor for his impression of the women's ministry. When one women's ministry group asked their pastor to share his evaluation of their ministries, he replied,

> "The women's ministry of our church is an integral part of our ministries. I find several strengths:
> 1. It is balanced. There is an excellent blend of evangelism and missions, the fun and the serious, the young and the old, self-improvement and service to others.
> 2. It is biblical. At the heart of our program is our women's encounter with the Word of God.
> 3. It is supportive. Our women's ministry leadership want the ministry to fit squarely into the overarching goals of our church.
>
> As a pastor, I cannot imagine our church functioning effectively without our ministry to and with women."

CONCLUSION

Just as it's needed in various physical aspects of a woman's life, balance is needed in women's ministry to assist women in their desire to become what God created them to be.

Leaders should not be discouraged if they cannot develop a full-blown, well-balanced women's ministry at the very outset. Instead, they must develop what they can, making sure that courses and activities are a valid part of the master plan. Each year they can focus on additional activities which will help them come closer to the goal of balance. Leaders must keep their eyes on Jesus, who is "the author and perfecter of our faith" (Heb. 12:2). They are a significant link between God and the precious women with whom they travel toward maturity in Christ. What a responsibility! What a privilege!

> "Honest scales and balances are from the Lord;
> all the weights in the bag are of his making" (Prov. 16:11).

---

[1] Gene Mims, *Kingdom Principles for Church Growth* (Nashville: Convention Press, 1994), 34.

[2] Benjamin S. Bloom, ed., *Taxonomy of Educational Objectives: Handbook I* (New York: David McKay Company, 1956), as quoted by Daryl Eldridge, ed., *The Teaching Ministry of the Church* (Nashville: Broadman and Holman Publishers, 1995), 270.

[3] Ibid., 271.

THE TEAM THAT JESUS BUILT

JANET THOMPSON

"When is it time to give away your ministry?" I toss this question out to the audience during leadership trainings, and it is also the title of a chapter on building an Administrative Team in my "Woman to Woman Mentoring Coordinator's Guide." Some answers I often receive are:

- When you lose your passion.
- When God calls you somewhere else.
- When you are no longer effective.
- When it becomes too big for you to handle on your own.

When is it time to give away your ministry?

All negative responses—did you notice? Yes, even the one that God is calling you somewhere else. I do not believe that God ever calls us out of an area unless we recruit and train a capable person to replace us. Throughout the Bible we see that when God removed one of His leaders or moved them somewhere else, He always had an apprentice ready to take his or her place. Moses trained Joshua as his replacement. Elijah mentored Elisha. God raised up Solomon to carry on after David. When God called Jesus back to heaven, Jesus left a team of trained disciples ready to carry on His work.

Jesus did not give away His ministry because He lost His passion, stopped being effective, or the job was too big for Him to handle. No, instead, He systematically selected and trained a team in preparation for His planned departure. From the very day He called the disciples into service, He groomed them as His replacements. Jesus progressively gave away His ministry.

The answer to my opening question "When is it time to give away your ministry?" is the minute you start the ministry. That's right. Just like Jesus, from day one we continuously seek and train qualified women to whom we can delegate and share the load. Otherwise:

- We become prideful.
- We and our team members think only we can lead or perform key tasks.
- It becomes harder to let go.
- We will not think anyone can do it as well as we can.
- We won't trust anyone but ourselves.

If you want to do women's ministry all by yourself, most people will let you. But eventually, you'll grow passionless, overwhelmed, and ineffective. You'll get tangled in a web of our own creation. Feeling trapped, you'll start looking for a way out. You may feel sure God is calling you somewhere else, when actually you just don't want to do it any more. I see so much of what I call the "corporate two weeks notice" and sometimes not even that. Women just pick up and walk out on their ministries with no concern for the gaping hole they leave or the hardship it puts on everyone else. That is not how Christian women should serve God or treat each other. It certainly does not reflect what Jesus did. Jesus is our example of perfect leadership. He left a far different model for us to follow and emulate as leaders and team builders.

When Woman to Woman Mentoring began at Saddleback Church in January 1996, my mission was to create a ministry that would outlive me. I want Woman To Woman Mentoring to be going strong long after I am gone. Hence the title of my Leader Kit is not just "How to Start a Mentoring Ministry," but instead, "How to Start, Grow, and Maintain a Mentoring Ministry." That means the ministry cannot center on me or any other person. From the very beginning, I trained and mentored others to replace me if and when the time came. Indeed, the time came in November 2002 when I was diagnosed with breast cancer. But we never missed a beat because a "Team That Jesus Built" was in place and took ownership of each ministry area. The team stepped in and continued in my absence. When I recovered, we all realized the value of my having systematically and progressively given away the ministry to them.

Equally important was that once I gave away the ministry, I did not take it back. Instead, the team capably continue while I became a consultant and helped them fine tune their respective areas. They learned what I had been telling them all along—they really could do it without me. That should be every leader's ultimate goal. Even if you stay on as leader until your homecoming with Jesus, having a well trained, equipped, and capable team keeps you from becoming prideful, losing your passion, becoming overwhelmed, wanting to leave, or becoming ineffective.

Do I feel sad watching my team carry on without me? Do I feel a sense of loss? Absolutely not in the least! I am overjoyed. There is no loss, only gratitude that what I have worked for, prayed for, and taught to others is now coming to fruition. The fulfillment of my core belief is that no ministry should ever be about one person. Today, while I still function as the Ministry Leader, my official title has always been "Ministry Visionary." Now, I can truly take on that role. I am free to develop and fine tune Woman to Woman Mentoring to its fullest potential and globally share with other churches what we learn at Saddleback.

I do not claim to have team building figured out. Like you, I am continually learning. As with our faith, leadership is a lifetime process. Let me share with you from my book, *The Team That Jesus Built,* a few highlights of what God has taught me along the way. I would also suggest reading the Book of Mark in the Bible as a great scriptural study of Jesus' leadership style.

If we want to do it all ourselves, most people will let us.

Scripture says, "Jesus, full of the Holy Spirit, returned from the Jordan and was led by the Spirit in the desert, where for forty days he was tempted by the devil (Luke 4:1-2, NIV). Reading on in Luke 4:3-12, we learn that Jesus was tempted by the same things that tempt us today:

- using our own ability to feed our hunger for success, popularity, recognition, possessions.
- retaining all authority and splendor for ourselves.
- doing something foolish and expecting God to rescue us.

Pride is at the heart of each of these temptations. It is pertinent to note Satan tempted Jesus just before Jesus started His public ministry (Luke 4:13-15).

Lesson to Learn

If Jesus was tempted, we will be tempted. Pride fools us into thinking it could not happen to us or we can resist temptation single-handedly. Pride sets us up for failure. God hates pride because He knows it destroys us and our ministries. Yet pride is at the center of almost everything we do unless we recognize and fight it the same way Jesus did—by knowing God's Word and hiding it in our hearts so that we will not sin against Him.

Surround yourself with godly people who are willing to keep you accountable.

Surround yourself with godly people who are willing to keep you accountable as you launch a ministry or take on a leadership role. Ask them to listen for you referring to "your ministry" or "your team." Give someone permission to point out times when you are:

- not including others in decision making.
- reveling in the limelight.
- seeking the praises of others.
- doing everything yourself.
- becoming too controlling and inflexible.
- being a perfectionist.
- doing something foolish.
- not respecting authority in your church.
- doing something against church policy.
- focusing more on your own good than the good of the ministry.
- not developing a capable team to assist you.

Make the Bible your Bread of Life. You would not go a day without eating unless you were sick or fasting. If you go a day without the Lord's Word, you will surely be sick in heart and spirit. There is no other way or substitute. If Jesus truly is to be at the center of your ministry and leadership, He must truly be at the center of your life.

Taking It to Heart

Everyone who goes into leadership, even Jesus, is at sometime tempted by Satan. Knowing this, what is your game plan for when that happens? Do you have trusted accountability partners in place? Think through steps you can take now to ready yourself for the inevitable temptation of pride, greed, selfishness, bending the rules, lying, rejecting authority, impatience, anger, lust, or misplaced ambition. Pray for God's guidance as you put these steps into practice.

"Jesus returned to Galilee in the power of the Spirit, and news about him spread through the whole countryside. He taught in their synagogues" (Luke 4:14-15).

The Scriptures tell us that immediately after the temptation in the desert, Jesus drove out evil spirits while teaching and healing (Luke 4:14-44). The first disciples were not recruited until chapter 5 in Luke. Jesus did not wait until He had a team together before launching into the call of public ministry the Lord had given Him.

Lesson to Learn

I call it the upside-down method. Traditional thinking says we need to have a leadership team in place before starting a ministry. I disagree. When I received the call to start Woman to Woman Mentoring, I didn't know anyone to ask to be on an administrative team, but I did know that:

- The women helping me lead the ministry would first need to participate in a mentoring relationship in order to understand from experience the ministry they were leading.
- I needed to observe them serving before asking them to serve on the administrative team.
- I needed to step out and start anyway.
- The administrative team would develop as the ministry developed.

You must start the ministry before you can give it away. Let the leadership team evolve out of women who step up to help you. Instead of putting a plea out for leaders and team members, plea for women who would like to serve in the ministry. Give them assignments and then observe. Those who are dependable, reliable, demonstrate follow through, and show commitment are the ones you want to groom for your leadership team.

This takes a while, but it is well worth the time and effort to have women on your team who can truly assist with the activities and operation of the ministry. In the meantime, lower your expectations of what the ministry will accomplish. Take on only a couple of projects and invite many women to participate. Then wait for God to raise up leaders. If this is a ministry He is blessing, He will meet your needs in His time frame.

You must start the ministry before you can give it away.

Taking It to Heart

If you are just starting a ministry, are you brave enough to begin it alone? Do you believe that God will meet you there and provide until He brings the workers to the harvest? Will you follow the call no matter what and let Jesus be your example? Will you start small and let the ministry evolve as the right women reveal themselves as true leaders who could help you take the ministry to the next level? Do you have the courage? Do you trust your faith? Do you believe that God wants this more than you want it yourself? I pray that your answer is "Yes!"

"One of those days Jesus went out to a mountainside to pray, and spent the night praying to God. When morning came, he called his disciples to him and chose twelve of them, whom he also designated apostles" (Luke 6:12-13).

Selecting His team was such an important decision that Jesus secluded Himself and prayed about it all night. When He came down from the mountain, Jesus chose His team—the twelve apostles. Perhaps during prayer God revealed the twelve names from the numerous disciples following Jesus, so that they might be with Him and that He might send them out to preach (Mark 3:14b). Jesus knew He would pour Himself into this team of men who would be with Him till the end of His earthly ministry and then carry on after Him.

An important point in this passage is that Jesus designated them apostles. Read what the Revell Bible Dictionary says about the term 'apostle.'

> One who is sent out; specifically applied to Jesus' twelve disciples, Paul, and other NT missionaries. By NT times, apostle meant an envoy, one sent on a mission as the personal representative of the one sending him. The word was used in the Greek OT for messengers who were sent by God and who spoke with his authority. In the NT, the word apostle serves both as a title and as a general description.

As a specialized title, *apostle* designates Jesus' twelve original disciples, who had a unique role in founding the church. They were given authority and personally trained by Jesus Himself. Jesus also commissioned them to " 'go and make disciples of all nations, baptizing them in the name of the Father and of the Son and of the Holy Spirit, and teaching them to obey everything I have commanded you' " (Matt. 28:18-20). The commission is restated in Acts 1:8: "You will be my witnesses in Jerusalem, and in all Judea and Samaria, and to the ends of the earth."

Lesson to Learn

Pray for who God would have on your prospective team. Pray for patience with this process because it will take time. My error in the beginning was to rush ahead of God instead of waiting on Him. When your team is selected, continue praying for them often. Discover their needs, both personally and in the ministry, and let them know you are lifting them up in prayer. Incorporate ways for them to pray for each other.

Taking It to Heart

It is impossible to be an effective leader without a faithful daily quiet time, regular attendance at your home church, and participation in a group that encourages spiritual growth.

If you want to lead a ministry and do not spend daily quiet time worshipping, praying, and studying God's Word, then incorporate it into your life immediately. Schedule God into your activities or your activities will squeeze Him out. Don't even consider adding a new role until you have a firmly established quiet time. There is no way around this—no excuses suffice.

If you currently have a daily quiet time, how can you take it to the next level? Maybe it is having one in the morning and evening or adding a new depth. You

Schedule God into your activities or your activities will squeeze Him out.

are about to take on a significant role for God that requires you to spend significant time with Him.

JESUS CALLED HIS TEAM

"He saw James son of Zebedee and his brother John in a boat, preparing their nets. Without delay he called them, and they left their father Zebedee in the boat with the hired men and followed him" (Mark 1:19-20, NIV).

Jesus handpicked His team and said to them, " 'Come, follow me' " (Mark 1:16-20; 2:14). We do not see Him taking just anyone who wanted to come on board. Jesus went to those He wanted to be His trusted teammates. The key is He did the choosing, not the reverse. Without hesitation, He intentionally called them. Jesus chose some seemingly unqualified people; yet, He obviously had discernment to see beyond their outside appearance into their hearts and potential. How did He do that? He prayed.

Lesson to Learn

We need to follow Jesus' example by:
- praying for the persons God wants on our teams.
- listening for the names He reveals.
- Risking rejection.
- Approaching them to serve.

Don't feel as if you need to put every woman who says she wants to serve with you on your ministry team. Do some homework. Interview her. Give her assignments and see how she performs. Remember, it is much easier to gently tell her she is not a fit than to later deal with having someone on your administrative team who is not ready for leadership.

Taking It to Heart

Do you have some women in mind? Have you prayed and asked God to reveal who He wants on your team? Ask God to give you discernment and courage to approach them. Are you willing to ask women who God reveals that would not be your own personal choice? Think about ways to intentionally select your administrative team.

JESUS CHOSE A SPECIFIC NUMBER

Jesus chose twelve team members and designated them apostles (Mark 3:14a). We don't know why; perhaps the Father told Him to choose these men. Even after Judas' betrayal and suicide and Jesus' death and resurrection, the remaining apostles recruited a twelfth. That was the perfect number for Jesus' team.

Lesson to Learn

Often we think the more people on the leadership team the better—more accomplished, more ideas, more hands to do the work. However, you have probably found as I did that more on the administrative team actually causes more chaos, confusion, and distractions. The bigger the team, the more

Ask God for discernment in choosing potential leaders and the courage to approach them.

difficult it is to manage. Instead, select a number for your administrative team that you can efficiently and effectively nurture and lead.

Taking It to Heart

I found the following suggestions helpful in determining how many women I needed on my administrative team.

1. Determine the major areas your ministry will be covering-limit six to eight.
2. Group similar areas together.
3. Choose a leader for each area.

For our discussion, let's say you are the Visionary Leader of a Women's Ministry comprised of:

- Bible Study
- Retreats and Conferences
- Woman to Woman Mentoring
- Support Groups
- MOPS
- Small Groups

These six areas need leaders. I call these leaders Shepherd Coaches. Your administrative team would be comprised of six Shepherd Coaches with whom you will meet and invest time and training. Often, teams become committees with far too many people to be effective. I found that out the hard way when I once had twelve Shepherd Coaches on my Woman to Woman Mentoring administrative team. I realized that while Jesus could handle twelve on His team, that was far too many for me. I find that six to eight is a nice size for a productive team. Once you go beyond that, start consolidating ministries together under one Shepherd Coach.

JESUS RECRUITED UNLIKELY PEOPLE

"As he walked along, he saw Levi son of Alphaeus sitting at the tax collector's booth. 'Follow me,' Jesus told him, and Levi got up and followed him" (Mark 2:14, NIV).

When we look at the rag-tag group of men Jesus chose for his team, we can be encouraged that with Christ as our Ultimate Leader, we all have potential to lead. Jesus saw potential in common fishermen, telling them soon they would be fishers of men (Mark 1:17). Then He added Matthew, a shrewd and hated tax collector, along with Matthew's political opposite, Simon the Zealot.

Lesson to Learn

Every Christian is a leader whose life should lead others to Christ. As news of corrupt leadership daily bombards us, many women tend to look at leadership as a bad thing. They do not see themselves as leaders. The word *leader* intimidates and scares them. Yet many of them run complicated households—working, home schooling, juggling and balancing many areas of a family's daily life. They *are* leaders. They just need someone to believe in them and show them how to apply their daily leadership skills to ministry.

With Christ as our Ultimate Leader, we all have potential to lead.

Taking It to Heart

I had no real credentials for starting Woman to Woman Mentoring except being comfortable as a leader. Otherwise, I was an unlikely candidate. Yet several pastors saw my vision, passion, and potential to lead and gave me an opportunity. Because of their belief in me, Woman to Woman Mentoring has flourished.

Don't be fooled by outside appearances (Gal. 2:6) or someone who talks and seems right for the position. Think outside the box and inside the heart. Often, the same group of women do all the work. Keep a vigilant eye for those who show leadership potential even though they may not fit the mold.

JESUS CHOSE PEOPLE DIFFERENT FROM HIMSELF

"These are the twelve he appointed: Simon (to whom he gave the name Peter); James son of Zebedee and his brother John (to them he gave the name Boanerges, which means Sons of Thunder); Andrew, Philip, Bartholomew, Matthew, Thomas, James son of Alphaeus, Thaddaeus, Simon the Zealot and Judas Iscariot, who betrayed him" (Mark 3:16-19).

Jesus was a carpenter, a religious teacher, a prophet, a rabbi. His team members were fishermen, a tax collector, and a political zealot. Jesus was a scriptural scholar, and the disciples He designated apostles were spiritual neophytes. Jesus was the meeting of grace and truth; His disciples were quick tempered and doubters. Yet, Jesus chose them as His replacements. They represented the people to whom the twelve would be ministering after Jesus departed. People needed to relate to them, and so He chose a band of extremely ordinary men. We are Christians today because of this varied team.

Lesson to Learn

Humanly, we migrate towards people who think and act the way we do. Teams comprised of people just like the leader will be ineffective, cliquey, and will only excel in areas in which they all are comfortable and knowledgeable. A well balanced team will have members representing:

- different ages.
- all seasons of life.
- varied personalities. At least one of every personality type and several who are the exact opposite of you should be included. Give everyone on the team a personality test. (I use Florence Littauer's *Personality Puzzle*, available from CLASServices, Inc. 1.800.433.6633.) Let the team members know about each other's personality and discuss the different facets of each one. This information will help you and them understand each other better.
- different spiritual gifts and talents. Give everyone a spiritual gifts test. (I use Peter Wagner's "Finding Your Spiritual Gifts," available online http://buildingchurch.net/g2s.htm.) Again, discuss the results with the team and try to maintain a varied representation of both spiritual and creative gifts.

Healthy, well-balanced teams are diverse.

Taking It to Heart

As the team adds or replaces members, new members take the personality and spiritual gifts tests. The team learns the results, and the new members learn about the team. This utilizes understanding and communication in the getting to know each other phase. The more varied the group, the more versatile and creative your team. It also challenges you, the Ministry Visionary, to work with women different than yourself. Knowing their comment or action might just be a personality difference facilitates tolerance and peace. Each personality has perceived good and bad sides depending on who is looking. Understanding how personalities affect relationships is important. Reading *Personality Puzzle* helps with understanding how personalities affect relationships. I recommend giving this book to each team member as required reading.

JESUS RECRUITED WITH A PURPOSE

"As Jesus walked beside the Sea of Galilee, he saw Simon and his brother Andrew casting a net into the lake, for they were fishermen, 'Come, follow me,' Jesus said, 'and I will make you fishers of men.' At once they left their nets and followed him" (Mark 1:16-18).

Jesus recruited each team member for a specific reason—a unique role and purpose. He knew their specific gifts and talents. Each one had something to contribute that was different from the others. Jesus' role than became to take this group of seemingly misfit individuals and mold them into a synergistic, unified team that loved each other and worked together as a whole.

Lesson to Learn

Determine the objectives of your ministry. Our Women's Ministry example is comprised of six focused areas. Each of those areas needs a Shepherd Coach gifted in the specific area.

Women's ministry teams are much like the varied team that Jesus compiled. For example, the MOPS leader will be a young woman with preschool children. She may not be as spiritually mature as the woman you select as the Bible Study Shepherd Coach. The Conference and Retreat Shepherd Coach will have strong organizational skills which might even occasionally clash with yours because she may be a lot like you. The Support Groups Shepherd Coach might be a deeply sensitive and compassionate woman, and the Small Group Shepherd Coach might be very outgoing and gregarious. Some may be single, others married. Some working, some not.

Taking It to Heart

I love this quote from the *Leadership Bible*, "Teams by their nature, require specialists. Specialists often differ in personality and view. Team members combine their strengths to help one another to grow and to change their world. Such a diversified team may be tougher to lead—but then training lions is more exciting than feeding goldfish!

JESUS CAST HIS VISION

"Then Jesus said to Simon, 'Don't be afraid; from now on you will catch men.' So they pulled their boats up on shore, left everything and followed him. ...

Jesus went out and saw a tax collector by the name of Levi sitting at his tax booth. 'Follow me,' Jesus said to him, and Levi got up, left everything and followed him" (Luke 5:10-11,27-28).

Jesus was a visionary who boldly and effectively proclaimed the plans He had for His team. Jesus was going to heal, preach, teach, cast out demons and evangelize the world, and He invited His team to join Him in that grand and glorious purpose. They literally left their professions and livelihoods to follow Him.

Lessons to Learn

- Why was Jesus' vision casting so effective with His team? What can we learn for our own vision casting?
- Jesus started His ministry before calling the disciples, therefore, establishing credibility—news about Him spread through the whole countryside (Luke 4:14). They knew of Him and His incredible work.
- Jesus told them they would be doing something bigger than themselves-something only God could do in and through them.
- Jesus spoke their language. To the fishermen He talked of fishing for men, not global evangelism—terms that would have been foreign to them. Fishing they understood.
- Jesus told them not to be afraid—He had a plan and He would equip and train them to be part of it.

Taking It to Heart

My title in Saddleback's Woman to Woman Mentoring Ministry is "Ministry Visionary." That is what it started out as and continues to this day. My team calls me by that title, and it is on my official church nametag. This accomplishes two very important objectives:

1. It puts my role into proper perspective. My team and others see me as a visionary. I don't call myself the ministry leader, and neither do they. The term *visionary* conveys my openness to the great things the Lord is going to do in our ministry and the team's role in following that vision. I have never had to relinquish or formally pass on my leadership because I never had it in the first place. This reminds us this ministry is not centered on me. We are a team—I am the Visionary, and they lead the ministry.
2. Visionaries dream dreams of what can be done. Life will never be static with a visionary on the team. My being the visionary establishes the atmosphere for future changes—growth, mobility, maturity, improvement, new ideas, reaching out above and beyond what we think we can do.

JESUS TRAINED HIS TEAM

"One day Jesus was praying in a certain place. When he finished, one of his disciples said to him, 'Lord, teach us to pray, just as John taught his disciples.' He said to them, 'When you pray say …' (Luke 11:1-2).

Throughout the Gospels, we see Jesus situationally answering questions, teaching, and performing miracles in front of His team and often stopping to explain what He did or said (Mark 2:15-3:6; 4). Although they typically did not understand everything He taught at first, Jesus displayed patience and persistence. He later told them they had the power to do everything He did (Mark 16:15-20). He didn't add that He could do it better and faster; nor did He step in and do it Himself unless it was a teaching opportunity such as when He cast out demons because they lacked faith and had not prayed (Mark 9:17-29).

Jesus consistently worked Himself out of an earthly job. From the very beginning, He equipped the team to replace Him because soon He would be gone and they would have to carry on without His physical presence. He wanted them to succeed. He did not show them up or make them feel inferior. The closer He got to the cross, the more He taught them.

A secure leader embraces her team's talents.

Lesson to Learn

A secure leader is not threatened by talent on her team—she embraces it. I am not a creative person, so I surround myself with women who are. Otherwise, we would be very organized but also very boring. Encourage others to use their gifts, and work with them to develop the areas where they need to grow. Provide your team with opportunities to cultivate areas where they excel and teach them how to lead. Here are some ideas, and I am sure you can think of more:

- Give leaders leadership and spiritual development books.
- Research affordable conferences on leadership that you can attend as a team.
- Do a Bible Study together so they continue growing spiritually and as leaders. Important note—don't lead the studies yourself. Rotate the leadership throughout your team.
- Take time to answer questions and explain the reasons you have for making your decisions.
- Use situations that arise as teaching opportunities.

Taking It to Heart

Helping the team work through a suitable strategy provides problem solving skills that support the ministry philosophy and are applicable to other areas. However, remember that the apostles never stopped asking questions and usually did not understand Jesus' explanations, but He didn't give up. They got it when they were on their own.

JESUS MET WITH HIS TEAM

"When he was alone, the Twelve and the others around him asked him about the parables. He told them ..." (Mark 4:10-11).

Many Scriptures refer to Jesus gathering His apostles together, often in a home or quiet place. They would ask questions, and He would answer or explain the miracle He had just performed or the meaning of the parable He had told. He invested time in them.

Lesson to Learn

Developing a team that can carry on without you is going to take an investment of time and energy. It won't happen quickly, but if we visionaries are willing to patiently mentor our teams, it will happen. I recommend a bimonthly administrative team meeting. Here are some guidelines:

- Distribute to each team member an agenda of the topics to be covered at the meeting.
- Vision cast for upcoming events.
- Each of the team members should give a concise report from her area of responsibility.
- Set a beginning and ending time and stick to it.
- Don't allow team members to address individual issues.
- Regularly communicate with each team member outside the meetings to conduct discussions pertinent to their areas that do not affect the rest of the team. I tell the team that our group meeting is not the place to throw something new at me, ask for my opinion, or use the other team members' valuable time discussing something that really only pertains to them. Cover those items in individual meetings so you use the group meetings to present decisions and action plans that affect the whole ministry.
- Do not take votes. Jesus never took a vote! He didn't say, "Well disciples, what do you think we should do about this?" Or "Do you think we should go here or there?" Had He done that, we know enough about the disciples to know that they all would have had differing opinions. Much time is wasted in meetings discussing what color the tablecloths should be—even people not affected by it will have an opinion. Unless votes are unanimous, there is always an unhappy person. Not allowing votes does not mean that you are a dictator—certainly no one would characterize Jesus that way.

Taking It to Heart

I will never forget the team meeting where the Publicity Shepherd Coach made the mistake of asking the other team members what they thought of the new coffee cup logo design. Some thought it shouldn't have steam, others thought it was too small, others too big. Although the cup logo did not affect any of the team members personally, they spent a good half hour discussing it. Had the Publicity Shepherd Coach instead presented the finished work of graphic artists, the team would have exclaimed how great it looked.

JESUS FELLOWSHIPPED WITH HIS TEAM

"While Jesus was having dinner at Levi's house, many tax collectors and 'sinners' were eating with him and his disciples, for there were many who followed him" (Mark 2:15).

The Gospels mention many times that Jesus and the apostles ate and broke bread together in homes (see Mark 1:29-31; 2:15; 3:20). His very last meal was with all of them in the upper room (Mark 14:12-26).

Lesson to Learn

The first few years of my leadership were all business. We met every month and stuck to the agenda. Then I realized we might be missing out on fellowshipping with each other and getting to know more than just what we did for the

Developing a team that could carry on without you requires an investment of time and energy.

ministry. Jesus certainly did eat with His apostles, and it was not always for work purposes. So I initiated a fellowship/Bible Study night that features studies on leadership. We alternate each month with a business meeting one month, Bible study the next. On Bible study night, we meet in a team member's home, eat dinner together, do our study, and pray. Rather than leading the group myself, we rotate facilitators amongst the team.

Taking It to Heart

Can you see the benefit of spending relaxed, casual, but still meaningful time with your team? If you are an 'all business' kind of person, give yourself permission to get to know your team members on all levels of their lives. Pray to see value in truly knowing someone and not just valuing what they can do for you. Remember that even playful times together still have a purpose—developing relationship with the whole person.

Pray to see value in truly knowing team members and not just valuing what they can do for you.

JESUS CONFRONTED DIFFICULT SITUATIONS

"When evening came, Jesus arrived with the Twelve. While they were reclining at the table eating, he said, 'I tell you the truth, one of you will betray me—one who is eating with me.' They were saddened, and one by one they said to him, 'Surely not I?' 'It is one of the Twelve,' he replied, 'one who dips bread into the bowl with me.' " (Mark 14:17-20).

Jesus confronted Judas and told him He knew of his plot against Him. He did not mince words, avoid it, or tell others behind Judas' back. Later, Jesus confronted Peter and said that he would deny Him before the end of the night in spite of Peter's protest he would never do such a thing (14:29-31). When Jesus came upon two of His disciples arguing, He asked them, " 'What were you arguing about on the road?' But they kept quiet because on the way they had argued about who was the greatest. Sitting down, Jesus called the Twelve and said, 'If anyone wants to be first, he must be the very last, and the servant of all' " (Mark 9:33-35).

Lesson to Learn

I have had a Judas or two on my team—how about you? When this happens, it is important to address the situation. Most of us hate confrontation, but as leaders our role is to confront a disloyal team member or someone causing a disturbance. Often, we mistakenly think that as Christian women we must simply endure someone who is obviously working against us, but being a Christian does not mean ignoring problems or problem people. Jesus certainly didn't. Jesus confronted problem people and dealt with issues. It is best and biblical to follow the guidelines in Matthew 18:15-17.

Use this same model when team members argue. When Jesus heard the two disciples arguing, He immediately addressed the issue with both of them and then used it as a teaching experience for the others. Sometimes differences evolve from personality clashes, but allowing a problem to fester is not in anyone's best interest. Infighting can never be tolerated or pushed under the carpet because it will eat away like a cancer at the unity of the team and the work of the ministry. You as the Visionary must deal directly with it on your own team of Shepherd Coaches, teaching them how to address conflict on their teams.

If conflicts cannot be resolved to the best interest of the ministry, you may need to remove the problem team member. Not from your life or your church or even your ministry. In fact, just the opposite, because they need extra attention in their spiritual walk and in understanding what it means to selflessly serve the Lord. Perhaps they can serve in another place in the ministry, but leaving them on the leadership team will most certainly lead to dissension and to God's work being compromised. No one wins in that scenario.

Audiences always tells me they need to hear how to resolve conflict more than any other talk I give. I also write about this in my *Mentoring God's Way Bible Study*, "Euodias and Syntyche: How to Resolve Conflict."

Taking It to Heart

How would you rate yourself when it comes to dealing with conflict? Do you avoid it? Ignore it? Let someone else deal with it? Tell others about the problem instead of telling the problem person? Take it personally? Deal with it biblically, directly, and resolutely?

If confronting conflict is an uncomfortable area for you, seek help to objectively and biblically deal with it. Conflict is an inevitable part of leadership. Some suggestions include:
- Read Christian books on conflict resolution.
- Consult with your pastoral staff.
- Practice what you learn from reading and consultation.
- Have an accountability partner who does not let you run from conflict.

Remember that as a leader, you are a point person and not everyone is going to like you all the time—in fact, if they do you are probably not being a decisive and effective leader. Many people measure their leadership success by the number of critics they have.

JESUS RETREATED WITH HIS TEAM

"Jesus withdrew with his disciples to the lake" (Mark 3:7, NIV).

Mark 3:1-6 records Jesus' encounter with the Pharisees regarding His healing a man on the Sabbath. The very next verse (3:7) records Jesus' retreating with His team. After a big ministry event of teaching, preaching, healing, or performing a miracle, Jesus often retreated with them. He also retreated with them right before a major miracle (4:35-36; 6:31-32). The Book of Mark records five separate places where Jesus took His team to a quiet retreat to recharge, refuel, refresh, and strengthen their relationships with each other. Jesus often said to the disciples, " 'Come with me by yourselves to a quiet place and get some rest' " (Mark 6:31).

Jesus knew the Lord's work requires stamina, courage, energy, and time!

Lesson to Learn

Jesus knew His work requires stamina, courage, energy, and time! We can't give what we do not have. Sometimes we get so busy planning the event that we forget to plan time together to spiritually fuel up and refuel afterward.

Always schedule time before and after an event to rest, affirm, encourage, pray, and evaluate.

Taking It to Heart

Each Fall, I take our Woman to Woman Mentoring administrative team on a planning weekend retreat. We go at least two hours away from home so no one is tempted to go home for the night or run to a soccer game. We find a nice large cabin or condo in the mountains or at the beach and settle in for a time of fun, calendar planning, vision casting, lessons, girl time, and relaxation—although the team would laugh at that last word since I usually have the weekend packed pretty full. When we leave this retreat, we have evaluated the current year and planned all our events for the next. Everyone brings their personal, school, and church calendars. Working out the schedule requires a few grueling hours, but when it's completed, the team knows the upcoming year's plans and has the dates booked.

Mid-year we have a Saturday mini-retreat locally, and each administrative team member brings her apprentice. There we work on things like role playing conflict, recruiting help, and interviewing someone for a leadership position. If you cannot get away for an entire weekend, start with a mini-retreat.

Each team member contributes $15.00 a month toward the annual retreat, and we use the collected funds to pay for our retreat house. I plan an agenda and pray the Lord will give me a theme. Several years ago, the Lord gave me "The House That Jack Built" as a theme. I scratched my head trying to figure that one out until I realized He wanted me to rewrite the jingle. It became "The Team That Jesus Built," and I share this version in my book of the same name. We were in the mountains at that retreat. The girls took a walk during one of the breaks and came back all excited that I needed to go see something. They took me to a cabin on the next street that had a sign in front that read, "The House That Jack Built"! We knew God was confirming that He had truly blessed us with the theme that year—as He does every year. He will for you too.

JESUS EMPOWERED HIS TEAM

"He appointed twelve—designating them apostles—that they might be with him and that he might send them out to preach and to have authority to drive out demons" (Mark 3:14-15).

Not only did Jesus appoint and designate the disciples to be apostles, but He also empowered them with the authority to carry out the jobs of preaching and driving out demons. Jesus gave the disciples, now apostles, assignments to do the work He had been doing and sent them out to do it without Him! He married responsibility with the all important binding thread of authority. Sometimes the apostles did well. Other times they failed miserably, but Jesus used their failures as teaching opportunities and then sent them out again. The idea was not for Jesus to jump in and do the ministry Himself but to continuously remind them He had passed on the authority and now His role was their cheerleader!

Lesson to Learn

The key to developing a responsible team that could function in your absence is a continuous process of …

- delegating,
- letting go,
- granting authority, and
- stepping aside.

Many leaders readily delegate and give assignments but don't grant the accompanying authority and responsibility to complete them. Admittedly, this is really difficult. Often, like the apostles, our team disappoints us by not doing something the way it should be done or the way we would do it. However, if we take back the task, we miss the opportunity for a positive teaching experience. Our team will never learn to do things themselves. Instead, you should …

- let the person to whom you are assigning a task observe you first
- split the task between the two of you.
- critique and evaluate her performance.
- progressively assign more of the task to her until she is doing it completely. Observe, evaluate, suggest improvements, and encourage her.
- Release the task and let her do it on her own.
- check back a couple of times.
- start the training process over again if needed, always with the goal of passing it on completely. If she is the right person for the task, she will eventually 'get it.' If not, assign her another task and recruit another person to train for this one.
- let go!

Many leaders readily delegate and give assignments but don't grant the accompanying authority and responsibility.

Taking It to Heart

We call our Woman to Woman Mentoring administrative team members *Shepherd Coaches* because *shepherd* entails nurturing and *coach* encompasses teaching and training their teams to perform. I often hear the comment, "I can do it faster and better myself." That is probably true, but it is not team building. A leader who feels she has to have her hand in everything will cut off helping hands. There will be little growth or new vision because she is task oriented rather than equipping oriented.

JESUS WAS NOT DISCOURAGED WHEN HIS TEAM DID THINGS WRONG

"After Jesus had gone indoors, his disciples asked him privately, 'Why couldn't we drive it [the demon] out?' He replied, 'This kind can come out only by prayer' " (Mark 9:28-29).

Initially, the disciples were not skilled in ministry. Actually, they became more effective after Jesus' death. Even when they bumbled and questioned and at times seemed not to believe in Jesus' vision, He did not lose heart. He did not give up on them. He continued to patiently and deliberately teach, train, and release. Jesus helped them see where they needed improvement and then sent them out again.

Lesson to Learn

Our team members are going to make mistakes—maybe even big ones. We have a choice. Are we going to berate them, make them feel like failures, and step in and do the tasks ourselves? Or are we going to ...

- applaud what they did right?
- ask where they see they can improve?
- gently point out areas we notice they need to change?
- discuss a plan for improvement?
- send them out to try again?

Taking It to Heart

When I first started Woman to Woman Mentoring, I filled every position and took care of every task myself. Soon, I began recruiting, training, and passing on much of the work.

One of the areas I held onto the longest was Prayer Day. That is the day when we go through the process of matching pairs of Mentors and Mentees through intercessory prayer. I felt the team could not do it without me. After all, I created that day and wrote the guidelines for it. I had the gift of discernment that helped in the matching. I just could not let go. Then one day the Lord reminded me that churches all over the world were having Prayer Day without me, and they were doing just fine. What made me think I was so important that my own church could not do it without me?

That was a wake up call. I did not back out of Prayer Day immediately. Instead, I practiced the steps I described under "Jesus Empowered His Team."

- I participated in Prayer Day with them.
- Then I arrived later—after the team had started praying about and matching the Mentor/Mentee teams.
- Next, I progressed just to checking in at lunchtime.

Before long I was not part of the day at all; they faxed me the final matches. Now, I don't see the final matches and no longer attend the selection process.

Yes, I questioned some Prayer Day matches, However, the team's decisions did not bring about the end of the world, and members learned from the process and were more experienced for the next time.

I used the same procedure in passing on other ministry responsibilities. Another area I felt I would always be a part of was our administrative team meetings. I led them in my home for eight years and thought I would continue doing so forever. Then I had breast cancer and later took a sabbatical to write a book. My friend Jane Crick, our Publicity Shepherd Coach, pointed out that there was no way I could remove myself from the day-to-day operation of the ministry as long as I was leading the meetings. I call her my Jethro, Moses' father-in-law who reminded Moses that he too must let go for the greater good of the ministry (Ex. 18:13-27).

Tonight as I write, the team is having a meeting and I am not there. They don't need me to help work out the details of the upcoming events. They may miss some points I would address, but they are learning to take ownership of their areas without relying on me to tie it all together. This is every leader's ultimate goal—to decrease that the team would increase.

"Then Jesus directed them to have all the people sit down in groups on the green grass. So they sat down in groups of hundreds and fifties" (Mark 6:39-40).

Jesus displayed organizational skills to His team when He gave His disciples specific instructions on how to seat the people: Instead of randomly feeding an out-of-control crowd, He had the people divided into groups of specific numbers.

Jesus did not feed the people in the crowd all by Himself, either. Instead, He told the disciples, " 'You give them something to eat' " (Mark 6:37). Scripture records Jesus doing only two things: thanking God for the food and breaking the bread. Then the apostles delivered the food and cleaned up.

Lesson to Learn

Effective leaders are organized. They follow a system and procedure that everyone understands. It needs to be simple, functional, and effective. I have found the organization chart to be all three.

Effective leaders are organized.

When I first presented the organization chart to my team at a retreat, many of them rolled their eyes and remarked that it was way over their heads. Just like your teams, my team members range from stay-at-home moms to teachers to business women. Unless they work for a company, they may be unfamiliar with Organization Charts. However, the charts show the flow of responsibility and delegation better than anything else I have found. In ministry, the Organization Chart is not a discriminating or hierarchy tool. Rather, it is simply a method of organization that God introduced as early as the days of Moses to help instill leadership order and responsibility.

" 'Select capable men from all the people—men who fear God, trustworthy men who hate dishonest gain—-and appoint them as officials over thousands, hundreds, fifties and tens. Have them serve as judges for the people at all times, but have them bring every difficult case to you; the simple cases they can decide themselves.. That will make your load lighter, because they will share it with you. If you do this and God so commands, you will be able to stand the strain, and all these people will go home satisfied.' Moses listened to his father-in-law and did everything he said. He chose capable men from all Israel and made them leaders of the people, officials over thousands, hundreds, fifties and tens." (Ex. 18:21-25).

Taking It to Heart

In our hypothetical Women's Ministry, the Organization Chart starts like this:

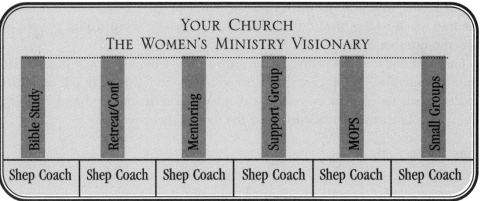

Shepherd Coaches are the first level of leadership under the Ministry Visionary and comprise the administrative team that you, the Visionary:
- meet with,
- council,
- train,
- love,
- teach,
- serve as a role model, and
- retreat with—they are your team.

The Shepherd Coaches learn from you, the Ministry Visionary, and develop their own team of leaders in a like manner. Each Shepherd Coach determines the areas where leaders are needed and recruits women to fill those positions. These recruits are the leaders Shepherd Coaches will …
- meet with,
- council,
- train,
- love,
- teach,
- serve as role models, and
- retreat with—they are their team.

At this point, the Organization Chart becomes individualized for each Shepherd Coach. For example, let's take an area that I often encounter as a speaker.

It breaks my heart when I arrive at a retreat or conference and it is the frazzled and worn out Ministry Visionary who picks me up at the airport and takes me to the hotel while she continuously puts out fires back at the church via cell phone. Inevitably, when we get to the church only a handful of women are helping. When I ask, "Where are all the ladies who are helping with this retreat?" I am often given an answer: "Oh, they will be here tomorrow. They had things to do tonight." My heart breaks for the Ministry Visionary because I know she probably has not learned to delegate, and her ladies have not learned to serve.

Let me suggest a better plan. Let's break down the Organization Chart to the individual chart for Retreats and Conferences. For our discussion, these are the areas where the Retreat and Conference Shepherd Coach has determined she needs Leaders.

✣ GOD ✣

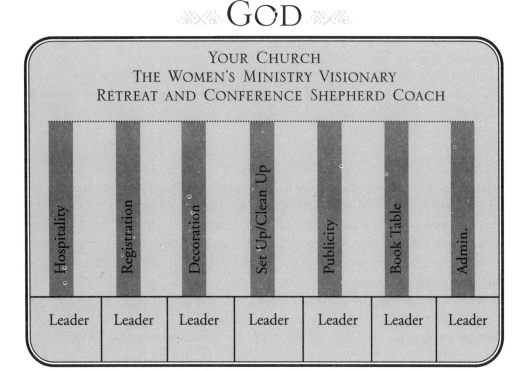

YOUR CHURCH
THE WOMEN'S MINISTRY VISIONARY
RETREAT AND CONFERENCE SHEPHERD COACH

Hospitality	Registration	Decoration	Set Up/Clean Up	Publicity	Book Table	Admin.
Leader	Leader	Leader	Leader	Leader	Leader	Leader

Each Leader has responsibilities in her area and recruits a team of Coordinators to assist her. The Coordinators then develop and recruit their teams of women seeking an opportunity to serve in the Women's Ministry.

In summary:
- The Ministry Visionary's team is made up of Shepherd Coaches.
- The Shepherd Coaches' teams are the Leaders.
- The Leaders' teams are the Coordinators.
- The Coordinators develop and work with a team of helpers.

Each level is a leadership role-Ministry Visionary-Shepherd Coach-Leader-Coordinator. This allows the Ministry Visionary to truly be a servant leader who touches more lives than she could ever do on her own. The Ministry Visionary mentors the Shepherd Coaches who teach what they have been taught to their Leaders who teach what they've been taught to their Coordinators. That is my definition of mentoring: Teaching what you've been taught so you can train those God puts before you so they can teach what you taught them to those God puts before them.

" 'Any of you who does not give up everything he has cannot be my disciple' " (Luke 14:33). Luke 5:11 tells us that the disciples did exactly that; "so they pulled their boats up on shore, left everything and followed him." Jesus set the standards high for participating on His team. He spoke often about the cost of being on His team (Luke 9:57-62; 14:25-33; Matt. 8:18-22). Luke 18:18-25 also contains the famous verses about the rich ruler who asked Jesus what it would take to inherit eternal life and be His follower. Jesus' words cut straight to the heart: " 'Sell everything you have and give to the poor, and you will have treasure in heaven. Then come, follow me' " (18:22). The rich man's response: "When he heard this, he became very sad, because he was a man of great wealth. Jesus looked at him and said, 'How hard it is for the rich to enter the kingdom of God' " (v. 24). When Peter pointed out: "We have left all we had to follow you! (v. 28), Jesus replied, 'I tell you the truth, ... no one who has left home or wife or brothers or parents or children for the sake of the kingdom of God will fail to receive many times as much in this age and, in the age to come, eternal life' " (vv. 29-30).

Lesson to Learn

The *Leadership Bible* comments on these passages: Jesus never hesitated to tell His followers that He wanted all or nothing. Indeed, Jesus said that their love for Him needed to be so great that all other human relationships would pale by comparison. While only Jesus qualifies for that kind of devotion, we can learn from this passage that skilled leaders don't blink when urging others to count the cost. They know that a follower who has a half-hearted commitment will never become a leader.

You might be thinking, "Women won't make that kind of a commitment." You are right; not all women will. But you don't need all women. You just need a few dedicated women who understand and embrace the cost of following in Jesus' footsteps. Not everyone in Bible times could be Jesus' disciple—He rejected the rich ruler's offer of service when he was not willing to pay the cost of giving away all he possessed. Seldom are we asked to give away everything, but often women feel that giving up their wants, personal desires, and time are too much to sacrifice. Just like the rich ruler, they miss out on the blessing of serving with Jesus.

Let me caution you that a woman with an unbelieving husband will find it difficult, if not impossible, to serve in a leadership role. She may be perfectly qualified and passionate about her service, but if her husband is not supportive of her ministry work, she will encounter stress at home and will be unable to keep her ministry commitments. I did not understand this at first. I always asked whether she had talked with her husband about the commitments, whether he knew the demands of the role, and was he OK with her service and time commitments? The response each time was, "Yes, he said I could do it." But then she was not able to come to required meetings, he wanted her home at a certain time, or he wanted her to do nothing in the evening or on weekends, and so on it went. She was not able to fulfill the responsibilities of her leadership role. In over 10 years of leading a large women's ministry, I have never seen it work. It puts unnecessary stress and pressure on her marriage, and that is not the way to win her husband to the Lord.

Because we do not want to exclude from God's service women whose husbands are not believers, consider these women for short- rather than long-term service commitments. They need to be and feel included in His service. Chris Adams gives excellent ideas for short-term service in the chapter, "Building Your Leadership Team" (see page 112).

I also often hear of recruiting leaders for only one year of service. You will never have a team of committed dedicated leaders if you follow that philosophy. It takes years to nurture a woman into a leader committed to the work of the Lord. If you want longevity, consistency, and commitment in your ministry, you must find women who are willing and who can count the cost of following you as you follow Jesus (see 1 Cor 11:1).

Taking It to Heart

Part of our job as Christian leaders is to help educate women on how to prioritize their lives so they always have time to serve the Lord. That means we need to know how to do that ourselves. Here is a quick way to have your life in step with God. Prioritize your life according to His priorities.

- Priority 1—Put Jesus at the center of everything you do instead of centering your life around Him. Then everything you say and do will come from a heart filled with Him.
- Priority 2—Just as your family is a part of your local family of God, your community of fellow believers is also part of your family. They are both priority. Jesus said, " 'Who is my mother, and who are my brothers?' Pointing to his disciples, he said, 'Here are my mother and my brothers. For whoever does the will of my Father in heaven is my brother and sister and mother' " (Matt. 12:48-50). We Christians should ask God to guide us to a healthy balance in meeting our personal family needs and the needs of our believing community.

We must prioritize our lives before we can help others set priorities.

- Priority 3—Follow Jesus' command to evangelize the world. Christ died for the unbeliever, and He chooses to work through us to accomplish His Great Commission (Matt. 28:16-20).

Until we are solidly grounded in Priority 1, we are not fit to lead. But once we are, nothing except ourselves can stop God from working in and through us. If we hear ourselves saying we are too busy to do the Lord's work, then we know Priority 1 needs work. Can you see yourself standing in front of Jesus Christ saying, "Sorry Lord, I have so many things to do, I can't serve You. I am just too busy."

Women too often use time as an excuse not to be about the Lord's work. We need to remind them that if they are too busy to serve, they are too busy. Something needs to change drastically or we will not be effective at the Priority 2 level of our life. Our ladies need to hear this message: if our family, health, relationships, and spiritual life suffer and our witness to the unbeliever is destroyed, there can be no Priority 3.

Many of today's Christian women have bought into the lie that they can "do it all," and each of us has our own definition of what "all" means. The truth is we cannot do it all. When we come to that realization, we too often forfeit God's work. Putting it aside may provide temporary relief, but what is it doing to our eternal life? We need to help women see that they are substituting the world's priorities for God's: working for man instead of God and putting the gods of things money can buy before the One and Only God. In America, we are all the rich rulers. Most of us live at a level far above our needs. We keep working harder and faster to raise our standard of living, which is the exact opposite of what the Bible tells us to do.

Many women today have made their families gods. Their children, instead of God, are at the center of their lives. They say they are doing things for the children, but what kind of children are they producing—self-centered, self-destructive, self-motivated? The family is falling apart at the fastest rate in history, and the church's statistics match the world's. Our too-busy lives, not focused on the Lord and His work, are leading to destruction instead of eternal life. Jesus predicted it. It is our job to turn the focus back to God by helping our women learn to die to themselves and live in Christ.

JESUS WAS SPECIFIC ABOUT THE JOB REQUIREMENTS

In Mark 6:8-11, Jesus proceeded to tell His team exactly how to travel and perform their duties. Jesus was organized, did not minimize the cost of being on His team, and was very specific about what He expected from them. Mark 14:13-15 is another example of Jesus giving two of His disciples specific instructions on how to go and find the house for the Passover meal.

Lesson to Learn

Woman to Woman Mentoring Ministry Coordinator's Guide uses the term "Opportunity to Serve" and has Service Opportunity Descriptions for each position and leadership area of the mentoring ministry. Very similar to job descriptions in the work world, they are comprised of specific:
- purposes
- requirements
- responsibilities, and
- durations.

The descriptions clearly provide information on what is expected and serve as a great interviewing tool. Everything potential leaders need to know about the positions is right in front of them, and you don't have to worry about forgetting to tell them something. They can easily determine whether this is the job for them. Once they accept the position, they have the Service Opportunity Description to remind them of what the job entails.

Taking This to Heart

In our ministry, we do not recruit without a Service Opportunity Description. The Shepherd Coaches, with the help of their Leaders and Coordinators, compile the specifics of each job on their team. This process provides a clear understanding of what the person is to do, and the person filling the role understands the expectation. For example, if someone offers to be a Hugger/Greeter and looks at the Service Opportunity Description and sees she has to hug instead of shake hands, she might say she cannot hug strangers. Wouldn't you rather find that out before the event rather than when she is standing at the door shaking hands instead of hugging? The Service Opportunity Descriptions allow you both to discuss such concerns before the event and find a role more suitable to her. This is a win/win ministry tool.

JESUS SENT HIS TEAM OUT IN PAIRS

"Calling the Twelve to him, he sent them out two by two and gave them authority over evil spirits" (Mark 6:7). This follows Solomon's wise advice in Ecclesiastes 4:9-10 that "Two are better than one, because they have a good return for their work: If one falls down, his friend can help him up. But pity the man who falls and has no one to help him up!" Mark 6:12-13 confirms this was an effective approach: "They went out and preached that people should repent. They drove out many demons and anointed many sick people with oil and healed them." Luke 10:1 says, "The Lord appointed seventy-two others and sent them two by two ahead of him to every town and place where he was about to go."

Lesson to Learn

Each leadership level needs an apprentice. On the Organization Charts we looked at earlier, the Shepherd Coach, Leader, and Coordinator positions would have an apprentice box off to the side. An apprentice learns by doing. She assists the person to whom she is assigned and prepares to step in and take her place if necessary. Amazingly, this has been the hardest concept for me to pass along to my own administrative team, yet it is essential to the longevity of a ministry. I am not sure if the leader's hesitancy to participate comes from:
- fear she will be worked out of a role,
- pride that she can do it by herself, or
- lack of knowledge on how to develop an apprentice.

I have not lost heart, however, and continue to council, encourage, pray, and train on how to develop the right apprentice. Some leaders have learned that a woman may want to be an apprentice just because she wants to spend time and hang out with her, but she has no intentions of ever replacing the leader. Such a person is not an apprentice.

Taking It to Heart

Essentially, every position in the ministry should have an apprentice. That way you always have a replacement trained and ready to fill in during an emergency, when someone moves, gets sick, or stops serving for whatever reason. Well-trained and capable apprentices can fill in for their leaders at meetings or complete tasks should the need arise.

Effective leadership at any level is servant leadership.

" 'Now that I, your Lord and Teacher, have washed your feet, you also should wash one another's feet. I have set you an example that you should do as I have done for you. I tell you the truth, no servant is greater than his master, nor is a messenger greater than the one who sent him. Now that you know these things, you will be blessed if you do them' " (John 13:14-17).

This famous passage tells the story of Jesus washing the feet of the Twelve—even those of Judas who would soon betray Him. Jesus used all His allotted time to invest in His team, but now it was time to take a step down and humbly serve them. In this great and memorable act of service, Jesus set an example of servant leadership for His apostles and us to emulate.

Lesson to Learn

Effective leadership at any level is servant leadership. Serve your team and they will follow you anywhere. As a servant leader you will …

- care about what they care about.
- be their cheerleader.
- pray for them and let them know you are praying.
- encourage them when they are down.
- let them know they mean more to you then just the job they are doing.
- be humble.
- often ask the question, "How can I help you?"

Taking It to Heart

I used the John 13 footwashing passage with my team at one of our administrative team retreats. I washed all their feet, and then they in turn washed each other's as they committed to love each other as Christ loved them.

This exercise was a very powerful and tearful moment for us all. For those committed to the service of the ministry, I believe it cemented a conviction to their role and to each other.

Asking for such a commitment may prove to be more than some leaders may be willing to give.

Serving your team may take many other forms in addition to the literal footwashing. Pray that God brings to mind what your team needs to see from you and to what length you are willing to go to put them first and yourself last.

JESUS RELEASED, GRANTED AUTHORITY, AND COMMISSIONED HIS TEAM

"Then Jesus came to them and said, 'All authority in heaven and on earth has been given to me. Therefore go and make disciples of all nations, baptizing them in the name of the Father and of the Son and of the Holy Spirit, and teaching them to obey everything I have commanded you' " (Matt. 28:18-20). "Then the disciples went out and preached everywhere, and the Lord worked with them and confirmed his word by the signs that accompanied it" (Mark 16:20).

You can serve your team in many different ways.

After His death and resurrection and right before His assent into heaven, Jesus issued The Great Commission to the eleven remaining apostles. Jesus passed on His authority to His team, telling them, *everything I did you too can do on your own. Not only can you do it, I command you to do it.* Then He watched over them and continued to help them from heaven, just like He does for us.

Lesson to Learn

To commission others to serve in our place, we must also …
- grant authority,
- release, and
- step back and let them go.

As your Team That Jesus Built grows, you know increasing less about the details of the everyday operation because the ministry will outgrow what one person can keep a handle on. Isn't that great news? If you hold on tightly, your ministry only can be as big as your two hands. But when you equip, train, release, grant authority, and commission team members, there are no limits to the ministry your team can accomplish. Don't limit it to yourself. Let it go, and let it grow.

Taking It to Heart

Jesus' team was prepared for His departure. Is yours? If the Lord were to take you home today, are your team members ready to step in and carry on without you? Do you see that the time to prepare them for this is now, not in the urgency of some crisis? Are you willing to pass on to the next generation of leaders all that God has entrusted in you? Are you teaching them to do the same? This is the only way the Team That Jesus Built works.

Jesus' team was ready for His departure. Is Yours?

BUILDING YOUR LEADERSHIP TEAM

CHRIS ADAMS

*A*s you were growing up, whom did you follow? Who were your heroes? Whoever they were, they were your leaders. If you look back, would you follow the same leaders today? Do you think of yourself as a leader? What are you doing to build a team of godly leaders that others will desire to follow because of their commitment to Christ?

This chapter will help you build a strong team in your women's ministry as you encourage ladies to respond to God's call to leadership. All Christians are called to be leaders in one way or another. One of the privileges of being a women's ministry leader is helping women discover their giftedness and leadership abilities and matching those with ministry opportunities.

Since Satan often attacks spiritual leaders first, we must pray to discover God's direction before beginning a new ministry or seeking leadership for it. Then we need to continue in prayer for those leaders as they serve. Sometimes we are tempted to begin a new ministry that the Lord has laid on our hearts, but there seems to be no leader for it. Waiting for God to raise up the right person is sometimes difficult, but the results of following His plan will be much more effective than if we rush into a new ministry on our own.

As a leader, you must place high priority on your own spiritual preparation. Are you spending time daily alone with God in prayer, worship, and Bible study? Those you lead must be able to see your walk with the Lord and your desire to continue to grow spiritually. If you are not setting the example, those you lead may not see the importance of a continual, daily walk that draws women into a closer relationship with Christ.

Is leadership something you accomplish or acquire? Neither, it is a gift from the Heavenly Father. Leadership is the ability to influence people toward a common goal. In women's ministry, it is sharing the vision of reaching and discipling women for Christ.

Matthew 20:25-28 gives us quite a contrast between servant leadership and ruler leadership: "But Jesus called them to Himself and said, 'You know that the rulers of the Gentiles lord it over them, and those who are great exercise authority over them. Yet it shall not be so among you; but whoever desires to become great among you, let him be your servant. And whoever desires to be first among you, let him be your slave–just as the Son of Man did not come to be served, but to serve and to give His life a ransom for many" (NKJV). Rulers are "over" others. They exercise authority, tell others what to do, and coerce to get results. Servants are "among" others. They show and persuade in love. Servant leadership should be the goal for those in any position of leadership.

Rulers are "over" others; servants are "among" others.

PORTRAIT OF A LEADER

We could use many words to describe a servant leader. Let's look at a few.

- *Enthusiastic.* This leader has an obvious passion for the Lord, for women, and for ministry to and with women.
- *Encouraging.* She will encourage others to lead and serve the Lord through various ministries–not just women's.
- *Flexible.* She has learned how to make adjustments without allowing a situation to fall apart should things not occur as expected.
- *Innovative.* She is not afraid to take risks if God has led her to step out of the "norm" and do some things that "have never been done before."
- *Available.* She allows God to direct her time and priorities to serve Him wholeheartedly.
- *Delegator.* She knows how to allow others to take responsibilities without watching over each detail. She allows leaders the freedom to be creative.
- *Listener.* She knows how to listen to those she leads; she hears and understands their hearts. She affirms their contribution as important to the team.
- *Trainer.* She continues to learn so that she can train others as well as keeping them informed of training opportunities offered by others.
- *Nurturer/Discipler.* She is as concerned about the spiritual growth of her team as she is in developing leadership skills.
- *Transparent.* She is transparent about her own failures and weaknesses so those she leads will be able to come to her when they struggle.
- *Accountable.* She allows and expects the Lord and her team to hold her accountable for her leadership and spiritual walk.
- *Evaluator.* She continually evaluates activities, studies, leaders, and ministries to make sure they are effective and current.
- *Dependable.* She will stand by her commitments to the best of her ability.

What does a leader look like? You! Unique and gifted to serve wherever God leads. If God has called you to lead, He has equipped you to do all He asks:

"We are His workmanship, created in Christ Jesus for good works, which God prepared beforehand that we should walk in them" (Eph. 2:10, NKJV). God has already prepared beforehand all He wants us to do to serve Him. God's indwelling Holy Spirit provides the power to be obedient when He calls.

MOBILIZING A LEADERSHIP TEAM

A Christian team could be described as a group of people who serve each other under Christ. In women's ministry, a team is made up of leaders who have responsibility for various aspects of the ministry to ladies in their church. Just as Jesus was a team leader and member, the women's ministry coordinator/director/team leader serves in both capacities. She works alongside her team, but also understands that she assumes final responsibility.

Because women are so busy and sometimes hesitant to commit to many things, it is not easy to enlist leaders and volunteers to meet ministry needs. However, it can be done, and women will serve. The *Indiana Baptist* reported these reasons people say yes to volunteer opportunities:

"It sounds like fun.
I want to be where the action is.
They really need and want me.
It is a chance to learn new skills.
It could help me with my personal life.
I have gotten a lot of help; now it is my turn to repay.
It is a critical need; I have got to do my part.
I will have a chance to really influence what happens.
Service is a tradition in our family. It's expected.
My best friend is asking me.
I will make new friends."[1]

Mobilizing a leadership team is essential for effective ministry to women.

As we begin praying for leaders, it will be wise to consider these reasons.

Mobilizing a leadership team is essential for effective ministry to women. Brad Smith says that a lay mobilization system works with existing church programs if it includes the following components: assimilation, context, discovery, matching, placement, coaching, and recognition.[2] Let's look closely at each one.

Assimilation means becoming a part of the church. As women join the church, we must be sure they find their niche, a place they can grow as well as serve. Providing a ministry for women new to the church speeds up assimilation and makes sure new women do not feel forgotten.

Context refers to helping women understand the biblical basis for volunteer service. Jesus commissioned His followers to go and make disciples of others (see Matt. 28:19-20). We must teach women that throughout Scripture we are instructed to share, go, serve, and witness.

Discovery of spiritual gifts and interests is an important part of developing women into leaders. We can encourage the use of spiritual gifts inventories and studies to help each woman discover how and why God has uniquely gifted her.

Matching shows women how to connect their gifts and interests with service opportunities.

Placement is selecting the best opportunity for service based on gifts and interests. This is much more effective than just filling an empty position.

Coaching should continue for each woman as she serves. As a team leader your responsibility is to offer training and encouragement.

Recognition happens as you offer times for celebration of service. This could be an appreciation service or banquet to say thank you for their willingness, sacrifice, and hard work.

Discovering Leaders

As you pray, you may discover several ways to identify and choose team members for specific assignments. Ask your pastor and other staff members for suggestions. They come in contact with many potential leaders and can point you to them. Other leaders in your church may also be able to provide suggestions.

Surveys can be helpful to discover talents, interests, and gifts needed for each area of service. If your church does not encourage surveys, discover leaders on your own by praying and watching women as you attend worship, Sunday morning Bible study, and other church activities.

A leadership team should be made up of women from different life stages and generations. This way you will get input from various groups like single and senior adult women, young moms, empty nesters, professionals, women sandwiched between aging parents and children at home, full-time homemakers, and so on. Remember that all these women will take the excitement of women's ministry and promote activities in their circles of influence.

Your team should also include people with different leadership styles. If you only choose women like yourself, there will not be balance in your planning or ministry. You need drivers who provide energy and excitement to complete the task at hand. Initiators enjoy beginning new ministries. Detailers will spend much time making sure all the bases have been covered. Listeners tend to listen quietly to discussion and then share an important conclusion. The innovator is not afraid to take risks.

Respect and value all leadership styles, gifts, knowledge, experiences, and personalities. Including various types of leaders will help ensure an effective team for ministry. Every woman has something to contribute. Help her find her passion and discover how to use it to serve Christ. Remember, God uses ordinary, inadequate people to accomplish extraordinary ministry through His power.

With all these different types of leaders, what should you look for? Look for *faithfulness* in their walk with the Lord. Are they growing spiritually? Are they spending time with Christ each day in prayer and Bible study? Look for *teachability*. Those leaders willing to listen and learn will continue to grow in service. Look for *availability*. Ministry takes time and willingness to be available.

Enlisting Leaders

In approaching potential leaders, ask for a time when you can visit with them. You might even conduct an interview to discover any interest in the ministry. Define job expectations in detail. Always allow them to pray and seek God's direction before responding to your request. Be supportive of their response—whether or not they accept the leadership position you offer.

Respect and value all leadership styles, gifts, experiences, and personalities.

Mary Frances Bowley, First Baptist Church, Peachtree City, Georgia, uses the following criteria for selecting new leaders. They must:

1. Have a God-planted desire to be a member of the team.
2. Display team building qualities.
   - Love Jesus.
   - Love people.
   - Know God's Word.
   - Know what authority is.
   - Be able to take responsibility.
3. Demonstrate depth of commitment.
   - Participate in an in-depth Bible study.
   - Pray for the same 30 families (from Sunday School and church rolls) on a continuous basis (five per day six days a week); on the seventh day, pray for team members and their families.
   - Understand the vision God has given your church to use women's ministry as an outreach to the community and to strengthen the body of believers; communicate this to the women of your church.
   - Be willing to meet monthly for planning, fellowship, and prayer.

Training Leaders

Once you discover and enlist leaders to be on your leadership team, they need to be trained. The degree of training you provide will be reflected in the effectiveness of your women's ministry. Consider the following elements as you set up your training.

PRAYER

The most important area in training your leaders is prayer. This is the key to all you do in women's ministry; it even ranks above developing leader skills. Model the importance of prayer by beginning and concluding each meeting with prayer. Teach your leaders to be pray-ers and not just do-ers. Schedule times strictly for prayer and praise. A good question to ask is, "What is God doing in your life?" These times of prayer may be retreats lasting a few hours or overnight. Prayer will help avoid burnout among your team members and keep them focused on God's will for the ministry. Assign team members prayer partners for continued prayer for specific needs between planning meetings. Encourage your leaders to become involved in the intercessory prayer ministry of your church. Pray for your team regularly, and let your team members know that you do. Making prayer a priority will teach leaders to continually seek and respond to the Lord's guidance in all aspects of their lives—especially as they lead the women of your church and community.

STUDY

Studying *Experiencing God: Knowing and Doing the Will of God* as a group can enhance and encourage spiritual growth among your team members. As you learn that ministry is what God does and not what we do, you will begin to see where He is already at work. When God invites you to join Him in ministry, your team is ready and willing to obey His call.

The degree of training you provide your leaders will be reflected in the effectiveness of your ministry.

PURPOSE AND VISION

Keeping your ministry's purpose and vision in front of the team at all times will help focus the ministry. Check to make sure all plans will accomplish the purpose God has given the team. Many people die without Christ every day. Ask, "What will this activity or event do to reach women for Christ and disciple them?" If this is not going to be accomplished, maybe your plans need to be changed or replaced.

ONGOING PLANNING

Ongoing planning encourages team members and shows accountability. This means not only meeting once or twice a year for strategic planning for the future but also conducting monthly planning meetings to carry out the strategic plans. As you share important information with the team, allow for feedback from each person. What is happening in their areas of ministry? Do they have any special praises to share? What about problem areas? Are plans proceeding according to the schedule, or do adjustments need to be made? This is a time for team members to report to the rest of the team both their needs and their joys.

ASSISTANCE

Each team member should always seek others to assist her with her area of ministry. The more people the team member involves, the greater the outcome of each event or activity. As committees and work groups share responsibilities, the circle of influence involves more women.

Teamwork is not hierarchy. As team leader, you may need to give specific instructions about an assigned task, but you should give ownership to those on your team by allowing decisions to be made at the lowest possible level. This empowers your leaders to make decisions about change and to accomplish tasks; it validates their responsibilities. William Easum says, "Today's leaders focus on permission-giving rather than control or managing. They network individuals and teams through a shared vision of a preferred future. They facilitate ministry in others. They do not 'give' orders, or dictate how people must operate within the organization. They cast the vision that creates victory, that frees people to make on-the-spot decisions and then get out of the way. In this role they model an open and free environment in which ordinary people are encouraged and equipped to do extraordinary ministry. Their passion is to develop other leaders who will develop other leaders."[3]

ENCOURAGEMENT

As team leader, you are the head cheerleader for the team. Encourage your leaders often. Share with them Ephesians 2:10: "We are His workmanship, created in Christ Jesus for good works, which God prepared beforehand that we should walk in them." God will equip them for everything He calls them to do. Recognize their service–the job itself and what it took to do it. Send thank you notes to your leaders and to their families for supporting them. Continue to remind them of your prayers for them, their areas of service, and their families.

As team leader, you are the head cheerleader for the team.

Encourage them to be innovative and to take risks. Remember, Jesus was pretty radical, too! If they experience failure in some aspect of their ministry, help them regroup and carry on. We often learn more from failure than success.

LEARNING STYLE

As you train your leaders, be aware of their different learning styles. Some learn best by listening to others talk in person, through radio, television, and audio tapes. Some learn best by reading books, newspapers, and magazines. Visual aids will enhance their learning. Others best learn through hands-on experience. Some can work without assistance. Discover what types of learners you have on your team, and check to see if your training includes all types of teaching so that each woman will learn according to her style.

NETWORK

Maintain contact with the network of people who provide leadership training on an associational, state, and national level. Take your team to the training events that will be most beneficial to them as individuals and team players.

LEADERSHIP TEAMS

Women's ministry includes many types of leadership teams. Even though your core leaders may provide the foundation for the ministry and may serve for two or three years, you must also establish other types of leadership teams. Let's take a look at some of these teams and the benefit each one offers.

- Co-leaders: This approach offers two busy women the opportunity to join together to accomplish a task.
- Short-term: Short-term responsibilities mean there is closure at the end of a set time period (perhaps 4 to 12 weeks).
- Project: Committing to a single project means there is closure once the project has been completed.
- Ongoing: This team lays the foundation for the daily and weekly ministries. Leaders generally serve from one to three years.
- Dream Team: This team, made up of women from all seasons of life, may only meet once or twice a year. It may be called the assessment or think-tank team. These women provide the stimulus to continue to look to the future for growth, change, and ministry development. In "The Mindset of Today's Changing Woman," Denise Farrar says,

> There will be one striking characteristic of third generation Women's Ministries. They will incorporate a group into their ministry that could be called a 'think-tank group.' The purpose of this group will be to focus on emerging trends and patterns. Most women's organizations have some type of decision-making group, but their focus is on implementation and coordination. Ministries on the cutting edge will have a separate group focused on the current trends and patterns affecting women as well as their needs. ... These women need to be innovative, change-agent types of leaders.[4]

- Leader/Learner: This team is made up of a leader and an apprentice. The leader mentors the understudy as she carries out her responsibilities. The one learning is expected to take the leadership position after a specific time period when the leader steps down or into another area of service. William Easum says, "If you are able to see in people more than they can see in themselves and are willing to equip them and set them free, you have the ability to be a leader in the Quantum Age. Mentors always have interns or apprentices and they take the long term view instead of looking for the quick fixes."[5] These leaders are concerned about the future of the ministry and who will carry on after them.

TEAM MEMBER ASSIGNMENTS

Following are some suggestions for team responsibilities. Use these as a beginning point as you design your ministry team to meet the needs of your church.

Women's Director/Coordinator/Minister

The director is the administrator who:
- oversees planning, coordination, and implementation of all discipleship, outreach, evangelism, and fellowship activities, leaders, and volunteers for women's ministry;
- provides training and motivation for women's ministry leaders;
- prepares, sets the agenda for, and chairs all planning meetings and retreats;
- prepares and oversees the annual budget and calendar; works closely with other church leaders.

Suggested Teams

In consultation with the core leadership team, the women's ministry director will oversee all teams. The number and size of each team depends on both the size of the church and the extent of the women's ministry. You may not need all of these; you may want to combine some of them. Use only those that apply to your ministry. Your women's ministry will not need all of these it is fairly new. The following teams may be composed of a group of women or one person.

HOSPITALITY

Greets and makes each woman feel welcome at all women's activities.

FACILITIES

Makes sure proper procedures have been followed for securing buildings and rooms needed for each activity or event.

PROGRAM

Helps develop effective ministry through ongoing weekly studies and groups such as electives, personal choice studies, and Bible studies; previews each study; secures leaders for each group.

CHILD CARE

Provides quality child care and learning opportunities for children while their mothers are participating in women's ministry activities.

SPECIAL EVENTS

Secures special committees that join together to plan and implement retreats, conferences, banquets, luncheons, seminars, and other special events.

REGISTRATION

Works with church support staff to take reservations and sell tickets; is responsible for receiving and handling money for ticket sales at events; provides registration for weekly program activities; provides name tags at all functions.

MISSIONS EMPHASIS

Works with missions organization (Women on Mission, WMU) to coordinate missions education ministries; provides missions information and prayer calendars; provides information on special missions prayer emphases to the church.

OUTREACH/EVANGELISM

Is aware of community needs and offers ministry to meet those needs (short- and long-term); encourages seeker-sensitive activities to reach the unchurched.

PRAYER

Specifically prays about details and decisions regarding the plans and activities of women's ministry to ensure the stated purpose is accomplished according to God's will; sets up prayer groups as needed; oversees emergency prayer chains.

ART/DESIGN

Helps create appealing flyers, brochures, and news clips for publicity; provides ideas and assistance for platform settings.

PUBLICITY

Handles printing newsletters, and announcements for events and programs (see "Publicity and Promotion," p. 208).

SPEAKERS

Oversees the selection of speakers for special events and conferences; contacts with and hosts speakers.

MINISTRY NETWORK

Oversees the network of ministries (both inreach and outreach) within the church and community in which members may involve themselves in reaching out to others in Christ's name.

NEW MEMBER SHEPHERDING

Coordinates teams who visit women new to the church to help acquaint them with their new church family, offer assistance as needed, and inform them about areas of interest and service. Team members agree to have at least five "touches" with each new member assigned to them (visit, phone, mail, invitation to lunch or women's activity, and so forth). To learn more about New Member Shepherding, read the chapter "The New Member" in *Transformed Lives: Taking Women's Ministry to the Next Level.*

CORRESPONDENCE

Leads a team of women to write personal notes of condolence to bereaved families, notes of welcome to newcomers, and congratulations to women who have just delivered babies, as well as letters of support and encouragement to home and foreign missionaries.

FOOD

Plans for refreshments, meals, and beverages at events and programs.

DECORATIONS

Works with special events and art/design teams to plan decorations around the theme of the event or study.

BULLETIN BOARDS

Works with women's ministry director and publicity committee to promote events and programs.

ENCOURAGEMENT/LAY COUNSELING

Coordinates ministry for women with special needs (crisis, evangelism); provides training for lay counselors.

SECRETARY

Keeps records; orders materials; serves as historian by keeping scrapbook.

JESUS' MINISTRY

We have the perfect example to follow as women's ministry leaders. Jesus was not only a team leader, He was a team member. Jesus ministered with and trained His disciples to carry on His work. He fellowshipped with His team. Jesus prayed with and for them. He did not do everything, but He trained others to serve with Him.

Jesus' priority was His relationship with God. Jesus had interruptions as He served, but He met the ministry at hand and accepted it as God's assignment.

Selma Wilson, former editor of *Journey,* a monthly devotional magazine for women, shares the following regarding Jesus as leader:

Jesus was not only a team leader, He was a team member.

Mission Statement

"I have come to do the will of the Father." As leaders, we need to always keep our mission in front of us. Our mission is never about a program, an event, or a resource. It is always about doing the will of the Father. Jesus said the greatest commandment is to love the Lord our God with all our hearts, souls, minds, and bodies (see Deut. 6:5).

Vision

"I have come that [you] might have life and that [you] might have it more abundantly" (John 10:10, KJV). Jesus had a vision for reaching people. We in leadership need a vision for reaching people with the good news of Jesus Christ. That must be central to all we do. Often our vision is limited to having a great event or a great women's program. When this happens, we are not being the leaders God has called us to be. Have a vision for people, not programs.

Focus

Vision and focus are very similar. Vision is about the future. Focus is about what we see right in front of us, that ever-mounting "to do" list. It's all the interruptions we get, all the detours on the journey to our vision. Jesus modeled the journey well. Jesus was frequently interrupted. He had to deal constantly with the religious system. Yet, He never lost His vision. Jesus was a servant leader in everyday life. He took time to minister, listen, heal, and share. Interruptions became opportunities for Jesus to carry out His vision. The interruptions were the will of the Father for His life for that time.

Prayer Life

Jesus modeled the need for prayer and a quiet time with God. If Jesus, the Son of God, needed that time, who are we to think we can live without it? We can not. We must schedule time each day to be alone, to be quiet before God. Spending time with God and praying are keys to staying on mission, to keeping our vision, and to staying focused on what's important. Without this time, we can shortly find ourselves far away from God's will and mission for us. We must make this a top priority and a regular part of our lives.

View of Eternity

Jesus had a clear perspective of eternity. He knew His destination. One of the greatest things we can do as leaders is remind ourselves and those around us of eternity. We are truly only passing through this life. This is not our home. If we have an eternal perspective as we live each day, we will be better equipped to stay focused. We are less critical of others, eager to share our faith, better able to give wise advice, and have the energy to do what is before us today. Stop and think on heaven. Read the Scriptures that confirm that we have a home prepared for us. We need to lead with our sites set on eternity.

Commitment

Jesus was committed to do the Father's will all the way to the cross. His last words, "It is finished," have such profound meaning. Jesus had completed the mission the Father had called Him to do. Is that our prayer? God has truly called us to be on mission. We are a part of kingdom business. It is a high and worthy calling. Is it your prayer to have the Father say at the end of your journey in this life: *Well done thou good and faithful servant?*

As a women's ministry leader, ask yourself, *Who will carry on when I am gone?* Reproducing yourself in others as you follow Christ will ensure that the ministry continues.

---

[1]Charles Willis, "Volunteer enlistment critical to meet ministry needs," *Indiana Baptist*, August 30, 1994, 6.

[2]Information in this section is adapted from Brad Smith as reported by Ferrell Foster, "Leadership Network nurturing Churches' 'lay mobilization,' " *Baptist Press*, 6 October 1995, n. pag.

[3]William Easum, "Sacred Cows Make Gourmet Burgers," *NEXT* Volume 1, Number 3, July 1995, 1-2.

[4]Denise Farrar, "The Mindset of Today's Changing Woman" *Symposium II: Building Bridges Between Christian Women and Their World* (Pasadena: The Women's Ministries Institute®, 1995), 57.

[5]Easum, 2.

INVOLVING THE UNINVOLVED

KAREN FINKE

I remember standing on the playground of Proctor Elementary School, dreading what was to come. Captains picked for the ball game (kickball, softball—it didn't matter) were choosing teams. I was always the last chosen. I also remember being taken to Sunday School by well meaning parents who did not attend church but occasionally felt the need for us children to go. I remember walking into a class where everyone knew each other, and they all knew the routine of the morning. I knew no one. I desperately wanted to be part of that group, but I wasn't and didn't know how to make that happen.

Every Sunday women come into our church buildings and sit on the fringe. They are married, unmarried, with children, and childless. They are senior citizens, young adults, and all ages in between. They all have one thing in common. They are waiting for someone to pick them to be on their team, to become part of the "group."

Church leaders are well aware of the 80/20 rule. Twenty percent of the people do eighty percent of the work, while eighty percent of the people sit quietly in the pew, seemingly content to do nothing to contribute to the life of their local church body. But are they really content, or are they uninvolved because no one has asked them to contribute? Because no one has asked them to be on their team?

Involving the uninvolved in ministry and fellowship is one of the greatest challenges in women's ministry today. All across the country leaders are asking the same question—how do we get the women involved? An answer that rolls all too quickly is "Women today are too busy." While this is a legitimate reason and certainly one that should be considered, I'm not sure that is the sole answer to the question. Reality shows us we have time for the things we value. We will repeat activities in which we are fulfilled and make meaningful contributions. And we are likely to encourage someone else to join us in these.

So the question remains—why do so many women remain uninvolved in ministry and the events planned specifically to meet their needs? Although as many reasons exist as there are women, here are a few we often see.

1. Women today are busier than in years past.

We are involved in careers, raising active families, and civic affairs. We have

We likely will invite others to join us in meaningful and fulfilling activities.

crammed as much into our schedules as possible. Very little time remains for church activities, especially those that don't meet needs. Rarely will women show up for an event or meeting simply because it is on the church calendar. This fact challenges us to be purpose driven and plan ministry that is needs based rather than event based.

2. Events are scheduled at times when women are not available to attend.

Now is the time to think outside the box as we plan ministry events. Survey the women in your church to decided whether daytime or evening is best. Do they work outside the home, or are they stay-at-home moms? Are the majority older women who don't drive in the evening? Maybe options at both times fit your needs. Does your community or school have activities that compete with the time when you always have Bible Study? If so, you may need to acknowledge that the chosen day may not be the best time for your particular church to offer Bible study.

3. Lack of quality child care.

Women's ministry has always needed to provide child care. Today's mom demands qualified workers and safe environments. Also, providing child care only during the day time is not enough. Busy family schedules demanding Dad's time as well as single moms with no one at home to help with the children call for quality care for evening and weekend events as well.

4. Some women are not interested in women's activities in the church.

For whatever reason, some women have never come to an event or become involved in women's ministry. Perhaps they have seen past women's events as "fluff" and not worth their time. Our responsibility is to become creative and to investigate the real needs of these women. Use written or spoken testimonials from women proclaiming how a Bible study, fellowship, or a special event has ministered to them. Sharing how women have been served through the ministries will dispel some preconceived notions of the uninvolved. Perhaps a focus group of a select group of women who are not active in the women's ministry will give some insight into why they don't participate.

5. There is no ownership in the event or ministry.

Few of us are interested in things we know nothing about. A rule of thumb when planning events states for every one person involved in the planning and implementing, four people will attend. The goal is to include as many people as possible, therefore expanding the circle of ownership.

The reasons for being uninvolved are valid and certainly need to be addressed. We would call these perceived needs. However, I believe that the following reasons may be, in many instances, the real reasons (or felt needs) why women do not become involved.

6. They do not know anyone involved.

Especially in larger churches, people may attend Sunday services regularly and only know by sight the folks who sit around them during the service. They do not attend a small group where connections would be made and are unlikely to respond to a bulletin invitation for an event where they will know no one.

7. Ladies are unaware of their giftedness.

If women do not know their spiritual gifts, they remain convinced they have nothing to offer. Too many of us believe that if we can't sing in the choir or

Include as many women as possible to expand the circle of ownership.

teach a class then there is no place for us to serve in the church. Paul begins 1 Corinthians 12 urging believers not to be ignorant about spiritual gifts. From his strong language we get the sense of the subject's importance. He goes on to explain how the Church needs each part to function the way God intended. Os Guinness writes in *The Call:*

> It [the call] argues that … purpose can be found only when we discover the specific purpose for which we were created and to which we are called. Answering the call of our Creator is the 'ultimate why' for living, the highest source of purpose in human existence. … To be sure, [this] calling is not what it is commonly thought to be. It has to be dug out from under the rubble of ignorance and confusion. And, uncomfortably, it often flies directly in the face of our human inclinations. But nothing short of God's call can ground and fulfill the truest human desire for purpose.[1]

8. Fear of not being accepted.

One lady in my Sunday School class said to me that she was considering joining the church. Her next statement was. "but I am afraid I would be rejected (not accepted)."

Individual backgrounds shape the way we perceive how others view us. Many women are sitting in the pews feeling left out and longing to be involved. Our job is to encourage and assure them of unconditional acceptance.

9. Real needs are not being addressed.

Can we emphasize enough the importance of planning activities and events based on the needs of the women in the church and community? We have an opportunity to minister to the real needs of women and have a huge impact on their spiritual growth. Consider divorce recovery, ministry to the single mom, post abortion issues, depression, eating disorders and addictions as small group opportunities. Providing ministries to the woman in the workplace has often been a neglected area. Again, this is where surveying the women in your church will provide valuable information.

We are often tempted to copy something fun and successful that another women's group has done. While sharing ideas is valuable, each women's ministry is unique and has its own individual needs. Providing a calendar full of activities does not insure involvement. Having a well-defined purpose statement and using it has a guide for everything planned will be a good place to begin meeting needs. The question we need to ask ourselves is "Will this make a difference in anyone's life?"

NECESSARY ELEMENTS TO INVOLVE THE UNINVOLVED

We must be intentional as we seek out the uninvolved. Being intentional means that involving the uninvolved becomes a ministry philosophy. This philosophy says that individuals are important and we are not recruiting folks only to fill a position. We are not inviting ladies simply to increase our numbers.

Adopting this intentional mindset will require leaders to ask some hard questions of themselves and their ministry teams. Do we really believe that every Christ follower in the body is gifted with a spiritual gift(s)? Do we really believe

"Nothing short of God's call can ground and fulfill the truest human desire for purpose."

that, because of these gifts, every believer can contribute in a way that benefits the entire body? Paul says in 1 Corinthians 12:18 "God has arranged the parts in the body, *every one* of them, just as He wanted them to be" (my emphasis) And further in the same chapter he says "those parts of the body that seem to be weaker are indispensable, the parts we think less honorable we treat with special honor." If we really believe what the Scripture says about each person's place in the church, then we would be amiss by neglecting to be intentional in searching for and calling out those who will not always stand in the front of the line. The entire body will suffer and the individual will be unfulfilled as a follower of Christ.

Ideas for creating an intentional ministry philosophy

1. Leaders should continually challenge the ministry team to look to the unlikely and to those who have not served before.

2. When enlisting new committees for special events include at least one person who has not served before.

3. Assign one person on the ministry team to have the responsibility for the uninvolved. A perfect choice would be someone with the gift of shepherding and/or mercy and with a passion for seeing women grow in their relationship with Christ.

4. A new member ministry could be established. One church I know has ministry team members personally deliver one of their women's ministry mugs along with information about the ministry to each new lady that joins the church. This gives them the opportunity to get face to face with her and discover any ministry needs as well her interests and gifts. Consider using *Transformed Lives* for training that includes New Member Shepherding.

The second necessary element is to identify the uninvolved. In 2 Timothy 2 Paul introduces us to his good and faithful friend Onesiphorus. Paul is in prison in chains. He is cold and lonely and probably dirty and stinky. All of his friends have deserted him—except one. The scripture tells us that Onesiphorus "searched hard" for Paul until he found him. He was not ashamed of Paul's situation and ministered to him in many ways.

Twenty percent of the people will continue raising their hands to volunteer. Some will always show up at an event simply because the church doors have been unlocked. As leaders we tend to turn to these same people over and over when we are looking for servants. It's always easier to ask someone we know will say yes. Identifying the uninvolved will challenge us to open our eyes and look for the folks who aren't quite as noticeable. My church's women's ministry is implementing an ambassador plan. A representative from each Sunday Bible study group will serve as an Ambassador to their class. Their responsibility will be to keep the women in the class aware of ministry events and opportunities. In addition they will be able to relay to the ministry team those women they see that could potentially serve and ladies who need special ministry attention.

"Searching hard" within that uninvolved eighty percent is not easy but worth the return as we discover gifted women. Women who will help to strengthen the Body and grow in their relationship with Christ as they serve and experience fellowship.

Identifying the uninvolved will challenge us to look for folks who aren't as noticeable as frequent volunteers.

Inviting the uninvolved to be involved is probably the single most effective tool. There is nothing like a one on one invitation to help a person feel valued and accepted. Jaye Martin of North American Mission Board writes in *Women Reaching Women, Revised and Expanded:*

> All these women and many more are just waiting for someone to care, waiting for someone to stop and notice they exist. Through events, we can reach out to women and show them a new world where Christ can provide them a new perspective, allow them to meet new friends, and give them meaning to life. (p. 193)

Too often we depend solely on mass mailings, Sunday bulletins and pulpit announcements to do our work for us. While these venues are a necessary means of communication they should never take the place of one individual seeking out another.

Consider Jesus' example. There was a man named Zacchaeus who was a chief tax collector and hated because of it (Luke 19: 1-10). When Jesus entered Jericho, Zacchaeus was in a tree. Talk about trying to stay in the background! Jesus purposely called to this unlikely host and chose to visit the pagan tax collector instead of a religious man. As a result Zacchaeus repented and became a Christ follower, returning half of his earnings to the poor.

Finally, being intentional, identifying the uninvolved and then extending one on one invitations to events and activities is only the beginning to an important end. The real purpose and goal is to integrate the uninvolved Believer into meaningful fellowship and active ministry where the gifts that God as given them can be used.

Too many people sit in the pew week after week thinking they are not qualified and convinced they have nothing to offer the church. As leaders, we are responsible to help others discover their giftedness, "to prepare God's people for service" (Eph. 4:12). Many resources are available to help in gift discovery (see p. 224). Also, providing opportunities for service in various areas gives an individual the chance to "try on" different ministries.

We as leaders are responsible to help others discover their giftedness.

INVOLVING THE UNLIKELY

Insignificant and unlikely are words that come to mind as we see Jesus choose His inner circle. In his book *Twelve Ordinary Men,* John MacArthur describes the twelve apostles as lacking spiritual understanding, lacking humility, lacking faith, lacking commitment and lacking power. Not exactly who I would choose to be on the team that would be expected to spread the gospel to the ends of the earth! Jesus entire ministry was marked with His encounters with unlikely people. For example, the rich young ruler, the Samaritan woman, and the woman caught in adultery were all people who were forever changed by the attention of Jesus.

The first year of my married life my husband and I spent the summer selling Bibles and other publications door to door. Each Sunday we would gather with other salespeople and have a meeting. One thing that I remember being repeated often—"Don't believe the myth that only brick houses buy." As I would go down the streets I would check out the houses and make assumptions about the buying potential based on the look of the house. I would be tempted to skip those houses that I thought would not buy. Many times I was surprised when a house that I had decided would not purchase anything became the biggest sell of the day.

There are many women that we look at through our leadership eyes and classify as an unlikely candidate for service. Our tendency is to skip over them and call on someone we deem more qualified. Jesus gave us a good example as He sought the twelve disciples. He knew better than anyone how unskilled they were. But Jesus knew something else too. He knew that the Holy Spirit would gift and equip these men to do the work they could never do on their own. Jesus intentionally chose these men because He knew that their ultimate victory and power would come from Him. Again we have to ask ourselves, do we really believe what the Scripture says about everyone having a significant purpose in the body?

Involving the unlikely women in service and fellowship in your church may be one of the most difficult things you do in ministry. You will encounter women who have security issues, women who lack people skills, and women who are just—how should we say it?—difficult.

An interesting verse in Proverbs 14 says, "Where there is no oxen, the manger is empty, but from the strength of an ox comes an abundant harvest." Think with me for a moment about what besides oxen would be in the manger, remembering that the are fed daily. Not a very pleasant sight (or smell)! If we are involved with ministry then we will deal with people that are difficult. People that are needy and demanding. People that drain our energy. Does that mean that these folks can not contribute in a meaningful and edifying way? What this does mean is we are going to have to depend on grace that only comes from abiding in Jesus as we interact with these women.

Here's the good part. The verse also implies all that smelly stuff will eventually produce an abundant harvest. I have a feeling the harvest will not only be a result of these ladies finding a place of service that suits them but also growth in the lives of the leadership as they become conduits for God's grace.

Our victory and power come from the Holy Spirit.

OBSTACLES TO INVOLVING THE UNLIKELY

1. It is not easy. Leadership never is! But the rewards are worth it.

2. It will involve many hours of investing in the lives of these women. Some of the women we encounter have a multitude of life issues that have a tremendous impact on their lives. Many of them have no other objective person with whom they can share and receive counsel. Part of leadership is being available and helping to provide ways she can grow in her relationship with Jesus.

3. It will not be popular. In years of leading women in my own church, one of the most difficult things I encountered was getting committee heads to include those outside their own friendship circle and women who have never before served. It is an understandable reaction but demonstrates again the need for ongoing encouragement and urging to change our philosophy on involvement.

Some persons who should be invited to serve may seem incapable or that what they have to offer is not "good enough." Luke 7 is a beautiful picture of

Jesus' acceptance of the unlikely. A sinful woman came into the place where Jesus and the disciples were dining. She began anointing his feet with her tears and expensive perfume. Those around Jesus were outraged, but Jesus gave value to her offering. We know from other Scriptures that this woman became Christ's devoted servant and follower. Had it been left up to the other dinner guests, she would have been turned away and forgotten.

SURVEY RESULTS

I created a survey for two churches investigating how a person becomes involved in ministry. Although not extremely scientific, this survey provided great insight. Here are some of the questions:

Are you currently serving in any capacity? If yes …

Did you respond to a published need?

Did you see a need and offer to serve?

Did you serve as a result of being asked by an individual?

To become a future servant would you most likely …

Respond to a published need?

Volunteer your services?

Respond only if someone asked you?

Overwhelmingly, most said they are currently serving only because someone asked them. That was not as surprising to me as this next fact. Most people responded that, while initially they began serving only after being asked by an individual, they said that in the future they would respond to a published need or volunteer their services. They no longer needed someone to invite them individually. That tells us two things. These folks discovered their gifts and found meaningful service. They now feel confident to step out and become involved, knowing they have made a meaningful contribution.

Jesus' example of calling individuals into service is our best model. Countless women discover their God-given purpose and experience fulfillment after being invited to serve. Service often followed a personal invitation to an event.

I recently led a weekend retreat in Texas. They had a great theme and the lady who was responsible for the decorating did an incredible job of carrying the theme throughout every aspect of the event. All weekend she reached out and included all of the ladies in attendance. I thought to myself what a valuable part of the weekend she had been. During the reflection time at the end of the weekend, I was surprised by this woman's testimony. Through tears she explained that this was the first time she had participated in any women's activity. She thanked the one responsible for asking her to serve and said that single invitation changed the way she sees herself in relation to the church. She was ready to yield to God and serve wherever He wanted her. And that, my sisters, is the reason we do what we do.

[1]Os Guinness, *The Call* (Nashville: Thomas Nelson, 1998), 4.
[2]Chris Adams, *Women Reaching Women* (Nashville: LifeWay Press, 1997), 93.

Service often follows a personal invitation.

WOMEN'S MINISTRY IN SMALLER CHURCHES

MARTHA LAWLEY

T love that God makes each local church unique. We find in today's churches countless variations including size, location, facilities, leadership, cultural practices, and ministry styles. Even within these categories we find wide diversity. For example, so-called smaller churches (less than 250 members) are each unique. Some gather in rural settings while others meet in urban or suburban areas. Some have older members while others have more young people. It's easy to become overwhelmed by all this diversity. Wouldn't it be simpler if all churches were alike? I admit I used to think one ministry goal was to help churches look more alike. However, I've come to believe diversity among local churches is part of God's great plan to build His kingdom. He has a unique plan for each church, strategically positioning and equipping her accordingly. I also believe ministry to women is an important part of this divine plan.

Diversity among local churches is part of God's great plan to build His kingdom.

This chapter is designed to encourage women in smaller churches as they seek and follow God's direction for ministry. My desire is to offer a balanced approach that recognizes the unique dynamics of a smaller church—her strengths as well as her struggles. I've discovered that some of the greatest obstacles we face in smaller-church ministry spring from our own attitudes. Therefore, we'll begin by examining some common attitudes that can hinder women's ministry in smaller churches. We'll then consider some tender words of encouragement from Jesus and conclude with practical suggestions for women's ministry in smaller churches.

SMALL TALK

When I attend a women's event at a larger church, I cannot help but be impressed with what I see—the facility, the ministry opportunities, and the staff. "If only we had these resources in our small church," I've often thought. It can be mind numbing to visit a church that employs more people than the entire membership of your church! I don't think I'm the only one who has felt this way. Big churches often have this kind of affect on those of us from churches with smaller congregations.

If we were totally honest, many of us would have to admit that, deep down, we've bought into the notion that bigger really is better. And who could blame us? Just about everywhere we turn, we're bombarded with a thousand variations of the bigger is better theme. For example, "A bigger home makes a family happier." "The more stuff I have the better my life will be." "Would you like to super-size that?"

The belief that bigger is always better usually produces an unhealthy ministry mind-set that destines women's ministry in the smaller church to mediocrity. Comparing ourselves to larger church women's ministries can cause us to doubt the value of our own ministry and resign us to a future of limited impact void of any great expectation. I'm convinced that God desires to accomplish great things through every church, regardless of size. As we will see, the real problem may be our definition of success.

As members of a smaller church, we must critically examine the bigger is better philosophy. Begin by asking yourself, "what does the Bible have to say concerning size?" I pray this chapter will help you discover or affirm God's perspective of ministry in the smaller church. Doing so will allow us to move forward in effectively ministering to women.

God desires to accomplish great things through every church, regardless of size.

THREE IMMOBILIZING MYTHS

Let's begin by examining three common ministry myths that can immobilize women's ministry in a smaller church. As we consider these myths, please do not become discouraged. Most of us in smaller churches continually struggle against these mindsets. I once heard someone say the two greatest things about God are that He loves us right where we are and He does not want us to stay there! Unmasking these myths helps us more clearly see God's perspective of ministry, allowing us to join Him where He is already at work.

Myth 1: Women's ministry was meant to be easy.

This myth is rooted in the mistaken belief that freedom from difficulty is evidence of God's blessing. In other words, if I'm doing God's will, things should be easy. Interestingly, I have yet to find sound biblical support for the idea that the center of God's will is problem free. In fact, just the opposite. In His earthly ministry, Christ faced every challenge you and I face in ministry (and more). God's precious, one and only Son—who did only what the Father told Him—ministered without sin, yet He faced every challenge imaginable. Why should we expect anything different?

Ministry, although a marvelous privilege, was never intended to be easy. It enriches our lives and strengthens our relationship with God and others, but it can be difficult. Many of my frustrations in ministry are the direct result of my mistaken expectation that ministry should be struggle free. God desires for us to minister from His perspective—to have the mind of Christ concerning ministry (Philippians 2: 1-11). I'm learning to seek daily God's renewal of my mind concerning ministry.

The myth that true ministry is struggle free leads to disappointment, discouragement, and defeatism. This particular myth also sets us up for another smaller church ministry pitfall—the grass is always greener (or the carpet newer) in the larger church.

Myth 2: Women's ministry in larger churches have greater impact.

After years of ministering among women in a smaller church, God helped me see that much of my distress stemmed from a bigger is better mindset. In some ways, I saw our women's ministry as inferior because it was small. God challenged me to carefully evaluate my standards for measuring the success of our women's ministry by asking a few basic questions. What kind of impact does God care about? What would a successful women's ministry look like to Him?

Jesus taught many lessons on kingdom economics, clearly illustrating that the economy of God's kingdom is intentionally different from the world's. For example, the first shall be last (Matt. 19:30), the least shall be the greatest (Matt. 18:4), and we must lose our life to gain eternal life (Matt. 10:39; 16:25). Kingdom ministry should not be measured by the world's standards for measuring success.

As ministry leaders we must ask ourselves whether we will choose to operate under the principles of the world's economy or the principles of God's kingdom economy. God can change our minds about how we measure success in women's ministry. His Word provides the only valid measure of success. Think about the women in your church and consider the following questions:

God's Word provides the only valid measure of success.

- Are the women in our church being transformed into the image of Christ (2 Cor. 3:18)?
- Are they equipped to view every aspect of their daily lives as ministry (Col. 3:17, 1 Cor. 10:31-33)?
- Do they know and use their spiritual gifts (1 Pet. 4:10)?
- Are others hearing and experiencing the message of salvation through them (Philem. 6)?

These biblical measurements guide us toward a women's ministry that God will bless with eternal impact.

When I think about the many ways smaller church ministries can have a significant impact on the kingdom, I immediately think of my home church. I'm astounded at how God has used our little church in northern Wyoming to impact the world. God progressively transformed many believers, and they lived out God's kingdom agenda. From within our midst God has raised up missionaries, ministers, and countless lay leaders who serve around the world. My church is not alone. Many of today's missionaries, ministers, and other lay leaders are the product of smaller church ministries. Don't let the enemy deceive you—women's ministry in the smaller church can have similar eternal impact for the kingdom!

Myth 3: Women's ministry in the smaller church is more challenging.

This myth is rooted in the sinking sand of self-centered focus. When I lament over my own personal struggles, I (like Elijah) eventually convince myself that I'm the only one. No one else has it as difficult as I do (1 Kings 19:10). Isn't it interesting how coming to that conclusion somehow makes us feel better?

In reality, women's ministry in a smaller church is no more or less challenging than women's ministry in larger churches. Each size church faces unique struggles, and each possesses unique strengths. That is not to say that smaller-church women's ministry is no different than women's ministry in larger churches. Important differences create unique opportunities for each.

A women's ministry that is self-centered in focus suffers limited vision. Self-focus promotes defeatism—"we can't do that" or "that will never happen here". Ministering in a smaller church, we continually face the challenge of limited resources. God is teaching me to resist my natural inclination to focus inward on what is lacking. With His help, my focus is shifted to Him, His will, His way, and His resources. I'm discovering God always provides what we need to do what He calls our women's ministry to do. (Although not necessarily what we have decided we should do.)

How do you see your women's ministry? What are your expectations for the future? I once heard a speaker say, "whether you think you can or you think you can't, you are right!" As leaders, our attitudes can limit the ministry of which God has invited us to be a part. God can do anything. Nothing is impossible for Him (Matt. 19:26). But whether we or our women's ministry will be a part of God's miraculous kingdom work depends in part on our focus. When we compare our women's ministry to that of larger churches, we give Satan a big foothold. Comparing leads to focus on self—our resources or lack thereof—instead of a God-centered focus. Complaining and complacency are its result. A God-centered women's ministry focuses on God's kingdom, His resources, and His standard for measuring success.

No matter what its size, any women's ministry clearly focused on God and His agenda can help transform women in all dimensions of their lives, equipping them to faithfully respond to God's call. The ministry will then have immeasurable impact on the kingdom through God's power.

A God-centered women's ministry focuses on God's kingdom, His resources, and His standard for measuring success.

WORDS OF ENCOURAGEMENT

As a member of a smaller church, I've found great encouragement and insight in something Jesus said in Luke 12:32. "Don't be afraid, *little flock,* because your Father delights to give you the kingdom" (emphasis mine). Even as I write the words of this verse, I am overwhelmed by their tenderness and concern. Let's consider for a moment the application of Jesus' words to women's ministry in a smaller church.

"Don't be afraid, little flock"—Jesus knows the struggles we face in ministering in the smaller church (Rev. 3:8; 2:9). He has not forgotten about us. I believe He watches with great interest as His bride prepares for His return. He esteems us even though others may not. He understands our fear and how disabling it is to us and the ministry to which He has called us. Only faith in God can drive out the fear we experience in smaller church women's ministry. Most of our fears come from our limitations as a small congregation—limited people, money, and facilities. I admit that at times I've placed my faith in the success of our women's ministry in myself and a few others. I've been afraid to attempt anything beyond what we can do with our visible resources. Jesus invites us to put our faith in Him and His Father (John 14:1). In reality, the success of any ministry is up to God—transforming lives, spiritual equipping, and salvation are all things only He can do. Apart from Him we can do nothing of eternal value (John 15:5). Basing our women's ministry on what God can and wants to do exercises a faith that drives fear away.

"[Y]our Father delights to give you the kingdom"—Giving us the kingdom pleases God. We do not have to earn it, He joyfully gives it to us. I lived much of my adult life under the mistaken impression that God needed my help. Over the past several years, God has been transforming my mind to see things from His perspective. He has lovingly showed me that He allows rather than needs my help. God invites us to be a part of His divine plan and to experience His power that accomplishes the work of the kingdom for our benefit. Joining Him in His work enriches our relationship with Him and furthers the process of our transformation into the image of Christ.

In Mark 4:26-27 Jesus said the kingdom of God is like "a man scatter[ing] seeds on the ground; he sleeps and rises—night and day, and the seed sprouts and grows—he doesn't know how." Sound familiar? You and I serve—planting, watering, and harvesting. We see evidence of kingdom growth around us, but we do not know exactly how God grows the kingdom. In 1 Corinthians 3:6-7 Paul addresses this same concept, "I planted, Apollos watered, but God gave the growth. So then neither the one who plants or the one who waters is anything, but only God who gives the growth." Putting great importance on our own work or the work of others ignores the truth that only God is necessary.

Our resources or lack thereof have never been the key to kingdom growth. Yet it's easy in the day-to-day challenges of women's ministry in the smaller church to behave as if God cannot do it without us. Successful smaller-church women's ministry is based on the understanding that it delights God to give us the kingdom.

Without a doubt God has happily given your "little flock" of women His infinite kingdom. Learning to embrace and live according to the principles of that kingdom—relying on God's plan accomplished in His time, through His power—cannot help but succeed (Acts 2:42-47, 4:23-35).

I've also noticed another way Jesus offers special encouragement to smaller churches. In Matthew 18:20, Jesus assures us that, "Where two or three are gathered together in My name, I am there among them." What a loving reminder that Jesus is in the midst of even the smallest group that gathers in His name. Jesus knows the dynamics of smaller-church ministry. He understands that we sometimes feel alone and discouraged. It's encouraging to know He is there. How sad it must make Christ when we ignore His presence among us! From His presence flows His power and provision for us. As leaders we must first recognize and respond to the presence of Jesus in our daily lives. Only then are we able to recognize and respond to His presence in our women's ministry.

Joining God in His work enriches our relationship with Him and furthers the process of our transformation into the image of Christ.

The ministry of Jesus provides one of the best examples of what God can do through a small group of people. Looking closely, we discover some important advantages of smaller size. Perhaps the most important strength we find in smaller churches is the strong sense of community. Our small size works to our advantage, allowing us to get to know one another better and providing the opportunity to build strong relationship. When women are absent, they are missed. This encourages greater involvement in the life of the church.

A strong sense of community also provides an excellent environment for ongoing discipleship. Discipling is most effective in small groups where women develop trust and mutual accountability. Remember, Jesus ministered to many but chose to disciple only 12 people.

Jesus understands the challenges we face in ministering to women in smaller congregations. He offers valuable examples of successful ministry and needed words of encouragement. Most of all, He offers Himself to guide and grow according to His divine plan.

PRACTICALLY SPEAKING

Most of our discussion thus far has focused on issues of attitude and proper focus because I truly believe that allowing God to transform our thinking about kingdom ministry is a vital prerequisite to effective women's ministry in the smaller church. But we also need practical suggestions for everyday ministry. Keep in mind that, without the proper perspective, even the most practical tips have limited effectiveness. Keeping in mind what we've learned about God's perspective of ministry, let's consider an action plan for women's ministry in a smaller church.

ACTION PLAN FOR THE SMALLER-CHURCH WOMEN'S MINISTRY

1. Begin where you are. I've found it easy to get overwhelmed when I start something new. Beginning or fine-tuning a women's ministry can seem over-whelming in any setting. Do not try to do it all. We encourage all leaders, regardless of church size, to start small and follow God as He opens new areas of growth. Trying to do more than God intended will hinder your women's minister and may waste valuable resources. If you are just beginning a women's ministry, consider starting with weekly Bible study and a few fellow-ships during this next year. If you already offer women's Bible study groups but want to add more opportunities, discover what most interests and excites the women in your church. Encourage ministry opportunities that channel these interests and passions.

2. Trust God's timing. An important aspect of God's plan for women's ministry in your church is His perfect timing. As leaders, we must prayerfully seek to understand God's timing. Getting ahead of God—doing too much too soon—limits the impact of your women's ministry. When we run ahead of God, we can find ourselves spread too thin and outside of His provision. Falling behind God—failing to obediently respond to opportunities He places before us—can be just as devastating. Effective ministry happens when we join God where He is working—when He is ready for us.

3. Use what you have. Trust God to supply what may be lacking. He always provides exactly *what* we need to do everything He calls us to do *when* He is ready for us to do it. Many of us fail to recognize some of God's provisions because they arrive wrapped in unfamiliar packaging. Ask God to open your spiritual eyes to see His provision for your church's women's ministry. Then believe God has provided exactly what it needs.

Scripture teaches God's power is made perfect in our weakness (2 Cor. 12:9). Hebrews 11:34(b) reminds us that our weakness is turned to strength through faith. Yet, we tend to structure our women's ministry to hide our weaknesses. Doing so reveals a lack of faith, and we may deny God the opportunity to turn our ministry weaknesses into strength. Always expect God to do something miraculous through the weakness of your women's ministry. Keep in mind that God is sovereign and He acts according to His will and timing, not ours.

4. Find others to serve alongside you. I have a friend whose family have been sheep ranchers for several generations. She has shared many helpful insights from her experience with sheep. One thing her father taught her was to "always mend fences in pairs." Working in pairs is more effective and more fun. Ecclesiastes 4:9-10 reveals that "Two are better than one because they have a good reward for their efforts. For if either falls, his companion can lift him up; but pity the one who falls without another to lift him up."

Ask God to reveal whom He would have come along beside you to work among women. I'm not just talking about your best friend or someone who is just like you. Instead, I'm talking about a ministry companion—someone selected by God to work alongside you to complement your gifts.

5. See each woman individually. Another valuable lesson I learned from my sheep ranching friend is that to strengthen the flock you must see each sheep individually. Doing so allows the shepherd to respond to the unique needs of each sheep, strengthening the herd one sheep at a time. We can become so focused on the women as a group that we overlook the fact that they are individuals. To strengthen your women's ministry, see each woman individually. Strive to make decisions based on each woman's individual needs. Resist the temptation to generalize too much. Jesus demonstrated the importance of seeing each woman individually in the parable of the lost sheep (Luke 15:4-7). Leaving the 99 in a safe place, the shepherd went out to find the one that was missing. Jesus also reminds us in John 10:27 that He knows each of His sheep. We should strive to do the same. As we've already seen, it's much easier to get to know each woman more personally in a smaller church.

6. Find God's ministry niche for your women's ministry. I believe God has uniquely equipped each church for specific ministries. He has uniquely equipped the women in your church for the ministries He has planned for your women's ministry. Ask God to reveal His plans for your women's ministry. Consider the giftedness and passion of the women He has brought to your church. This will provide valuable insight into God's plan for your women's ministry. Focus on the needs God has uniquely qualified your women's ministry to meet.

Effective ministry happens when we join God where He is working —when He is ready for us.

7. Develop a network of other smaller-church women's ministry leaders. A final lesson my sheep rancher friend taught me has to do with learning from others. When she first began working in the family business, she wanted to impress others. In her enthusiasm, she made many mistakes that scared the sheep and made things more difficult. However, as she watched more experienced sheep handlers, she noted how they gently walked among the sheep, motivating certain sheep to lead others to the pens. If God is leading you to begin or grow women's ministries in your church, look around and find a few other churches that are effectively ministering to women. Seek out leaders from other smaller churches and learn from them.

HOW TO CUSTOMIZE FOR THE SMALLER-CHURCH WOMEN'S MINISTRY

This book and its companion resource, *Transformed Lives: Taking Women's Ministry to the Next Level* (which has tips in each chapter for adapting the principles to smaller churches), contain a wealth of helpful information. As leader of a smaller church women's ministry, you may need to adapt some of their suggestions to fit your church's size, strengths, and culture. I call this *customizing*. Think of it as a recipe. You may need to incorporate less of each ingredient so you don't end up with more than you can use. In other instances you may eliminate certain ingredients because your family does not care for them. Customizing is very similar. It gives you the freedom to choose and change as necessary to fit your church's unique circumstances and ministry.

As you read through a chapter, think about how the suggestions would fit your church. Ask God to help you answer these questions:

- Does this suggestion or idea relate to a challenge facing our women's ministry? If no, move to the next idea. If yes, then consider the next question.
- Would this idea or suggestion apply differently to a women's ministry in a smaller church? If no, then ask God if He would have you implement the idea in your women's ministry. If yes, then consider the next questions.
- How might this suggestion or idea work in our church?
- What adjustments might be needed to effectively adapt this idea to our women's ministry?

Now you try it. The chapter "Beginning a Women's Ministry" (p. 58) discusses the importance of gaining insight into the needs of the women of your church. Consider the suggestion of a written survey and the excellent example that begins on page 66. Use the customizing tool above to evaluate whether and how using a written survey would benefit your women's ministry.

Congratulations, you've just customized! Whether you decided your ministry doesn't need a formal written survey or you discovered a way to adapt the survey to meet your church's unique needs, you benefited from taking time to customize.

I believe God has exciting plans for you and your church's women's ministry. He is in the business of doing great things with very little. Women's ministry in the smaller church provides a perfect opportunity for God to reveal His power and glory. What a privilege we have to partner with God in preparing for Christ's return! I cannot think of anything more significant!

Customizing gives you the freedom to choose and change as necessary to fit your church's unique circumstances and ministry.

MINISTRY ONE-ON-ONE

VALERIE HOWE

Name at least one woman who has influenced your life spiritually. Women need women in their lives who can identify with their experiences and emotions. Evangelical Christian women's leaders need to know how to implement a mentoring ministry with women in their churches. Why have this sort of ministry? What's involved in beginning and maintaining it? And how will this program be set up in the local church? These questions will be answered in this chapter.

The Bible is our primary resource in implementing mentoring relationships among women in the local church. In keeping the Bible as our guidebook, we will be joining God where He is already working in the lives of women today.[1] Through His Word we can find out what a mentor is, why it's important to have a mentoring ministry in the local church, what type of women God is looking for as mentors, and what's involved in ministering effectively to women. In addition, we can explore the needs of women today and the how-to of meeting these needs through mentoring relationships.

WHAT IS MENTORING?

Let's define the word *mentor*. In his book, *Mentoring: Confidence in Finding a Mentor and Becoming One,* Bobb Biehl says that a mentor "helps a protégé reach her or his God-given potential. ... Mentoring is more 'how can I help you?' than 'what should I teach you' "[2] This does not mean a mentor does not teach. The Bible specifically says women are to teach other women. This will be discussed a little later, but keep in mind that teaching and modeling are involved in mentoring.

God has a plan for women that will stand the test of time. In some ways it seems that our modern generation has disregarded this teaching on mentoring.

Therefore, many young women, wives, and mothers have never been taught to live godly lives as examples which can be passed on to the next generation. But "down through the centuries, young people have learned most through careful observation of those who are more experienced,"[3] and "throughout human history, mentoring has been the primary means of passing on knowledge and skills in every field and in every culture."[4]

To support this concept of mentoring, Bob and Yvonne Turnbull suggest four keys for mentoring effectively.[5] I have adapted these for our discussion. Combined, they offer a definition of mentoring as well as a guide for us to follow.

There are four keys to mentoring effectively.

Key One: Share Your Successes and Struggles.

When I lost my temper with another church member, I confided my lack of patience to my senior friend, Faye. She had previously shared with me her own former struggle with controlling her temper. When I told her of my situation and that I wondered if I'd ever conquer my temper like she had, she replied, "Honey, just because you're 74 doesn't mean you still don't have to work at not losing your temper. It's just under control." Warning: Don't let sharing your struggles be seen as an excuse for sin. A shared common experience should be a way to move a mentoree toward Scripture for guidance on how to live.

Key Two: Share What You Do and How You Do It.

When I was searching for a way to have a short, meaningful quiet time, a lay renewal speaker came to our church and suggested using *Journey: A Woman's Guide to Intimacy with God.*[6] Mentors can suggest books they have found helpful on child-rearing, marriage, or specific subject matters in which the mentoree needs assistance.

Key Three: Build Skills to Meet Needs.

This is done in obvious and not so obvious ways. For example, my mother-in-law taught me directly how to make a pie crust, but she also taught me indirectly that Kenny, my husband, enjoyed eating her pies. That's why I wanted to learn her method—I had watched him eat her pies.

Key Four: Make Adjustments to Find What Works Best.

Elders have the authority to guide us in making adjustments as we submit to them in humility. They can see some of the pitfalls that lie ahead if we continue on a harmful course. A wise older woman who baby-sat for me once told me I was trying to do too much on my own. "Valerie," she said, "some day you'll learn to receive help." Her evaluation freed me to be able to do just that—receive help!

Each mentoring relationship will take on characteristics of its own, but teaching and modeling will always be involved. Mentoring is ministry one-on-one! It is a great place to start a women's ministry in the local church. But why is it needed?

1. THE BIBLE COMMANDS IT.

Scripture says, "Likewise, teach the older women to be reverent in the way they live, not to be slanderers or addicted to much wine, but to teach what is good. Then they can train the younger women to love their husbands and children, to be self-controlled and pure, to be busy at home, to be kind, and to be subject to their husbands, so that no one will malign the word of God" (Titus 2:3-5). We will look at each phrase of this passage later in this chapter.

2. GOD CALLS WOMEN TO IT.

"Those he predestined, he also called" (Rom. 8:30). God knew from the beginning that women would need some instruction on godly living, so He called the older, more spiritually mature women of His church to teach younger Christian women that which is good. This includes single, married, divorced, widowed, professionals, homemakers, and every woman of the church. In her book, *Between Women of God,* Donna Otto says,

> As I look back, I clearly see how God has faithfully provided other older women—messengers, models, mentors—to lead me along, to show me my Lord and Savior, to share the message of His love in flesh-and-blood, hands-on ways, and to help me with the nuts and bolts of every-day living. Woman after woman helped me find Christ and thereby discover rest and hope, peace and encouragement, health and fulfillment in all that God has for me. Each one delivered her message differently, and each one was effective.[7]

Women can minister with other women like no one else.

3. GOD QUALIFIES WOMEN FOR THE TASK.

If we "examine the biblical basis for a woman's worth and God's place for her in ministry from the perspective of women as *qualified* for ministry,"[8] we see that women can minister with other women like no one else.

Women are qualified for a number of reasons.
- They have been created in the image of God.
- They are qualified by redemption.
- They are qualified by Old Testament example.
- They are qualified by the example of Jesus.
- They are qualified by the example of the early church.
- They are qualified by Scriptural injunction.
- They are qualified by opportunity.
- They are qualified by the blessing their ministry brings to the entire church.[9]

4. A MENTORING MINISTRY WILL BUILD THE CHURCH.

Vickie Kraft, author of *Women Mentoring Women,* says,

> "I believe that God's promise to provide gifted persons for the equipping of the church includes His giving gifted women to local congregations. I believe God gives each congregation the gifted women it needs to minister to the unique needs of its women. When older women train

the younger women in a vital women's ministries program, not only are the women encouraged, but families and marriages are strengthened and stabilized. … A church without a vital ministry to women is like a home without a mother."[10]

5. THERE ARE BLESSINGS FOR THE MENTOR.

In a mentoring ministry, mentors help other women along in the journey of faith. They also equip younger women with the essentials they need to live godly lives.

In "Packing for the Journey," in *Christian Single* magazine, Deborah Tyler says, "You have to slow down enough to listen; to care. You will have to consider the needs of others and not just your own. But the payoff is significant. As you travel the feminine journey, take time to listen to the beat of another's heart. By doing so your own heart will grow stronger and you'll have more energy for the road ahead."[11]

There are other things that mentoring will do for the mentor. Their own answers become clearer; they will complement and clarify their own understanding; their mentorees will become teachers and mentors; they will refresh and rejuvenate the energy of youth; they will enjoy the satisfaction of a job well done; and they will work on a project with lasting value and eternal significance.[12]

Listen carefully. The Bible commands mentoring; women are called to it; they are qualified for it; it builds the church; and it benefits the mentor. How could Christian women possibly say no to mentoring when God says yes?

Oh, how younger women are searching for mature, godly role models—a Sarah, a Naomi, an Elizabeth—to guide them in the truth of God's Word. Women are ordained through Scripture, called of God, and in need of one another. A mentoring program is vital in women's ministry.

How could Christian women say no to mentoring when God says yes?

WHAT IS INVOLVED IN MENTORING?

Just how do women live out the task of mentoring in daily practical ways? Let's begin with an example. My mother is my mentor. She has given me a godly heritage that she received from her mother and grandmother. She says that her mother lived such a good life and was so kind that she "caught" godly lessons from her. My mother has done the same for me.

She has taught me many practical and spiritual lessons, such as how to pray and to study my Bible daily. These two things have led me to know God more fully and to lead others to discover the Jesus I know.

From my mother I learned to love my husband and five children. She taught me to set up a home routine and not to take on too many activities that would spoil my family time.

Mostly, I would say my mother taught me how to live; but mainly, she taught me how to die. For it was she who introduced me to my Lord and Savior. Her favorite verse of Scripture has become one of mine: "I know whom I have believed, and am persuaded that he is able to keep that which I have committed unto him against that day" (2 Tim. 1:12, KJV).

Yes, my mother is my *model*. My mother is my *sister in Christ,* and my mother is my *mentor,* a godly woman just a little ahead of me, cheering me on to victory in Him (see Heb. 12).

According to Lucibel VanAtta in her book, *Women Encouraging Women,* "Mothers and female relatives remain the time-honored and natural choices for role models. But too many miles or transient lifestyles or broken family relationships may separate them from us. ... [So] Christian women today are looking for mentors."[13]

What I learned from my mother about mentoring applies to all mentoring relationships. Love your protégé. Be an encourager, an affirmer, a cheerleader. Be open and honest in sharing with her. Pray for her regularly. Hold her accountable to God's Word. Seek what is best for her. Communicate often. This is what is involved in mentoring.

WHO SHOULD BE A MENTOR?

To become mentors, women need to pay special attention to the type of woman God calls to this task. "Likewise, teach the older women to be reverent in the way they live, not to be slanderers or addicted to much wine, but to teach what is good" (Titus 2:3).

Reverent in the Way They Live

The word *reverent* comes from the Greek language and describes a priestess serving in the temple of her god in the full-time service of worship. In other words, these women were willing to give their entire lives to serving a false god. Christian women who serve the risen Lord should be more willing than these women to count all of their lives as holy, living sacrifices (see Rom. 12:1). This means that cooking and cleaning, resting and exercising, speaking and listening, in addition to studying God's Word and praying are all of consequence in God's kingdom. The reverent life for the godly older women in the local congregation is lived out moment-by-moment and is certainly worth modeling for younger women. Potential mentors are easy to spot, for they truly are passionate about their relationship with God and want to share it with others.

Not Slanderers

Older, godly women make younger women feel they can safely communicate their struggles and problems without fear of others knowing their confidences. Christian senior adults communicate appropriate Scriptures instead of inappropriate stories, so that younger women will turn to God's Word instead of speaking in ungodly ways. For example, when mentorees have a problem (or a victory), they can learn to turn from sin (or to praise) and thank God by using God's Word instead of their own words. The more the Word is used, the less chance for gossip. The Greek word for *slanderer* or *malicious gossip* is taken from the root word *diabolus,* which means "devil." Satan uses broken confidences to divide believers. Vickie Kraft says, "A woman who is rooted in a deep relationship with God will not have the overwhelming need to pass on juicy tidbits to enhance her own popularity, and consequently her personal relationships will be protected."[14]

Love your protégé. Be an encourager, an affirmer, a cheerleader.

Not Addicted to Much Wine

The Greek term used in this phrase means "drunkard." It could also include other addictive behaviors such as abusing drugs, watching soap operas, excessive shopping, reading inappropriate materials, and overeating. If older women haven't learned how to live life in submission to the Lord rather than to compulsive behaviors, they will have little to offer younger women.

Recently through a Christian weight loss program the Lord revealed to me my own addictive behavior. Gluttony, to put it bluntly, was my weakness. Through Scripture study and learning to eat only when I'm truly, physically hungry, my focus has shifted from food to God. Now I'm gaining the victory (actually losing pounds) and will someday be free from my slavery to food. Any behavior that takes your mind and focus from God is not in His will. "Escaping reality does not promote biblical living."[15] Older women should avoid escaping reality and teach younger women of faith to avoid it, too.

Teach What Is Good

Like every form of teaching, passing on knowledge must have a goal—some principle or objective that needs to be taught. The goal of godly mentoring is for an older role model to teach a younger, willing student how to live a godly life. *Good* in Greek means "morally good, noble, or attractive." The mentor understands what is good and has a working knowledge of Scripture. She knows right from wrong as it is stated in the Bible. In addition, she knows it in principle. A mature woman of faith can guide a younger woman to depend on God's work in her own life to accomplish His purpose. This is the goal of mentoring.

WHAT SHOULD THEY TEACH?

What good things are mentors to train or encourage younger women to do to help them depend on God to accomplish His purpose in their lives? Scripture says, "Then they [older women] can train the younger women to love their husbands and children, to be self-controlled and pure, to be busy at home, to be kind, and to be subject to their husbands, so that no one will malign the word of God" (Titus 2:4-5).

Love Their Husbands

If married, mentors can encourage mentorees to love their husbands. The Greek word for love here is *phileo,* the love of human emotion, friendship, and enjoyment. *Phileo* means to truly be friends with their mates. They should have fun, laugh, and enjoy one another. When disagreements occur (and the mentoree needs to know that they will), the mentor can offer suggestions for solving conflicts in marriage. Bob and Yvonne Turnbull have an effective eight-step approach to resolving conflict:[16]

1. Deal with the anger.
2. Set a time to talk.
3. Establish ground rules.
4. Pray together.
5. Define the problem.
6. Look for a solution.
7. Develop a plan.
8. Close the issue.

Love Their Children

If they have children, mentors can encourage mentorees to love theirs. In today's society, women need to know that "children are a gift of the Lord" (Ps. 127:3, NASB). Children are not objects to be used or abused. Older women can use their personal experience as well as sensible wisdom to teach younger women "to bring [their children] up in the training and instruction of the Lord" (Eph. 6:4). One practical way to do this is to pray with them for their children and to teach them to pray daily for their families.

Younger women are instructed to teach their children God's Word "when [they] sit at home and when [they] walk along the road, when [they] lie down and when [they] get up" (Deut. 6:7). This takes time. Working moms who are trying to keep their families from drowning financially must be encouraged to find creative ways to do this. They need mentors to stand in the gap between themselves and their children.

Stay-at-home moms seem to have an advantage to teach their children all the time, but weariness and fatigue often set in after days of isolation. A mentor who can pray and counsel, even over the phone, can bring true spiritual healing through Christ to a broken woman.

Be Self-controlled

Jesus said, "I am sending you out like sheep among wolves. Therefore be as shrewd as snakes and as innocent as doves" (Matt. 10:16). Older women need to be alert while being discreetly open in their sharing. They must be willing to be vulnerable by showing younger women that they are not alone in their problems and struggles. Mentors are to guide the mentorees to follow the Holy Spirit's leading in everyday situations. This should include using the Bible to encourage the mentorees to give themselves completely to God, as well as to apply to needs as they arise. For example, Nancy, an older friend of mine, told me to praise God when a crisis arose because God inhabits praise, and Satan must flee.

Mentors are to guide the mentorees to follow the Holy Spirit's leading in everyday situations.

Be Pure

Another thing daughters of faith are to learn is "to be pure." Vickie Kraft speaks well to the issue of purity.

> This characteristic is very significant as it is related to the subject of loving your husband ... [by maintaining] sexual chastity before marriage and fidelity in marriage. ... Every biblical prohibition against sex is of sex outside the marriage relationship. Within marriage it is to be fully enjoyed and celebrated. Indeed, an entire book of the Bible, the Song of Solomon, describes in vivid detail the joys of the marriage relationship. However, marriage was designed as a commitment without alternatives.
>
> Sex within marriage is an important part of the ongoing relationship between husband and wife. Women need other women to encourage them to understand both the privilege and responsibility of the sexual relationship. A neglect of the physical aspects of marriage can put the relationship at risk. ... Physical relationship is to continue regularly except for a season of prayer for particular reasons (1 Corinthians 7:5).

The decision for restraint must be by mutual consent and for a brief time. (And, of course, there are times when for reasons of health there must be abstinence.)

A woman committed to purity and faithfulness in the sexual area honors the Lord and is a blessing to her family.[17]

Be Busy at Home

Managing the home may be a forgotten art in the church. However, it makes a tremendous difference to a woman's family as well as to God, or He wouldn't have included it in Titus 2:5 as an area for training younger women. Women are to "manage their homes" (1 Tim. 5:14). In the Greek language, this means to be the house despot, total ruler, or to manage the house in such a way that the family is kept in order. In a controlled home environment the husband/wife relationship will have a better chance to thrive and grow, and the children will be more at ease.

Basic household skills can be taught by a mentor who has already been there and done that. Skills such as cooking, cleaning, ironing, sewing, planning meals, and managing time wisely are highly useful to young women. For example, scheduling nap time and picking out clothes on Saturday night for church have been invaluable suggestions to me. Laying clothes out the night before a school day also lessens anxiety in the morning. This counsel sounds simple, but what a gift it is to the woman on the go!

Whether married or single, women (and their families) benefit from a well-run home. Just as cups of cold water given in Jesus' name will one day earn a reward (see Matt. 10:42), so too the mundane tasks of household chores are of eternal consequence.

Be Kind

Being kind involves words that encourage husbands, children, friends, and strangers. It also involves actions that say "I care" to those around.

Mentors find creative ways to express their love. A card, a word of encouragement, a meal, or caring for children are only a few ways to model and instill kindness. They live the command, "Be kind and compassionate to one another, forgiving each other, just as in Christ God forgave you" (Eph. 4:32).

Being kind involves words that encourage.

Be Subject to Their Husbands

If married, mentors can encourage mentorees to submit to their husbands. The Greek word for *obedience* used in the commandment for children (Eph. 5:1) and slaves (Eph. 6:5) is different from the word used for *submit* or *subject* (Eph. 5:22). This is *voluntary submission*—submission given willingly to a husband's leadership. It does not suggest nor state that women are in some way inferior to men, only that they have a different role. It does say that women are to respect their husband's role as head of the house.

This kind of submission is possible only as younger women learn to obey Christ and submit to His authority. Then and only then will they see the benefits that respecting their husbands can bring.

Jesus—the ultimate mentor—chose to submit His will to the Father. When women learn to obey God by submitting themselves to their husbands, the blessing of God will rest on their homes. The home then becomes a place of security, protection, and peace where the women, under their loving husbands' direction, are allowed to grow to their highest potentials.

A wife's submission to her husband includes all the other areas in Titus 2:4-5 that God instructs older women to teach. In loving her husband and children, in being self-controlled, pure, and kind, and in managing the affairs of her home, a woman shows her submission to her husband and to the Lord.

Live So the Word of God Will Not Be Dishonored

When older women model and teach the commands given in Titus 2:3-5, "the Word of God may not be dishonored" (NASB). This is true because the younger women who have learned these truths will be beacons to others. The world needs to see good examples passed on from one godly woman to another. Psalm 103:17 says,

> But the lovingkindness of the Lord is from everlasting to everlasting on
>   those who fear Him,
> And His righteousness to children's children
> To those who keep His covenant
> And who remember His precepts to do them.

The world needs to see good examples passed on from one godly woman to another.

To a world that is lost and dying, mentors and mentorees alike can honor God's Word and witness to others. Now that's evangelism!

HOW DO WE GET STARTED IN OUR CHURCH?

Form a Mentoring Committee

The best place to start is to form a Women's Ministry Mentoring Committee. If the church is not large enough to support a full committee, select two to three dedicated women who are willing to guide the program.

Determine a Time Frame

Select a time to begin that is most convenient for the church. September or October are optimum times. Various schedules will work. Partners can meet once a month for a year. A shorter time frame may fit your situation better. They might meet for six to eight weeks at a time and study the Bible and/or learn some skills which can be taught by one of the mentors or a special guest. Or, the church may want to offer an in-depth study such as *A Woman's Heart: God's Dwelling Place*, or *A Heart Like His: Seeking the Heart of God Through a Study of David*, both by Beth Moore.[18] Or, you may choose from a number of studies that fit this purpose well. Many are listed in "Tapping Resources for Women's Ministry" beginning on page 222.

These studies provide an excellent opportunity for mentoring pairs to study together during the week and then attend the weekly group session.

Donna Otto and Vickie Kraft have developed different plans for maintaining mentoring ministries within the churches. Donna suggests a 24-week series in segments from September through May, skipping holidays and school breaks to accommodate moms with kids in school. Vickie recommends a daytime and a nighttime schedule with different course offerings for various interests. It runs in three segments: a fall session from mid-September to mid-November; a winter session from the week after New Year's to mid-March; and a spring session from late March to mid-May. Planning one or two summer events that include families is nice. The ideas are limitless.

Publicize the Program

Determine to use the most effective forms of publicity. The mentoring program should be publicized and sign-up opportunities given for at least a month prior to the designated start time of the program.

Possibilities for publicity include newsletters; verbal announcements; church bulletins; brochures; posters; flyers; and newspaper, radio, and television ads.

Compile a Profile Sheet

Prepare a profile sheet for each mentoring participant which will allow older women to be paired with younger ones. This profile should include such things as name, address, phone number, personal interests, areas needed in spiritual growth, and what participants want from a mentoring relationship.

It may be helpful to establish age limits. Vickie Kraft suggests that seniors be over 45, while juniors be under 35. Women between 35 and 45 qualify for either category. Once participants return their completed profiles, the committee can pair women according to their answers. Much prayer must go into this part of the process.

Just Do It

From here on out, just about anything goes. For the pair's first meeting, consider a tea or some other get-acquainted session. A list of "getting-to-know-you" questions may come in handy. Some basics might include: What is your favorite color? food? activity?

Encourage participants to pray for each other regularly and to do things together such as developing a skill, going to lunch, and meeting for Bible study. The important task is to build the relationship. Stay in contact with juniors and seniors to make sure both are fulfilling their commitments.

At the end of whatever time frame you choose (whether 6 months or a year), close with a special time of testimony and celebration for the relationships that have developed. When you begin the next series, some partners may choose to be paired together again.

If you see that no one else is interested in mentoring in your church, don't be discouraged. Ask God to show you a mentoree or a mentor and get busy. Lucibel VanAtta's book *Women Encouraging Women* is helpful for this one-on-one ministry. (This resource is no longer in print but might be found in your church library or online.)

Mentoring involves time and effort, but it yields great rewards.

As women build relationships with one another, a women's ministry, as well as the entire body of Christ, blossoms and grows. Women are led to the Christ who is their Soon-and-Coming King. Jesus Himself leads them to one another to do the work of building each other up in the faith until He returns. As Christian women, we must heed His command, answer His call, and meet the needs of women inside and outside His church. We must live godly lives so that we can motivate and teach other women to be about His business. No matter what age we are, we should always be seeking a mentor as well as others we can mentor.

Mentoring takes time and effort, but it yields great rewards for all involved. It can and should be an incredible adventure!

Note: For more information about beginning or maintaining a mentoring ministry in your church, see *Transformed Lives: Taking Women's Ministry to the Next Level* and *Woman to Woman Mentoring: How to Start, Grow, and Maintain a Mentoring Ministry.* To order these resources: write LifeWay Church Resources Customer Service, One LifeWay Plaza, Nashville, TN 37234-0113; FAX order to (615) 251-5933; PHONE 1-800-458-2772; order ONLINE at *www.lifeway.com*; or visit the LifeWay Christian Store serving you.

---

[1]Adapted from Henry T. Blackaby and Clyde V. King, *Experiencing God: Knowing and Doing the Will of God* (Nashville: LifeWay Press, 1990), 32.

[2]Bobb Biehl, *Mentoring: Confidence in Finding a Mentor and Becoming One* (Nashville: Broadman and Holman, 1996), 19.

[3]Drs. Les III and Leslie Parrott, *The Marriage Manual* (Grand Rapids: Zondervan Publishing House, 1995), 7.

[4]Ibid., 12.

[5]Material in this section adapted from Bob and Yvonne Turnbull, *Marriage Mentors* (Nashville: Lifeway Press, 1995), 19-20.

[6]To order or for more information call 1-800-458-2772.

[7]Donna Otto, *Between Women of God* (Eugene, Ore.: Harvest House Publishers, 1995), 17.

[8]Vickie Kraft, *Women Mentoring Women* (Chicago: Moody Press, 1992), 16.

[9]Ibid., adapted from 16-22.

[10]Ibid., 12.

[11]Deborah Tyler, "Packing for the Journey," *Christian Single,* December 1995, 31.

[12]Parrott and Parrott, 66.

[13]Lucibel VanAtta, *Women Encouraging Women* (Portland: Multnomah Press, 1987), 18.

[14]Kraft, 29.

[15]Ibid., 30.

[16]Turnbull and Turnbull, 68-69.

[17]Kraft, 34. Author, Denise Farrar, *Women's Ministry Symposium IV:* The Women's Ministries Institute®. Used by permission.

[18]For more information about women's enrichment ministry resources contact LifeWay Church Resources Customer Service at 1-800-458-2772.

MEETING NEEDS THROUGH GROUPS

RHONDA H. KELLEY

*W*omen need other women! This statement shouldn't surprise any of us. After all, we realize how much we need each other and prove it every day by our actions. For example, women go together to the ladies room. If a woman goes alone to the restroom, she often starts a conversation with a stranger and leaves with "a new best friend." We desire to build new relationships and nurture old friendships.

When the church recognizes that women need other women, the door is opened for exciting new ministries. One way to help women interact with other women is by providing group experiences. Small groups within the church can strengthen the individual woman as well as the corporate body of the church. Through groups, the needs of believers in the church and unbelievers in the community can be met. Let's examine the role of groups in the women's ministry of the local church.

THE THREE A'S OF GROUPS

Why do most women benefit from group interaction? The support and love of a small circle of friends can nurture a woman in a unique way. Personal relationships help meet several basic needs—acceptance, affirmation, and accountability. These three A's serve as the primary purposes of any women's group within the church.

Acceptance

Women need a sense of belonging, a confidence that they are a significant part of a whole, an important member of a body. Statistics and trends in divorce, spousal abuse, and sexual harassment in the workplace indicate many women are not finding acceptance. Loneliness becomes a woman's greatest enemy when she senses isolation. Small groups, especially within the church where beliefs and lifestyles are similar, can provide women with acceptance. In words and actions, other women in the group express love, concern, and understanding. Women are strengthened by the acceptance of others.

Elizabeth, mother of John the Baptist, accepted her unmarried cousin, Mary of Nazareth, who later gave birth to Jesus Christ the Messiah. Elizabeth loved Mary despite what other people thought. She praised Mary for her faith in God and befriended Mary while awaiting the birth of her own child (see Luke 1:39-56). Christian women today can offer acceptance and love to others.

Affirmation

A grateful word, a loving hug, or a kind gesture goes a long way with a woman. Encouragement is not just appreciated by women, it is necessary for them to thrive. Members of a group can offer encouragement to one another and promote personal growth. In Scripture, Phoebe was an encourager to Paul (see Rom. 16:1-2) and Priscilla, with her husband Aquila, was an encourager to Apollos (Acts 18:24-26). During the trauma of the crucifixion, a group of women supported Jesus and each other by standing together at the foot of the cross. The affirmation of godly women was crucial to the establishment of the early church. Christian women today are strengthened by the affirmation of others.

Accountability

A woman may wish to change or desire to reach a goal, and if she senses support from others it may be easier. Whether she is seeking personal or spiritual growth, a woman's self-discipline is developed in part by accountability to others. A Bible study group, a weight control program, or a life support group provides an external checks-and-balances system to supplement internal discipline. Naomi became Ruth's accountability partner in her search for God and a fulfilling life (see Ruth 1:6-22). Women today are strengthened by their accountability to others. Small groups can actually encourage believers to grow closer to each other and closer to God.

Encouragement is not just appreciated by women, it is necessary for them to thrive.

DISTINCT NEEDS

Almost everyone agrees that life is filled with crises and challenges. While the women of the world face hurt and despair, even the most godly woman has her own needs. These needs are personal and real. They are universal and yet unique to her. They are life-changing and life-ending. The needs of a woman affect every area of her life—physical, social, emotional, and spiritual. Both the churched and the unchurched have needs that can be met by God and through the ministry of His church.

In a seminar titled, "The Needs of Women Today," the following were identified as women's six most significant needs.

1. Salvation and spiritual growth
2. Acceptance and self-worth
3. Family unity
4. Friendships
5. Financial security
6. Crisis care

In his book *His Needs, Her Needs,* Willard Harley suggests the five most common needs of women in marriage are:[1]

1. Affection
2. Conversation
3. Honesty and openness
4. Financial support
5. Family commitment

While you may agree with these conclusions, don't just accept a list of needs developed by another person. If God is leading you to develop a ministry to women, identify the needs of the women in your world and allow God to meet those needs His way. As you perceive common needs, small groups may be a way to effectively meet them.

The needs of women around you can be determined in several ways. First, you may be aware of "seen needs." Obvious needs of women may be very clear to you or your leaders. The women in your church may need fellowship, encouragement, and spiritual development. Seek the opinion of a staff member or an outside consultant to help identify these general needs.

Personal perceptions and expert opinions are helpful, but often you must seek more specific information. "Surveyed needs" add objective data to the personal opinion of "seen needs." It is useful to survey or canvas individuals about their perceptions of what they need most.

A survey can be formal or informal, general or specific, written or verbal. The objective of a survey is to gather data from persons other than yourself. You may choose to gather information informally from a small number of women by calling them or meeting in a focus group. Or you may decide to obtain data formally from a larger number via a written survey or church-wide meeting. (See Survey for Small-Group Ministry, p. 151.) After you conduct your survey, be sure to use the results in your leadership team as you plan activities. Remember to report your findings to your women and other church leaders.

No matter what method you use to determine the needs of women in your church and community, identify *specific* needs. If you do not clearly define your target, you will never hit it. Always focus your ministry on the needs of the people, not the impact of the program.

In her book *Designing Effective Women's Ministries,* Jill Briscoe says, "All I had to do was figure out 'my' needs and how God could meet them and then learn how to press the need button for other women as well."[2] That is the challenge for each of us in developing a ministry for the women of our church. First, we must understand how God is meeting our needs. Then we must realize how God wants to meet the needs of other women through the activities we offer.

DIVERSE GROUPS

There is more than one way to effectively implement a women's ministry. Therefore, there is not just one list of appropriate groups for women. In order to offer groups that truly meet the needs of the women in your area, answer the following questions.

- Who are the women in your church?
- Who are the women in your community?
- What are their needs?
- What are your available resources?

If God is leading you to develop a ministry to women, identify the needs of the women in your world and allow God to meet those needs His way.

- What has worked before?
- What has never worked?
- What are other churches doing to address similar needs?
- What is God leading you to do?

While it is helpful to listen to other people and learn from other churches, be careful to avoid inappropriate imitation. It is essential to the vitality of your work to personalize your ministry. Let your women's ministry be unique. Establish a one-of-a-kind mentality. Another church is not your church; their needs may not be your needs; their gifts may not be your gifts. Seek wisdom from the Lord to establish groups that will effectively meet the needs of the women in your church and community. Among the most common types of groups are special interest, Bible study, prayer, and support groups.

Special Interest Groups

Churches today offer a variety of groups specifically for women. Special interest groups often form when a consensus of opinion is shared by several women. They join together to discuss issues relating to political or social concerns, professional involvement, or personal interests. Some churches have advocacy groups, business organizations, or home management classes. A citizens' awareness group may help inform the women of your church and community about local, state, and national issues as well as suggest appropriate actions to take.

Bible Study Groups

Bible study groups are key to a growing women's ministry. Christian women who have a personal commitment to the systematic study of God's Word benefit from group interaction and accountability. Ongoing and periodic Bible studies are both effective. Some churches provide more general study while others provide in-depth study. Weekly or monthly, daytime or evening Bible studies can be established. Once the need for a group Bible study has been identified, seek a dedicated teacher, find an ideal time, and determine an appropriate topic for study (see "Tapping Resources for Women's Ministry," p. 222). Group discussion and teacher interpretation greatly increase a believer's understanding of Scripture.

Prayer Groups

Committed Christian women are women of prayer. While the practice of personal prayer is the privilege of every believer, group prayer is a dynamic way to experience the presence of God. Your women's ministry should call women to private prayer while offering opportunities for corporate prayer. Prayer groups typically share prayer concerns, form prayer chains, promote prayer events, coordinate prayer partners, and sponsor prayer rooms. The critical need is to pray—not to talk about prayer. Group prayer is a vital tool for personal discipleship and evangelistic outreach. Our prayers make our cares lighter!

Support Groups

Another effective type of group provides support. In recent years, support groups have been used in hospitals, schools, community centers, and churches

Let your women's ministry be unique. Establish a one-of-a-kind mentality.

to provide instruction and encouragement. A support group is actually a peer-led group of individuals who share a common need and who meet on a regular basis for interaction. Christian support groups are especially beneficial because members share similar biblical values and uphold Scripture as the definitive guideline for life decisions. In addition, these groups define a clear purpose, meet a specific need, and establish effective leadership.

Numerous nationwide Christian support groups have developed including Mothers of Preschoolers, Moms in Touch, National Center of Home Education, and Life Support Groups. Church-based programs may include support groups for women who are divorced, abused, terminally ill, single parents, or unemployed. Support groups can be ongoing or periodic. One church periodically sponsors a "Women in Crisis" series, addressing such topics as infertility, job stress, empty nest, mid-life crisis, blended families, death, and grief. These support groups respond to the needs of women in the church but also provide outreach to women in the community. Author Brenda Hunter noted, "Women always need other women to come alongside and speak their language: the language of the heart and of feelings. We shape each other's attitudes and self-definitions as we converse, and from each other we learn what it means to be female."[3] Look for opportunities to stimulate group interaction among women in your church and community so they can strengthen one another.

HOW TO BEGIN

Now that you better understand the importance of small groups in a women's ministry, you might be thinking, *How do we begin?* God may lay a burden on the heart of one woman in your church to start small groups for women. In other cases, the pastor or church staff may develop a vision for the women of the church. There is no "official" way to begin. When God reveals a want to, He will provide the way. The important thing is to start!

If your groups are staff-directed, be sure to include women of the church in the planning. Women's groups planned by women for women have proven to be most successful. While the church staff is an integral part of the planning, pray that God will raise up volunteers to coordinate the small groups. One woman or a few women may start a women's group. On the other hand, be sure to discuss all plans with your pastor and staff. Coordination with the church calendar will help prevent conflicts and assist in promotion of your groups.

Feel the freedom to structure the groups in your women's ministry your own way. Keep these suggestions in mind as you start small groups. Use the following checklist as your guide.

O 1. Pray for each other and become sensitive to personal needs.
   Prayer is key to any ministry—especially during the start-up stage when wisdom and guidance from the Lord are essential. A small prayer group may become the catalyst for other groups.

O 2. Survey the women of your church.
   In order to identify felt-needs and design appropriate groups, listen to the

Christian support groups are beneficial because members share similar biblical values.

women of your church and community. In doing so, you may choose not to duplicate other groups and start new ones. In any case, your local needs and not someone else's model should determine your agenda.

○ 3. Develop Bible study groups as a foundation.
A personal commitment to the Lord and His Word should be expressed through participation in systematic Bible study. Christian women are interested in spiritual growth and enrichment that can be promoted through group involvement. Bible study is the most common type of women's group.

○ 4. Keep missions and community outreach a priority.
Women's ministry should include missions groups with a focus on exciting and relevant education, awareness, and involvement.

○ 5. Work closely with your church staff.
Responsibility for leadership of the church has been assigned to staff members. Seek their wise counsel. Women's groups are part of the total church program.

○ 6. Find and train dedicated leaders.
God will raise up women to give leadership to the groups in your church. Be alert for willing workers and assist them in training for their jobs. Be particularly sensitive to women who have not held a leadership position before. New ministries often uncover new leaders.

○ 7. Hold a church-wide special event to promote the groups.
Many women will respond to a one-time activity before making a longer-term commitment. A special event attracts a larger number of women who can learn about small-group opportunities. Perhaps a "Preview Day" would be appropriate to overview options offered during this time frame. Offer information and register women on this day.

○ 8. Develop nurturing relationships.
Small groups, especially in a large church, encourage personal contact and close friendships. While your women's ministry will respond to the needs of the whole body, small groups can focus one-to-one on each individual.

○ 9. Work in harmony with other church groups or programs.
Your church may have ongoing groups in place. Try to complement the mission of other groups while clearly defining your group's purpose. A diversity of groups shouldn't compete with but should strengthen each other.

○ 10. Stay positive, focused, and pray, pray, pray!
Any Christian work can become overwhelming and discouraging. Keep your attitude positive and your vision clear. And, above all, pray without ceasing for yourself, your small groups, and your church.

When shared with a group, joys are multiplied and sorrows are divided. The blessings of group interaction among women are many. Don't let the ladies of your church and community miss the blessing of personal relationships!

Personal Blessings

Personal blessings are abundant to those involved in women's groups. A woman will experience limited growth personally and spiritually without interaction with other believers. When supported by members of a group, a Christian woman will flourish and be fruitful. Group meetings become a highlight of life, not just another calendar appointment.

Ministry Blessings

Churches with dynamic women's ministries that provide small groups are most often growing churches. If the women's groups are successful, then all other women's events will be strengthened. Specific blessings such as genuine enthusiasm, numerical growth, diverse participation, and prospective members are the natural result of well-planned women's groups. The blessings to individual women and the total women's ministry are unlimited.

Conclusion

As you develop women's ministry in your church, resist the temptation to start a group for every woman's need. Instead, seek God's guidance, pray for wisdom, be sensitive to needs, recognize helpful resources, and start simply. You don't have to do everything at once. The success of your women's groups will become an investment in the spiritual growth of women in your church and community. The needs of women in your area can effectively be met in large part through the development of appropriate small groups. God bless your efforts to reach women for His glory!

---

[1]Willard Harley, *His Needs, Her Needs* (Tarry Town, N.Y.: Fleming H. Revell, 1986).
[2]Jill Briscoe, et al., *Designing Effective Women's Ministries* (Grand Rapids: Zondervan, 1995), 17.
[3]Brenda Hunter, *In the Company of Women* (Sisters, Ore.: Multnomah Books, 1994), 23.

As a Christian woman, what is your greatest personal need or the area in which you would like to experience growth through being involved in a small group?

_____

_____

What are the three most prevalent needs of your closest non-Christian friends that we can address in a small-group ministry?

1. _____

2. _____

3. _____

Thinking about the women of our church, what concerns do you share for them and what do you feel are needs that can be addressed in small-groups?

_____

_____

List three pressing needs or issues our community is facing. How can the women of our church help address these problems through small-groups?

1. _____

2. _____

3. _____

What is your dream for the women of our church?

_____

_____

_____

_____

SMALL-GROUP MINISTRY PLAN SHEET

This plan sheet is designed to assist you in beginning small groups within your women's ministry. Once you conduct and compile the results of your survey, use this form to move forward in your planning.

Determine Priorities

Prioritize which needs expressed by the women in your church can be met through your small-group ministry.

1._____

2._____

3._____

4._____

5._____

Set Goals

Based on the priorities listed above, what will you focus on this year?

1._____

2._____

3._____

Determine Actions

What small groups will you offer that will help you reach your goals?

Small Group	Date	Person Responsible
_____	_____	_____
_____	_____	_____
_____	_____	_____
_____	_____	_____
_____	_____	_____

Future Plans

Looking ahead, what would you like to include in next year's plans?

1._____

2._____

3._____

Ministry to Women Whose Husbands Are Not Spiritual Leaders

Karla Downing

The goal of women's ministry is to meet the varied needs of all women, including those whose husbands are not spiritual leaders. Women in spiritually mismatched marriages face unique circumstances and have a unique set of needs. This chapter will provide you with information that will equip you to minister more effectively to them. Or, if you yourself are in a spiritually mismatched marriage, it will encourage you and provide you with practical ideas.

Spiritual mismatches result from a variety of spiritual inequities. The husband's spiritual state can be anything from ambivalent to hostile, atheist to agnostic, or casually to zealously committed to another faith. The husband may be saved but not fully serving the Lord or just not taking a leadership role in the home. While each situation is different, they all share some common aspects.

The ideal marriage is presented in Ephesians 5:22-29. The husband is the spiritual leader of the home and head of his wife. The woman submits to his leadership, and his love covers her, protects her, and provides for her. Together they create a godly home that prioritizes spiritual training as they rear their children in the Lord. A woman in a spiritually mismatched marriage knows her home isn't like this, and hearing the ideal can be a source of pain.

Spiritual mismatches aren't God's ideal plan for marriage for a number of reasons. God continually warned the Israelites not to marry outside their faith because their hearts could be turned away from Him (Ex. 34:15-16). Even King Solomon succumbed to his wives' influence and found his heart straying from God in his later years (1 Kings 11:3-4). Second Corinthians 6:14-16 warns us not to be "mismatched with unbelievers" in any close relationship (HCSB). Some versions call it being "unequally yoked," in reference to God's command not to "plow with an ox and a donkey together" (Deut. 22:10, HCSB). Animals pulling a plow wear around their necks a harness or yoke made of wood and metal. Putting together two animals with varying strengths, body builds, and abilities causes them to pull the plow inefficiently and results in pain. Similarly, disharmony exists between the righteous and lawless, light and darkness, and believers and unbelievers. Such disharmony in a marriage also causes pain. The Apostle Paul reminded believers to marry in the Lord because marriage has enough problems without additional division (1 Cor. 7:33-34,39).

But women find themselves in mismatched situations for many reasons. They may have gotten saved or recommitted themselves to the Lord after they were married. Or, their husbands may have fallen away, become less interested in spiritual things, or gotten involved in another religion. Perhaps a woman knew her spouse wasn't a committed Christian when they were dating but discounted the signs; or she may have pulled away from Christian fellowship as a result of his influence. A man may sense the importance of appearing to be spiritually strong while dating and may purposefully misrepresent himself to convince the woman to marry him. The woman who looks back on her decision to marry and sees that she was blinded to the problems, ignored the signs, or married knowing God didn't want her to may struggle with guilt. She may also see herself and her marriage as the result of sin and have regrets. It is important for her to remember God's love and forgiveness. He cherishes her as His beloved and wants the best for her marriage.

The Apostle Paul dealt with the question of whether a woman should leave a mismatched marriage in 1 Corinthians 7:10-16. According to him, the Christian wife ought not leave her husband simply because he is unsaved. Rather, she is encouraged to stay with him as long as he is willing so she can be a positive influence on him and their children. However, if he is unwilling to stay because of her faith, she can let him go. The more complicated question is: *How does she live with him, remain true to her faith in Christ, and be a positive influence on him and her children?*

God cherishes His children as His beloved and wants the best for them.

WOMEN WITH UNSAVED HUSBANDS

God warned believers against being spiritually mismatched because they have conflicting values and lifestyles. Christians and non-Christians have opposing worldviews that affect every area of life. Disagreements on how to raise and discipline children, entertainment, activities, lifestyle, values, priorities, and finances may add to those involving differences of spiritual beliefs.

A Christian wife has to handle these disagreements tactfully. She always needs to state her beliefs, values, needs, and preferences but cannot make her husband agree or abide by them. She must listen respectfully to her husband's beliefs, values, needs, and preferences and be careful not to cast judgment on them. Depending on the situation, she may face having to make adjustments she'd prefer not to make. For instance, going to places where alcohol is served may be uncomfortable; but unless it is a bar atmosphere or the amount of drinking is intolerable, she should not be too prudish and exclusive. She can attend family outings and work parties and choose not to drink. She needs to continue to be hospitable to her husband's friends, even if they aren't Christians. Yet, she may have to set boundaries and limits that will cause tension or discord. Some men will be angry that their wives don't do the same things they do. This is even more likely when the wife is a new convert and has changed her lifestyle.

When men disapprove of giving money to the church, women should evaluate their desire to give in light of their specific circumstances. Depending on their agreement with their husbands on finances, they may or may not be able to give what they'd like. They have to evaluate the effect on the marriage, how both spouses view the finances, how much freedom each spouse has to spend money independently, and whether both the wife and husband work.

Feelings of insecurity and insufficiency may make the unsaved husband resent his wife's devotion to the Lord and may cause him to be jealous of her attention to the church and Christ. He may be uncomfortable with his wife's admiration of the pastor and the time she spends at church. He may be suspicious and believe his wife is being brainwashed. He may feel inadequate to meet his wife's needs and fear their relationship could grow cold if they continue on different paths—yet he doesn't know what to do about the differences. Knowing his wife disagrees with his views and is unhappy with his choices may result in his feeling disrespected and devalued. Some men are hostile, defensive, critical, and sarcastic regarding spiritual matters—especially when they struggle with the internal conviction of the Holy Spirit. Light shines on darkness and has an effect (Eph. 5:13-14); as a result, unsaved husbands may feel uncomfortable and not know why.

Unsaved people often have unrealistic ideas about what a Christian should be like; they may expect perfection, piousness, or passivity. When wives fall short of these expectations, husbands may call them hypocrites, or ask, "What kind of a Christian are you, when you do that?" This is often a convenient excuse not to serve God, but it still puts additional stress and guilt on wives because they can't be perfect and will fall short even without unrealistic expectations. All a woman can do is try to do her best and show herself and others grace when she stumbles, as an example of the grace and forgiveness God offers to each of us.

Differing denominations or faiths can cause problems too, but differences in two Christ-based faiths can be dealt with more easily. Two faiths present a dilemma: Do both parents tell the children what they believe? Who takes the children to church? Does the wife go to her husband's church if she disagrees with the teaching? And what does she do if her husband forbids her to tell the children about her faith? What does she do if her husband is convinced her faith is wrong and even harmful and forbids her to go? The answers to these questions will vary depending on the specific set of circumstances. In general, a wife would want to be respectful of her husband's beliefs and not totally and outwardly opposed to what they are doing in the home and with the children. Unless she feels it is sinful and something she absolutely cannot support, she should show some interest in her husband's faith and attend some functions with him. When anything crosses the line and becomes a matter of disobeying God, wives have to follow God even when it causes dissension in the marriage (Acts 5:29). She needs to speak truthfully about her faith to her children in a way that doesn't openly disregard her husband or his position in the home.

A woman has the responsibility to make her home as "Christian" as possible. Often a woman sets the tone in her home, and she has opportunities to be a positive influence. Regardless of what her husband does, she is to live out her faith. When Paul discussed mismatched marriages in 1 Corinthians 7:10-16, he acknowledged the believer's lifestyle might cause problems in the marriage but assumed the believer would continue to live out his or her faith anyway. If the husband is hostile to his wife's faith and tells her not to listen to Christian music or programs, talk about her faith, or read the Bible in his presence, she can respect his wishes and do those things when he is not around. But she has the responsibility and option to tell him "no" to any request that is disobedient to God (see Acts 5:29). She must guard against any negative influence her husband's weaker faith or lack of faith has on her spiritual walk.

First Peter 3:1-4 reminds women in spiritually mismatched marriages to live out their faith quietly rather than flaunting, pushing, nagging, and forcing it on their husbands. Instead, they are to live "pure, reverent lives" and have a "gentle and quiet spirit." "Gentleness" and "quietness" refer to an inner peace and strength, not a spirit of passivity and weakness. A Christian wife is not to be a non-presence in the home or marriage; neither is she never to speak her opinion. She should strive to be like Christ who was not passive and weak, but strong, confident, sure of Himself, and very influential. Wives should explain and defend their faith, values, needs, opinions, and beliefs with gentleness and respect (see 1 Pet. 3:15-16).

A woman has the responsibility to raise her children in the Lord, but she has to use wisdom and discretion in how and when she does it. She should not put her husband down or minimize him. Her example to her children is powerful. My father was an unbeliever and regularly told us children that the Bible was wrong. He cut out Bible verses that he said couldn't be true and showed us how they contradicted other verses. My mother didn't try to control what my father said because she couldn't. But she took us to church every Sunday and made sure we knew what she believed. Mother could have taken a stand on many issues in her difficult marriage, but she chose her faith as the one on which she would not compromise. All four of her children are Christians today, and so is my father. Women should not use their children manipulatively to preach to an unbelieving spouse. However, the children can naturally talk to their dads and share their faith as they choose.

Understandably, a Christian wife experiences fear regarding her husband's salvation. To think of a loved one spending eternity in hell is sobering. If her faith is causing division, she may worry her husband will leave. She may experience sadness and loneliness when she cannot share such a vital part of her life. The believer's strength comes from doing what is right and trusting God with the outcome.

WOMEN DEALING WITH OTHER MARITAL PROBLEMS

Some marriages have other problems such as drug, alcohol, sexual and gambling addictions; abuse, anger, infidelity, pornography use, control, workaholism, general dysfunction, mental illness, personality problems, or irresponsibility. All of these complicate the spiritually mismatched dilemma. Women need to understand that they have a responsibility and right to set boundaries in these areas and are not required to passively tolerate their husbands' wrong behavior. First Peter 3:1-4 tells wives to quietly influence their unsaved husbands by their actions, rather than by nagging. However, these verses

Believers need to focus on doing what is right and trusting God with the outcome.

are often misapplied to these situations, inferring that a woman shouldn't say anything about the hurtful and sinful things her husband does. This is not true. She has to confront sin and speak the truth so she can bring light to dark areas and be an influence for good in her marriage and home (Eph. 5:1-14). Submitting herself and her children to destructive and harmful situations is wrong. She will have to make decisions that protect herself and her children and hold her husband accountable for what he is doing. She cannot make him change, but she can allow him to bear the consequences of his actions (Gal. 6:7-8).

Women don't need to live in fear (1 John 4:18). Some men who are particularly hostile and controlling toward their wives' right to follow their religious convictions and beliefs are also controlling in other areas. Sarcasm and hostility toward a wife's faith can also cross the line and become verbal and emotional abuse. These cases require discernment to determine whether submitting to the control is right or wrong. While spiritually mismatched marriages have a certain degree of pain and discomfort related to the lack of a spiritual union, wives can rejoice when they endure persecution for Christ's name (1 Pet. 4:14-16). However, women don't have to be martyrs and take anything and everything their husbands throw at them. Suffering for good might mean making a stand for what is right. Even though such a stand might cause more dissension, allowing their husbands to mistreat them without taking a stand would be the result of tolerating wrongdoing (1 Pet. 2:20). Factors such as physical, verbal, or emotional abuse call for counseling and may require separation for the wife and children's safety.

WOMEN MARRIED TO IMPERFECT SPIRITUAL LEADERS

Many women are married to men who are saved but don't take an active role leading their families spiritually. When we think of the man being the spiritual leader of the home, we think of him assuming the responsibility for the spiritual training of the children and the wife. This would include leading Bible devotions, administering godly discipline, praying with and for the family, having a godly character and example, loving and nurturing his wife, training the children in the Lord, making wise decisions for the family, and serving God with all his heart, mind, and soul. This perfect picture of a spiritual leader is set as the standard for the Christian man, and the wife compares her husband to it. When he falls short, she feels disappointed in him and her marriage.

Men are generally not as relational, communicative, or spiritual as women. By nature they often have difficulty doing the very things they are expected to do as spiritual leaders. In addition, personality styles affect how a man interacts. If he is more outgoing and talkative, he will naturally interact more with his family. But, if he is quiet and tends not to talk about what is going on, he may try to connect in ways that his wife might not recognize. Many men struggle with providing financially for their families and don't interact with their families in an emotional and personal way, possibly because their fathers weren't involved with their families outside of their role as providers. Some men are not natural leaders and will defer to their wives things that are hard for them to do. Others lack the self-confidence they need to be a spiritual leader. Still others are stressed and beaten down from other areas of their lives and withdraw from the family when they come home as their way of coping with the pressure. Others try their best, are criticized by their wives, and eventually give up.

It is important that wives not force their husbands into a "model husband" suit. Focusing on things a man doesn't do will increase a woman's discontent with the marriage, will cause the husband to feel disrespected, undervalued, unappreciated, and may even result in his being less loving toward her. Men take disapproval, nagging, and criticism as signs of personal failure and withdraw more and interact less. A wife's instructions on how to do things right will seldom motivate a man to try harder.

A husband may not be as spiritually mature or as knowledgeable as his wife about the Bible; therefore, he may feel intimated. A wife cannot force her husband to mature in his faith, but she can encourage him to be a spiritual leader in subtle yet positive ways. She can compliment him when he interacts with the family. She can express confidence in him and speak positively about his importance to the family. She can appeal to his values and ask for his help shaping the marriage and family. She can set up times to have a family devotional and ask him to take part. Rather than expecting him to initiate and organize the devotionals (which lots of men don't do), she can consult him in the decision-making process of how, when, and what materials to use. Regardless of what he does and doesn't do, she must guard against critiquing his efforts and implying that they fall short.

Deuteronomy 6:6-7 tells us that God's truths are to be in our hearts and that we are to repeat them to our children: "talk about them when you sit in your house and when you walk along the road, when you lie down and when you get up." We impart spiritual truths to our children throughout the day, not just in planned devotions. Wives should give their husbands credit for what they do. Putting them into molds and only being pleased with their influence when they fit that mold is bound to result in wives' overlooking positive things about their spouses.

When our children were young, I tried to get my husband to lead family devotions. It didn't work. It wasn't his style; he didn't like to read or do object lessons out of a book. I was disappointed and dissatisfied, but years later I realized he had a positive effect on their spiritual training in a way that I couldn't. He loves science, geology, archaeology, and history. He showed them geological formations and explained how they proved the existence of Noah's flood or how a fossil record disproved evolution. He looked at the wonder of creation and pointed to how God had to have been behind it. He could explain history and timelines that proved the Bible was real and answer questions about how Christianity shaped world events. None of those areas are strengths for me, and I would have ignored them.

Because women are naturally nurturing, they likely will provide much of their children's moral and biblical teaching. But men also can be strong influences by reinforcing character traits of discipline, responsibility, strength, and work ethic. Life lessons are often more powerful than a planned discussion.

Letting go of the cookie-cutter approach to a family's spiritual life is one of the best ways to maximize a husband's spiritual headship. When a wife sees her

A godly wife can encourage her husband in subtle yet positive ways.

husband's abilities and allows him to lead in areas that are natural, she can affirm and appreciate him rather than criticize him for his lack. She can fill in the gaps as his helpmate and bring her strengths to complement his. She can encourage and invite him to be a part of things she is doing, without judgment and criticism. For instance, she can ask him to do specific tasks that he might not otherwise do such as put the kids to bed with prayers and a story. She can encourage the kids to ask their father questions, giving him an opportunity to respond and expressing confidence in him as the family's spiritual leader. She can ask him to explain things at the dinner table or ask him to pray for her and the children throughout the day. If he is uncomfortable praying aloud, she can ask him to agree with her as she prays.

His lack of spiritual maturity may be evident in other areas also. He may not read the Bible, attend church regularly, or apply biblical truths to his life. A wife needs to avoid the tendency to nag and push. She can occasionally suggest a Bible study or other "together" activity and bring flyers or dates of events to his attention, but she should not be angry or judgmental if he doesn't want to go. Women need to avoid the impulse to preach and lecture their husbands about what is right. Instead, they can share their concerns and convictions and then let their examples shine. God will convict their husbands in His way and time. Women are not to function as the Holy Spirit in their husbands' lives.

Women are not to function as the Holy Spirit in their husbands' lives.

MINISTERING TO WOMEN IN SPIRITUALLY MISMATCHED MARRIAGES

Many women in spiritually mismatched marriages are acutely aware their marriages fall short of the ideal Christian marriage and their homes fall short of the ideal Christian home. This realization often results in their feeling disappointed, different, and sometimes inferior to other Christian women. They experience confusion about how to handle dilemmas resulting from the spiritual mismatch. Along with practical guidance and understanding, they need to be reminded God desires to give them victory in their marriages and to help them grow and mature.

Oftentimes, the teaching we offer to women includes examples of only ideal marriages. Being aware of these needs will enable you to adapt your teaching materials to their needs on an ongoing basis. Offer examples and applications to their unique situations. For example, when teaching on spiritual leadership, talk directly to the women whose husbands aren't spiritual leaders. (Take care not to single out any one person.) Or, when talking about raising children with godly values, talk to the women whose husbands don't endorse and enforce spiritual values, allowing the children to do things that these women are uncomfortable with, such as watching PG-13 and R-rated movies. Balance your teaching about submission with realistic issues women deal with. Remind them that submission is voluntary and can and should be withheld when submitting enables sin or harms them or their children.

Another misconception a woman may have is the idea that she is responsible for her husband's salvation. Subtle reinforcement comes from statements such as: "Love your husband to the Lord." "Pray him into the kingdom." "When you are right with God, He'll start working on your husband." First Peter 3:1-4 tells women with unsaved husbands to win them over by the way they live. Wives know they have an influence. They need to be reminded they are neither responsible for how their husbands react to that influence nor can they be perfect. God is ultimately the One who convicts through the Holy Spirit (John 16:8-11) and draws men to Himself (John 6:44). The responsibility for one's spiritual state rests on the individual; each of us will give account of our own choices to God (Rom. 14:10-12).

A woman in a spiritually mismatched marriage often overly focuses on the couple's spiritual differences. She needs to be reminded that focusing on positive things she and her husband share will strengthen the marriage. She needs to spend time with her husband by supporting his interests, even if it means doing less at church. Keeping their marriage relationship a priority and continuing to need him is important. Also, she should keep in mind that sexual intimacy within marriage is pleasing to God.

Women sometimes rely on the Lord and other Christians to fill their needs, often without realizing they are pushing their husbands out of their lives. They need to continue to rely on their husbands to be the head of their homes and not make all the decisions without them—even if they believe they make wiser choices. Avoiding the trap of comparing their husbands to other "spiritual" men as well as discarding the belief that "If only my husband were saved or a spiritual leader in the home, we wouldn't have problems" will decrease discontentment and disillusionment. Christian marriages have struggles too; not all the problems in the spiritually mismatched marriage are caused by the different religious views. Some are related to differences in gender, personality, preferences, backgrounds, and styles—which would be there even if the husband had a strong faith.

When a wife respects her husband's right to believe differently, he will more likely respect hers.

As a leader, you must encourage a woman to accept, respect, and love her husband. Such training will show her obedience and submission to the Lord and commitment to her husband, regardless of whether he is leading the family to the wife's satisfaction (Titus 2:4; Eph. 5:24). Remind her to listen to her husband without being judgmental, superior, and forcing her values on him. When a wife respects her husband's right to believe differently, he will more likely respect hers. Encourage her to share honestly with her husband her concerns, needs, values, and opinions. She needs to admit and face her frustrations, disappointments, resentments, and hurts in the marriage and then realistically assess what she can and cannot change. She has to accept that she can't force her husband to be different and that she is responsible for her own choices. She will need to decide how to adjust to the situation while not taking over her husband's role and how to be responsible for her own spiritual growth. She must maintain a delicate balance between living her convictions, fulfilling her needs as a separate person, respecting her husband, and preserving her marriage. Each woman will find that balance in a slightly different way, depending on her circumstances.

Be careful to give her the freedom to figure that out for herself. Relationships have very complicated dynamics, and each couple finds their own way to function as a unit. She needs to do what works best for her marriage and life. Pressuring her to do something that doesn't work for her but seems right to you will only increase her frustration and pain.

A wife of an unbeliever may have to miss church at times to accommodate her husband and should feel free to be flexible with her attendance at events. After all, her relationship is with the Lord, not the church. She may need to choose not to attend weekend retreats or night meetings. Each circumstance will require different adjustments, depending on the husband's tolerance and the woman's circumstances. No absolute right or wrong exists in this area. One woman may need to attend church services and events even though her husbands isn't happy about it. Another may need to make reasonable adjustments so church doesn't become a divisive issue in the marriage or cause more dissension in the home.

Create an atmosphere in your women's activities and Bible studies that encourages women to truthfully tell about their struggles rather than pretend everything is OK. Stress the importance of being transparent and vulnerable with each other. James 5:16 says we are healed as we openly share our weaknesses with one another. This openness is refreshing; it ministers to the woman who is sharing and others as well. It allows women to use their gifts and past experiences to encourage and comfort each other (2 Cor. 1:4). This atmosphere will encourage the body of Christ to support each other (Eph. 4:11-13). You may need to start the sharing by being vulnerable and real about your personal struggles. Many women feel intimidated by the "other women" who appear to have it all together. Believing you are the only one with problems brings shame. One new Christian participated in a church Bible study on being a good wife. The study never addressed difficult marriages like hers. She said, "I watched everyone else who had it all together. I felt horrible that I couldn't be a good wife like them, but no one else said they had any problems. I decided a Christian either didn't have problems or was supposed to pretend everything was OK. I pretended but felt horrible about myself." We should not allow our women's ministry to be about pretending.

Plan events to meet these needs. Some husbands may not attend church preaching. Husband-friendly activities such as a Valentine's Day dinner, a Mother's Day or Father's Day brunch, or pertinent talks on life issues allow wives to invite their husbands without overtly trying to get them saved. When you plan church events, plan for singles and couples. Encourage women to come alone or with friends.

Support groups are an especially effective way to support women in spiritually mismatched marriages. You can invite a speaker, organize the meeting around a book or study, or allow it to be more informal. Also, have a list of women with past or present experience in a spiritually mismatched marriage, and make them available to mentor other women facing similar challenges. Provide additional referrals for women who are in difficult marriages and are dealing with issues such as addictions, infidelity, mental illness, abuse, and other dysfunctions.

You don't have to have all the answers for every woman's dilemmas. They will have to make most decisions on their own, but you can help each woman to feel more included, understood, accepted, and normal by adjusting your women's ministry to support her unique needs.

Note: All verses in this chapter were taken from the Holman Christian Standard Bible.

GIRLS' MINISTRY

(RAISING A NEW GENERATION OF WOMEN)

JIMMIE L. DAVIS

everal years ago God touched my heart, and I felt a clear calling to train women to minister to teenage girls. During 25 years of working beside my husband in youth ministry, I began to see a trend developing in curriculum and programming that was either gender neutral or male dominant. I began to notice that girls in our churches were often falling through the cracks and were not much different than girls who were unchurched. As I began to search for resources, I found very few written specifically toward the needs of teenagers. God gave me the opportunity to travel to many churches, to consult with girls and women regarding the need for girls' enrichment ministry, and to develop an intentional, organized plan for girls' ministry.

God is doing a new thing in women's enrichment ministry: girls' enrichment ministry!

Women's ministry is exploding across America. It seems God is stirring women to pour their lives into teenage girls. I weekly receive requests for information about this ministry. I'm pleased to respond that resources are emerging, girls' conferences are happening, and women are being called to minister to girls. God is doing a new thing in women's enrichment ministry: girls' enrichment ministry! This movement fills a significant need. Consider one girl's story:

Sitting on a street corner, 14-year-old Lynette sensed a hopelessness that reached beyond her hunger and loneliness. Her bright red hair spiraled out of the bandanna tied at the back of her head. The backpack crumpled beside her held her only worldly possessions. Feeling unloved by family, she had run away from home. The money she had stolen from her mother's purse was long gone.

Lynette, better known as "Squeaky," had always been somewhat eccentric and rebellious, but deep down she was like every other girl. Her need to be loved unconditionally transcended time, culture, and personality. Despair had finally overcome her stoic attitude, and tears began to stream down her dirty face. She was unaware of the man standing in the shadows like an animal waiting for the opportune time to pounce on its prey. He had seen her kind before. She would be an easy catch. At the moment of crisis he closed in. Pulling her close and wiping the tears from her face he said, "Come with me; I will take care of you." She believed him and over 30 years later remains his faithful follower.

The man was Charles Manson, crazed leader of the Manson Family Cult whose followers committed mass murders at his command. After Squeaky tried to assassinate President Gerald Ford at Manson's prompting, she was incarcerated for life. Later asked in an interview, "Why have you committed your life to follow Charles Manson?" she answered, "I decided when I was 14 years old that whoever loved me first could have my life."[1]

Times have changed; our society and culture are different; but this same thought still echoes in many teenage girls' hearts. Millions of "Squeakys" are looking for someone to love them. It can be the drug dealer down the street, the hormone-charged guy at school, or a godly woman who will teach them of God's love. Many will cling to the first person to show them attention. Teenage girls need a place to be loved, to belong, and to be accepted unconditionally.

GOD'S PLAN FOR WOMEN

God tells us in Titus 2:3-5 that older women should teach and train younger women. Teenage girls are included in this mandate. What better place to minister to teenage girls than through women's ministry? This may be happening by chance in our churches through Sunday school and discipleship programs, but because of their unique needs, teenage girls need a unique ministry that is organized, intentional, and purposeful. Often ministry to teenagers is left to the student ministry of the church. Dr. Allen Jackson, professor of youth ministry at New Orleans Baptist Theological Seminary puts it this way, "If you are a male youth minister, you must have female heroes for the girls in your church." Male youth ministers can be spiritual influences in the lives of teenage girls, but they will never show them how to be godly women. Whether ministry to teenage girls is under the student ministry or women's ministry of the church, training women to minister to the needs of teenage girls must be priority.

PREVENTION MINISTRY

Many adult women are in crisis across America today as a result of poor decisions made in their teenage and college years. Much of women's ministry is spent trying to help women through the crises they face. Women are facing drug and alcohol addictions, gambling addictions, divorce, problems with their children, eating disorders, domestic violence, relationship problems, and much more. Women who are living in bondage to sin may be turning to the church for help. What can the church do as a means of prevention ministry?

The church can make a difference in women's lives by guiding them to make wise decisions as teens. Mentoring and discipling girls before their values are set may make the difference whether they make a choice that changes their lives forever. Learning to make wise decisions through preteen and teenage years enables women to look back on their lives with less regret. Learning to depend on God and live in obedience to Him lessens the natural consequences of sin.

Many parents raise their children by telling them what to do and not to do. They overlook the responsibility to teach their children how to think. The result is a young person who is prone to peer pressure. The child spends her for-

Mentoring and discipling teenage girls before their values are set may make the difference whether they make a choice that changes their lives forever.

mative years doing exactly what her parents tell her to do. When she becomes a teenager, she doesn't know how to think through the process of making a decision. Automatically, she does what her peers tell her to do. The parents and churches have the responsibility to teach young women how to make wise decisions based on the truth of God's Word.

A concerted, purposeful effort to reach and enrich girls' lives will result in "a new generation of women" who will know truth and will not be bound by sin. Prevention ministry slowly will replace crisis intervention ministry.

The foremost reason to begin girls' enrichment ministry in your church is that God has chosen to use the church as the means to carry His message to the world and to bring people to a saving knowledge of Jesus Christ. Teenage girls are important to Jesus Christ and His kingdom. Who will the girls in your sphere of influence grow up to be one day? What part will they play in God's kingdom purpose? Intentional and well-planned girls' enrichment ministry can literally change the lives of women for eternity.

God accomplishes His Kingdom plan through the church and individuals. He has a unique plan for every person. He brings younger women across our paths so we may be faithful to Him and grow in Christ's likeness. By mentoring a teenage girl, you can make a difference in her life, can experience the joy of possibly changing the course of her life, and can have the awesome privilege of being a part of God's overall kingdom plan.

THE NEEDS OF TEENAGE GIRLS

Teenage girls' basic needs will forever remain the same, but the way we meet the needs of each generation must evolve. In other words, the message remains the same but the delivery methods change with each generation. For instance, this generation battles postmodernism, an ideology that says there is no absolute truth; each person must create her own truth. Postmodernism has subtly evolved through education, government, movies, radio, television, magazines, and the Internet and infiltrated our culture. In ministering to teenage girls heavily influences by such ideals, remember they need:

To know the truth of God's Word—Preteen and teenage girls desperately need to know the truth of God's Word and how it applies to their lives as young women. In years past, morals and truth governed most families. Today, instead of absolute truth, many teens base their decisions on personal preference and tolerance of others. In our world today, truth is thought to be relative, resulting in a society where there are no boundaries. As a result, many girls are prone to low self-esteem. Some are pressured into promiscuity and alcohol or drug use. Many find themselves dealing with eating disorders, self-mutilation, pregnancy, sexually transmitted diseases, unhealthy Internet relationships, and even confusion over sexual orientation. Given a fine China teacup, an old coffee mug, and a paper cup, many girls are likely to compare themselves to the throw-away item. Postmodernism contributes to these dilemmas, and many girls are in a downward spiral physically, emotionally, mentally, and spiritually.

To know boundaries—No real boundaries exist in the minds of teens today. Our world teaches our children that it is OK to make their own rules: "Whatever is right for me may not be right for you, and whatever is right for you may not be right for me." Parents reinforce the idea by not setting boundaries within the home. Many parents are busy, consumed with their jobs and their own problems. Setting and enforcing boundaries takes too much time. Some parents are afraid to set boundaries, thinking they will lose their child to the world if they do. Some parents don't agree on the boundaries, and the teen goes through life playing one parent against the other. Because of the high rate of divorce, some teens have one set of boundaries at one parent's house and another set of boundaries, or none at all, at the other parent's house. Some mothers want to be their daughter's best friend and fail to uphold the responsibilities of motherhood. Where no boundaries exist, the consequences of sin increase. It is no wonder self-esteem is lower today than ever before. Boundaries give teenage girls security. They may see how far they can push the boundaries, but they really are testing to see whether the boundaries are secure. Where there is no truth, there are no boundaries. Where there are no boundaries, there is no security.

To understand God has a plan for their lives—Girls need to know that God has a plan for their lives. If a young person gets through difficult high school and college years without making a life-altering mistake, then they will continue on the right track. To know God put them on this earth for a specific purpose can be the one thing that keeps them going in the right direction.

When teaching teenage girls, I often draw a timeline. The beginning dot is their birth. The second dot is their life now. The line continues, and the third dot is their death. I ask this question, "How much do you know about your life?" Of course their answer is, "From the first to the second dot." My reply is, "God knows everything from before the first dot through eternity. He has it planned specifically. Are you willing to follow Him to find your great adventure?" (See the following diagram.)

Boundaries give teenage girls security.

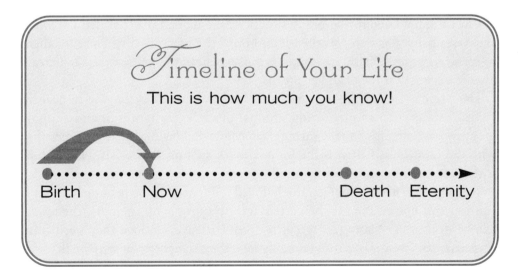

THIS IS HOW MUCH GOD KNOWS!

Low self-esteem, caused by many factors in a teenage girl's life, will deepen the feeling that God does not care about her. "If God doesn't care about me," she may rationalize, "then certainly He cannot have a plan for my life." A purposeful plan to enrich the lives of girls will enhance self-esteem and girls will begin to feel that God really does care and has a specific plan for their lives.

Teenage girls desperately need to experience a sense of family. In years past, the average family consisted of a mother, father, and two or more children who ate together, attended church together, and communicated daily. Today many families consist of a single parent or blend of two families who rarely sit down to eat a meal together and whose communication is often on the cell phone or not at all. Many girls live in homes where the mother is the custodial parent who works two and three jobs just to make ends meet. They spend every other weekend with the non-custodial parent and do not really feel at home either place. These girls are left with few boundaries, a fact that results in low self-esteem, anger, depression, emotional pain, and profound loneliness. Families with both a mother and father in the home are often filled with conflict, resulting in "emotional divorce."

Teens have an innate longing for a place to belong and to be accepted. When girls do not experience acceptance and belonging in their families, the tendency to seek acceptance in other places will increase. Boys as well as girls have this deep need, but they subconsciously seek satisfaction in different ways. Girls try to fill the need emotionally, and young men seek a sense of belonging physically. Girls tend to focus on how they look and feel (consider their obsession with makeup, hair, dress, nails); but boys focus on their physical strength, their manhood, their ability to win through sports, and other physical activities. Dating relationships, gangs, cults such as Wicca and Gothic groups, and even friendship groups provide a false sense of family for teenage girls. Many girls are willing to do anything to be accepted and feel loved. One 14-year-old girl wrote in an e-mail to me that she had a strong desire to have a child of her own. She continued that she would even be willing to be raped in order to get pregnant. When I inquired about her family situation, she replied that her dad left when she was a baby; her mom worked long hours, leaving very little time for them to spend together. Often girls subconsciously believe the lie that they can create a sense of family if they can get pregnant.

The church can provide teenage girls a healthy sense of belonging in positive environments such as mentoring groups, discipleship families, and support groups. Teaching girls to recognize their need to belong and that a relationship with the Lord Jesus Christ is the foundation for all of their other relationships is the starting point for girls' ministry.

Teenage girls need to be genuinely loved. The need to be genuinely loved is timeless and universal, but when a teenage girl's love bank is empty, the results can be disastrous. Many teenage girls do not receive the love they need from their parents. Even if parents genuinely love their daughters, it may be hard for them to show it. Many parents do not have the skills or ability necessary to love their daughters. Many focus on their jobs, personal problems, or addictions, and spend little time focusing on the needs of their girls. As a result, their teenage girls looks for love elsewhere.

You have probably heard the adage "Looking for love in all the wrong places." We must change the saying to fit the tendencies of teenage girls in this generation to: "Looking for love in dangerous places." Many teenage girls will jump at the first young man who shows her attention. The need to be loved overrides good judgment. In America today, statistics show that every nine seconds a woman is abused by her husband or boyfriend. Domestic violence is at an all-time high rate. Many young girls are willing to have sex with any guy who comes along because it causes them to feel loved. In the past a girl could get pregnant or contract an annoying sexually transmitted disease. Today unprotected sex can spell death. The American Association for World Health revealed the following statistics: Every day, more than 7,000 people between the ages of 15 and 24 are infected with HIV worldwide. Only one in four sexually active teens in the United States has ever been tested for HIV.[2]

Teenage girls need to know that true happiness, fulfillment, and love come from a relationship with Jesus Christ. When they receive His love and are totally secure in that love, they will be ready for earthly love relationships. Teaching teenage girls to set dating standards for their lives based on God's Word will help protect them from abusive, dangerous relationships.

Teenage girls need godly female role models. Many girls do not have a godly example to follow at home. Women in the church can fill in this gap by developing good relationships with, mentoring, and discipling them. Teenage girls are women and mothers in training. They learn how to be godly ladies by watching, walking alongside, and working with godly women. The following letter is from a teenage girl to her youth minister's wife.

Teenage girls need to know that true happiness, fulfillment, and love come from a relationship with Jesus Christ.

Dear Debbie,

I can't begin to thank you for all you have taught me. I have not really had a very good example to follow at home. My mom left a few years ago, and I don't really get along with my stepmother. I have watched as you take care of your children on youth trips and how you support Steve in youth ministry. I have noticed how much the two of you love each other. I have learned how to become a good mother and wife by watching you. I hope someday I might even make a good minister's wife. I know you probably didn't even know I was watching you, but thanks anyway.

Love,

Heather

Debbie was shocked—she had no idea the girl was watching her. This was a wake-up call for Debbie, and she began to intentionally reach out to the young girls. She has developed a heart for mentoring teenage girls and has started a mentoring program for girls in her church and community. You are a role model whether you intend to be or not. Girls are watching and learning.

Teenage girls need guidance to work through the unique problems of womanhood. In the past, girls began to mature physically around 11, 12, or 13 years of age. Today, many girls are beginning to mature physically around the age of 9 or 10, leaving a gap of three to four years between childhood and adolescence. Girls are reaping the consequences of sinful lives at younger ages because they are exposed to temptation earlier in life. Consequently, their hearts are becoming hardened earlier, making it difficult to reach them for Christ. Girls need help to sort through issues such as sexual and physical abuse, unwanted pregnancy, sexually transmitted diseases, hormonal issues, dating, understanding the male mind, dressing appropriately, eating disorders, self-esteem issues, friendship conflicts, family problems, spiritual issues, and the daily challenges of life as a female. I have folders full of instant message and e-mail questions from teenage girls. They are searching for answers. Unfortunately, they often find answers based on worldly standards. Females need someone who understands, and no one understands like another female! Who but another girl can understand the hormonal changes that take place each month in a girl's life, the heartbreak when a boyfriend walks away with her best friend, or the insecurity a girl feels when all her friends are going to the prom and she is the only one who doesn't have a date? Who but another female who has experienced similar violence can understand the violation and dirtiness a girl feels when she has been sexually abused or raped? Girls' enrichment ministry can provide an avenue to help girls work through the problems unique to womanhood.

Teenage girls need to be challenged intellectually. Teens have great potential! Often they are intellectually challenged at school and in every other area of their lives except church. We must teach girls how to study the Bible and dig deep into God's Word. If teens are not taught how to think and work through problems, they will depend on others to make decisions for them. Today's teens need to be challenged to take God's Word and search out the answers. Teenage girls need a godly woman to encourage them to use the guidelines in God's Word to work through everyday issues. They need guidance to learn to think and to discover the truth of God's Word and how it applies to their lives.

Teenage girls need three basic relationships. A relationship with God, relationships with significant adults, and healthy peer relationships are important for all young women.

Teens, especially girls, are seeking relationships more today than ever before. Often at events for teens, the boys will play some kind of sports while the girls sit on the sidelines in small groups. Often we think the girls need to be involved or we need to provide an activity for them to do. In actuality, social time is valuable time for the girls. They need to talk through their problems, share their dreams, and build relationships. We can capitalize on this time by looking for ministry and relationship-building opportunities. If any relationship area is lacking in a girl's life, her emotional and spiritual well being are affected. Internet relationships are replacing personal relationships. Instant messaging, text messaging, and cell phones are the most common forms of communication for teens today. Youth culture and the world do not easily promote a relationship with God, relationships with significant adults, or healthy peer relationships. Many youth think it is not cool to have a good relationship with parents or other adults. Younger adolescents tend to think adults really do not like them. Mentoring/discipleship groups will make building relationships with adults more comfortable for girls. Because her friends are there, the conversation is comfortable; she may begin to feel that "just maybe this adult really does like me." When a relationship is established between a girl and mentor, the adult has the right to hold her accountable for her relationship with God. Positive peer pressure is as strong as negative. Mentoring/discipleship groups foster all of these relationships, making a happier, healthier, more well-adjusted young lady who is able to make wiser life decisions.

THE INGREDIENTS FOR GROWING GODLY YOUNG WOMEN

Teenage girls' needs focus on five categories: spiritual, physical, mental, emotional, and relational. These categories can be compared to a tiered cake, each layer building on the one before (see p. 172). Have you ever made a cake that flopped? I have. I know from experience that if any layer, especially the bottom layer, is uneven and lacks the necessary ingredients, the entire cake will topple. If these areas are not well balanced with the necessary ingredients, her whole life will be affected. Let's take a look at the ingredients for growing godly women.

Spiritual

The bottom layer, or foundational building block, is the spiritual area of a girl's life. The foundation for her spiritual life is her relationship with God through Jesus Christ. If she has never accepted Christ's payment on the cross for her sins, then her whole life will be out of balance. Often girls will accept other people or things as their foundation. She may consider things such as position (cheerleader, class president, sports, honor student), possessions (car, clothes, nice house, money), and popularity (boyfriend, friends) as her foundation, but all of these can be taken away or lost in a minute. The only sure life foundation is one built on a relationship with God through Jesus Christ. He is the same yesterday, today, and forever.

A girl's relationship with God defines every other relationship she has. If she is not a Christian and has not allowed Jesus Christ to give her security and esteem, it will affect every other area of her life. She may have addictions, be filled with bitterness, believe Satan's lies, or give her heart and body away to any guy who comes along. However, if she is focused on learning more about God through Bible study and prayer, attends church to learn and worship, and is growing in her relationship with Jesus through discipleship, she will develop a strong foundation all areas of life. When a young woman has a strong spiritual foundation, she will be able to set solid standards that will keep her on the right track.

Mental

The second area of a girl's life that will affect how her needs are met involves her mind. A girl's mental state affects how she thinks and processes life. What she believes will determine how she acts. What a girl believes will affect how she dresses, what she does, how she feels about herself, others, and God, her relationships with others, and will determine whether she fulfills the purpose God has planned for her. If a young woman believes that God's Word is truth and bases her life on it, she will set her standards accordingly.

God's Word tells of His love and care for His children. His underlying motive for every principle is love, protection, and keeping us on the track He has planned for each of us. But a battle rages for the minds of young women. Through television, movies, magazines, music, and other media, the world says a young women must look, act, and think a certain way to be accepted, valued, and loved. Teenage girls are being exploited for money-making purposes.

The mind controls every other aspect of the body. Suppose a girl thinks she needs a boyfriend to survive and be happy. She believes if he asks her out or marries her, she will find contentment. If she believes her happiness and well-being depend on him, she will do anything to get him. She may spend all of her waking hours working toward the goal. She may exchange sexual favors for affection because she believes she "needs" a particular young man.

Likewise, if a girl believes drugs or alcohol will alleviate her emotional pain, she may do whatever it takes to get them. And since drugs and alcohol satisfy only for a time, she may believe she needs increasingly more to achieve satisfaction. Although addictions start in the mind, they affect every area of a girl's life. Addictions can ruin her reputation and cause her to lose others' respect. They affect spiritual, physical, mental, emotional, and relational areas of her life. Instead of alleviating emotional pain and suffering, addictions only increase problems and result in deeper suffering and depression.

Poor self-image is a problem for many teen girls. If a girl believes she must look a certain way to receive love and value, she will do whatever it takes to look that way. Media use models to portray the "ideal" girl. Even though magazines airbrush the pictures, teenage girls compare themselves and begin to believe they must look flawless to be loved and accepted. Comparing herself to others affects a girl's self-esteem. Many girls are obsessed with how they look. Eating disorders stem from an unhealthy view of one's body image among other emotional and familial issues. If a girl believes she has no control in her life, she may subconsciously believe the only area she can control is what she puts into her mouth. Food addictions, binge eating, anorexia, bulimia, and other eating disorders begin in the mind. But if a girl can change what she believes about her self-worth and the true source of beauty—a relationship with the Lord— she will be able to prevent or overcome many addictions and self-concept issues.

The mind is complex. When it is filled with garbage, sooner or later it will be evident. Have you ever noticed an unpleasant odor and could not quite figure out its source? As the days passed, the odor became stronger and stronger until finally you were led to the culprit? When a girl grows up filling her mind with garbage of the world, the evidence of it will eventually begin to emerge as bitterness, pride, anger, or instability. We must teach our young girls to recognize truth and to flee from the lies of Satan. When a girl fills her mind with the truth of God's Word and lives a life of obedience, her life will give off a fragrant scent to God and others! She'll be full of love, joy, patience, and kindness.

Many verses in the Bible deal with what a person believes. How a girl thinks and what she believes will affect what she does; what she does affects her emotions, our next building block.

Emotional

The third layer represents a girl's emotional dimension. Our emotions determine how we feel about others, ourselves, and God. Emotions determine whether we have healthy self-esteem. A girl's childhood and family life have a direct bearing on her emotional health. If she has been abused or neglected, she may feel emotionally unstable. Whatever sins she has learned will affect her emotional well being. When a girl's love bank is empty, her emotions will be a wreck. Learning to guard her heart is an important aspect of emotional health. Learning to give her hurts and pain to God is the key.

Not only does a girl's environment affect her emotions, but her growth as a young woman will have a direct bearing also. Only another woman can understand the hormonal issues a girl experiences during her transition into womanhood. Sometimes all a girl needs is another woman to sit beside her, listen, cry with her, and then have a good belly laugh at the appropriate time.

Physical

The fourth layer is the physical area. All of the other areas have a direct bearing on the physical. For instance, how a girl takes care of her body demonstrates what she believes about God and herself. Her beliefs will be expressed through daily activities such as diet, exercise, and rest. Unfortunately, how a girl feels about herself may also determine whether she uses harmful substances such as alcohol, drugs, and tobacco. It may also be reflected in how she presents herself and dresses. A mirror often reflects a young girl's beliefs and self-concept.

Likewise, a young woman's commitment to sexual purity is seen through her actions. A girl will usually give her heart (emotions) before she is willing to give her body, but once she has "fallen in love" with a guy, it is often easy for her to fall into sexual temptation. Low self-esteem, feelings of emptiness caused by separation from God, and not basing her standards on the truth of God's Word will get a girl into trouble. Teaching a girl that a relationship with Jesus Christ gives her direct access to God will help alleviate feelings of emptiness. When she is truly secure in her relationship with Christ, she will not be as vulnerable emotionally and physically. Teaching her to set her standards based on God's Word will help her to save herself sexually for marriage and to make healthy choices.

Another area of the physical building block is the tongue. Although it is small, it causes great harm when a girl becomes involved in gossip, slander, profanity, or negative talk. Teaching girls to be quick to listen, slow to speak, and slow to anger will enable them to have a healthier physical life (Jas. 1:19).

The physical deals with the way a girl's body looks too. Many girls constantly focus on looks. They compare themselves to others and desire to change their looks. This is a problem with teenage girls and women as well. "Extreme Makeovers" is a popular TV program that gives girls the idea that they can have surgery to change their appearance. The testimonies of those who have had extreme makeovers prove that how one wants them to take care of their bodies and to be satisfied with the way He created them. What a girl does with her body affects her physically, spiritually, mentally, emotionally, and relationally. Teaching girls to honor God with their bodies is a vital part of growing godly young women.

The Building Blocks for Growing Godly Young Women

Love the Lord your God with all your heart and with all your soul and with all your mind. This is the first and greatest commandment. And the second is like it: "Love your neighbor as yourself."

—Matthew 22:37-39

1 Corinthians 13:4-8   RELATIONAL   Proverbs 27:17
- Every area of your life affects your relationships: spiritual, mental, emotional, physical, dating, parents, friends, God, school, job, and even your future husband and children.
- Your relationships determine how effective you are for God.

Proverbs 4:23   Emotional—Feel   Proverbs 27:19
- Actions affect how you feel about yourself.
- Guard your heart by obeying God and following His commandments.
- Just because something *feels* right doesn't mean it *is* right.
- Follow God, not your heart.

1 Corinthians 6:18-20   Physical—Body   Proverbs 3:7-8
- Take care of your body—exercise, eat right, and get plenty of rest.
- Don't poison your body with drugs, alcohol, or tobacco.
- Dress attractively, not seductively.
- Lift people up with what you say. Don't bring them down with gossip.
- Keep you and your thoughts pure. Avoid sexual temptation.
- Glorify God with your body.

Proverbs 23:7   Mental—Think   Isaiah 26:3
- Look for the truth in God's Word. Thoughts lead to actions.
- Base your beliefs on the Word of God and not the word of man.
- Addictions start in the mind.
- Temptation starts in your mind because of a need or desire you have.
- Discover your needs and how to meet them in a godly way.

1 Corinthians 3:9-11   SPIRITUAL—SOUL   Romans 10:9-10
- If you want meaning and purpose in life, believe in God, confess your sins, and accept Jesus Christ's death on the cross for your sins.
- Daily prayer and Bible study are musts to keep your foundation strong.
- Get involved in a church. Find a small group of people to hold you accountable.
- Discipleship/Mentoring programs help increase your knowledge about God.

Relational

The fifth building block is the relational area of life. The relational area is supported and held in place by all of the other areas. For instance, a girl's relationship with the Lord Jesus Christ is the determining factor for every other relationship in her life. If she has "God esteem" rather than self-esteem, she will interact with others more successfully. When she finds security in her relationship with Jesus Christ, she will not put unrealistic expectations on others. As she grows mentally and bases her life on God's Word, she will make wise decisions that will foster healthy relationships.

Relationships with others determine how affective a girl is for the kingdom of God. If she is sexually involved with a guy, she will not be able to lead him to accept Christ. If she is using drugs or addicted to alcohol, she will not be able to be a strong witness. If she has low self-esteem, she will not have the confidence to be a strong witness or to fulfill God's plan God for her.

For success in girls' ministry, we must focus on all five areas of a teenage girl's life. By using the following tiered cake diagram, you will be able to address issues of accountability in small groups as well as ensure a comprehensive program that will meet the unique needs of preteen and teenage girls.

WHAT IS GIRLS' ENRICHMENT MINISTRY?

Girls' Enrichment Ministry is an intentional and organized method of enriching and spiritually transforming the lives of teenage girls, moving them from larger open groups to smaller closed groups to better focus on their individual needs as young women. This ministry can be organized and carried out within the youth ministry or under the umbrella of women's ministry.

Girls' Enrichment Ministry is not a stand alone program in the church. It must come under the approval and guidance of the pastor, the youth pastor, or the women's ministry coordinator. It must also fit within the overall mission statement of the church. It is not "another program" to take the time of the minister but a method to train women in your church to be involved in enhancing and enriching the lives of teenage girls. Girls' enrichment ministry is a piece of the puzzle that will create balanced ministry and help to build the Kingdom of God.

Five Aspects of GEM

Five areas need to be considered when beginning GEM in your church.
- Training women to minister to teenage girls
- Mentoring/Discipleship groups for teenage girls
- Special events for teenage girls: all girl conferences, retreats, mother/daughter events, girl-talk groups, father/daughter events
- Support groups for special needs
- Parent ministry

Many larger churches are considering hiring a staff member to focus on Girls' Enrichment Ministry. Your church may not be prepared to hire an additional person to focus on Girls' Enrichment Ministry, but you can take steps to organize your ministry to enrich the lives of girls in your sphere of influence.

RESPONSIBILITIES OF THE CHURCH STAFF MEMBER

As the staff person responsible for Girls' Enrichment Ministry, an important part of your work is to know your obligations. To be considered a church staff member, you should have direct responsibility for a certain ministry or portion of a ministry within the local church on a full- or part-time basis. Many churches choose to place GEM under the supervision of the youth minister or women's ministry coordinator. Girls' ministry fits effectively under either area. The youth minister and women's ministry coordinator may choose to work together to meet the needs of teenage girls. If this is true, your church will need to determine who is ultimately responsible for this area of ministry.

GEM must fit into your church's overall vision. It cannot be a stand-alone ministry; it must come under the supervision of the staff person assigned. In smaller churches, GEM may come under the authority and supervision of the pastor even though a volunteer may directly coordinate that ministry.

The church staff member is responsible for training and equipping volunteers, empowering them with the opportunity to lead, and allowing them to use their talents and skills. Setting up a mission statement and casting the vision for GEM with volunteers will allow all involved to understand and share that vision with others. The more volunteers who understand the purpose, the greater opportunity for outreach and ministry you will have through your ministry. Recruiting the director or co-director is the responsibility of the church staff person.

If you are serving in the church staff member role, begin to pray consistently for the person who is to hold the director position. Ask God to reveal to you whom He has chosen to carry out this important role. You will serve as a liaison between the director and the church staff and will provide resources to equip your director to carry out specific duties. The director will come to you with problems, and it will be your duty to provide resolution to those problems. Your attendance at all organizational meetings is also necessary, as you will be the provider of key information related to decisions concerning Girls' Enrichment Ministry.

Whether you are the supervising staff member, the staff member directly responsible, or a volunteer director, it is necessary to know how to effectively set up a girls' ministry. It is important to develop a leadership style to empower those working with you to complete the task. Many times you will simply provide resources for those carrying out the ministry. Other times you will be directly involved in the day-to-day task of ministry to teenage girls.

If you are working under the authority of a male staff member, applaud him for seeing the need and accepting the challenge of meeting the unique needs of teenage girls in your church and community.

Pray.

Prayer is the basis for every aspect of ministry. The vision for Girls' Enrichment Ministry must come from God and not you. The fact that you are reading this chapter indicates that God is already working and has put ministry to teenage girls in your heart. Seek His plan before you begin. Pray that God will show you who He wants to coordinate this ministry in your church. Pray that He will touch the lives of teenage girls and will open their hearts to be receptive and involved. Pray that God will raise up women who will become mentors and be willing to share their lives with teenage girls. Pray for a purpose and mission statement so you can communicate the vision to others. Pray that the pastor will embrace this vision and be supportive. Remember, prayer is not only the beginning step but is also the foundation for the path that will maintain and grow this ministry.

Invite others to pray with you about specific requests. Form a prayer team if your church does not already have one in place. Make sure you have God's permission before you proceed.

Share your vision with church staff.

The input of your pastor and other church staff is vitally important before you begin girls' enrichment ministry. The mission of Girls' Enrichment Ministry should not only fit into the mission of your women's ministry but also the mission of the entire church. The pastor and other staff members can give a vital perspective you may not see. Pray together as a staff for this ministry. If you do not have the permission of your pastor, this may not be God's timing. Submit to the authority of your pastor and watch God bless your ministry.

Choose a leadership team.

If you are the staff member in charge of ministry to teenage girls, choose a coordinator who has a heart for ministry to teenage girls and who will work under your supervision and authority. Titus 2:3-5 gives the qualifications of a woman who is worthy to teach younger women. You may not find someone who meets all of these qualifications perfectly, but if a woman is out of control in any of these areas, she may not be a good choice.

Form a team of godly women and diverse girls to study the needs of teenage girls in your community and church. The basic needs of girls are the same everywhere, but specific needs are based on the region in which you live, the family situations in your church, the social and economic status of the families in your church, and the culture of your community. This team can be short-term, or you may choose to use them long-term as an advisory team. You may need to meet with them occasionally or call them individually to get feedback and advice when needed.

Evaluate current programs, ministries, and events.

Your current ministries, events, and programs may already meet the needs of teenage girls adequately. Before you begin GEM, evaluate existing ministries. Do they simply need to be tweaked or do you need to begin something entirely new? Get feedback from teenage girls, youth workers, parents, and other churches that are ministering to the specific needs of teenage girls. Survey the girls in your ministry to find out what their needs are and how you can effectively meet them.

Set up a mission statement.

Design a mission statement and goals in line with the overall mission of your women's ministry and church mission statement, but focus on the specific needs of teenage girls. Under your supervision the GEM team will work with the GEM coordinator to set up the mission statement and decide how this mission will be met. Continually casting the vision for girls' ministry will help everyone to be on the same page and accomplish the purpose more effectively. Often the leader knows where she is going but forgets to inform others. When others get lost in the shuffle, the leader cannot understand why they are not doing their jobs. Many times, they simply do not understand the goal and how to reach it. Take responsibility as the leader to make sure everyone knows the destination and has the road map. Develop a leadership style to empower those working with you to complete their tasks. Often you will simply provide the resources for women who carry out the ministry.

Recruit, develop, and train leaders.

Finding leaders and equipping them to do their jobs adequately seems to be an age-old problem plaguing our churches. The keys to success in any ministry are recruiting and developing leadership, doing follow-up and evaluations, and fine-tuning the ministry on a regular basis. This is especially true in working with teenagers. Youth culture changes rapidly. Although the principles of God's Word never change, the methods we use to present the gospel must evolve continually.

Communicate, advertise, and publicize.

Publicity is important in attracting girls' involvement. If something looks fun, their friends are involved, and it is relevant to their lives, teens will be willing to give it a try. Personal invitations in the mail, e-mail newsletters, flyers given at youth events, posters placed in strategic places, and leaders talking to small groups about girls' ministry will communicate the beginning of a ministry focused on teenage girls. However, the very best method is personal invitations from friends. Girls love to be with their friends. If they know their friends will be there, they will want to go!

Also remember that instant messaging, e-mail, cell phones, and websites are a important forms of communication for teens today. Most teens have e-mail addresses and instant messaging screen names. Build an e-mail or instant messaging list and send an e-newsletter for Girls' Ministry. A page on your church's website devoted to girls' ministry may be an effective way to communicate with teenage girls. An interactive, updated site can be a point of contact. But I once heard someone say that a website that is never updated is a cobweb. If you develop a website, make sure it is updated weekly. Many teens are proficient in website construction. Involve the girls in your church who have this skill to publicize the girls' ministry. Look at other sites that focus on the needs of teenage girls for ideas and the kind of look that will be attractive to teenage girls. Most magazines catering to teenage girls have websites. Knowing what attracts teenage girls is their business. Get ideas from their sites and use them to your advantage on your web page for girls' ministry.

Have a kick-off event to begin girls' enrichment ministry.
An exciting kick-off event is a good way to generate interest in a new ministry focus. The vision for girls' ministry should be clearly and attractively communicated through a fun and informative event such as a banquet, dinner, or get-together. Inviting mothers and all female leadership will also create enthusiasm. Decorations should be attractive to teenage girls. The women and teenagers should feel ownership in the ministry, so involve as many of them in leadership and planning as possible. Also invite the youth minister or pastor to show his support for this ministry. Follow his leadership and communicate that he has the best interest of the teenage girls in your church at heart.

If you have a kick-off event, be diligent to follow through with developing girls' ministry. A kick-off event will create momentum, but if you let it die, recreating the excitement will be difficult. Keep the energy going with a follow-up event.

Evaluate and make necessary changes.
Evaluation of leadership and ministry to teenage girls is essential in a successful GEM. Continuing programs or events that are not effective waste precious time and energy that could be used to reach girls for Christ and grow them into godly women. Plan purposeful events and ministry. Every event, meeting, or group should fall in line with the mission statement God gave you.

Remember, each step we've discussed is vital in making the ministry to teenage girls successful, but prayer is the key. You can follow the steps perfectly, but the hearts and lives of teenage girls will not be touched unless God shows up. Your continual prayers will beckon Him to work.

RECRUITING AND DEVELOPING LEADERSHIP

Where do you find leadership for GEM? Are there qualifications for leaders? How do you train them, and what do you teach them? All of these legitimate questions to ask in building a successful ministry.

Qualifications for Leaders in Girls' Ministry

First, we will discuss the qualifications for leaders listed in Titus 2:3-5. Teenage girls learn best by example. I don't remember many of the Bible studies taught in my youth group, but I do remember the example of my Sunday school teachers. I remember how they loved me and how they treated their husbands and children. I remember funny things we did and times we cried together. I remember some of the trips we took and the times they rescued me when I felt lonely. I remember some of the notes they sent when I was in the hospital and the prayers they prayed for me.

Since girls learn from example, leaders should model the characteristics they are trying to teach. Titus 2:3-5 lists four qualifications for women who teach younger women. Women in leadership should be reverent in behavior, not be malicious gossips, not be enslaved to much wine (or addicted to any substance), and teach what is good.

Behaviors older women should teach younger women are best taught by modeling. Therefore, a woman in leadership should demonstrate and teach that a godly woman must …

- love her husband.
- be sensible.
- be a worker at home.
- be subject to her own husband.
- love her children.
- be an example of purity.
- be kind to others.
- not dishonor God.

Because of our sinful nature, no woman can measure up to each of these behaviors perfectly. Every woman may fail in one or more areas from time to time. A good question to ask when seeking leaders for girls' enrichment ministry is this, "Is this woman out of control in any of these areas in her personal life?" If so, she needs to be mentored by an older woman or counseled by a professional Christian counselor before stepping into the role of leadership for teenage girls. Girls are vulnerable to anyone who shows them love and attention. Placing into leadership a woman who would lead them in the wrong direction would be a tragic mistake.

Recently a woman declined my invitation to work with teenage girls because she felt she did not know enough about the Bible to teach teens. This common misconception among women prevents them from experiencing the joy and blessing of pouring their lives into younger women. They seem to believe that one has to be a Bible expert or a skilled teacher to work with teens. Nothing could be further from the truth.

Love for the Lord, good resources, a willing heart, a love for teenage girls, and initial followed by ongoing training will keep workers on the right track. However, women do need to be students of the Bible in order to teach biblical principles to teens. Passing on what God teaches them personally is a great start.

Sit down and talk personally with potential leadership candidates, especially if you do not know them well. Many churches require volunteer leadership to fill out a Leadership Application. These include questions about their previous experiences with youth, their personal testimonies, other churches where they have volunteered, references from former churches, and spiritual gifts and talents. This information is vital in selecting and matching volunteers with their best ministry fit. Questions should include . Consider placing women who have never worked with teenage girls or new Christians as assistants to more experienced women for "on the job training." Don't be afraid to ask each candidate questions and to lovingly evaluate her as she begins her work among the teens.

Also know that many insurance companies require churches to complete criminal background checks on all persons involved with minors in a church situation. This protects innocent teens as well as the church. If a volunteer abuses a girl, the church and staff are liable. Performing a criminal background check may not prevent abuse, but it will show your intent to protect the girls in your care.

WHAT SHOULD BE TAUGHT IN LEADERSHIP TRAINING?

Preliminary leader training sessions should involve:
- the information presented in this manual.
- a clear and regular communication of the Girls' Enrichment Ministry vision that will enable leaders to work together and stay focused on common goals.
- a spiritual gifts inventory and how they can be used to serve in the church.
- a personality test and how to teach girls according to their personalities.
- effective communication skills and small-group facilitating.
- using curriculum and effective teaching methods.
- a quick study of the rapidly changing youth culture.
- an overview of the church's policies and guidelines for working with teens.
- a presentation of the church program and doctrines.

Remember, ongoing leadership training is necessary for follow-up, evaluation, and fine-tuning of GEM. At least once a year, intense training and leadership development will strengthen even the best leaders.

SMALL GROUP DISCIPLESHIP AND MENTORING

Relationships are high priority in working with teenage girls. A teenage girl will receive the truth easier from a person with whom she has a strong relationship. Many definitions for mentoring and discipleship exist, but we will define these terms in relationship to Girls' Enrichment Ministry.

Mentoring can be defined as "coming alongside a young woman to model, teach, and train her through your life's experiences."

Discipleship can be defined as leading and training a young woman to be a follower of Jesus Christ.

Mentoring and discipleship go together like a car and tires. One does not fulfill its purpose without the other. Basing your mentoring and training on God's Word will help to mold and shape teenage girls into the likeness of Christ. If a teenage girl is mentored, but not taught biblical principles and truths in God's Word, she will not fulfill her God-given purpose.

Mentoring/Discipleship Groups are Best

One-to-one mentoring works well for women, but mentoring/discipleship groups have proven best when dealing with teens. Rare situations with exceptional women and teens will be appropriate for one-to-one mentoring, but as a general rule, mentoring groups are best for several reasons:

Teen girls' three basic relationship needs are met through mentoring groups. When a young girl is involved in weekly discipleship and held accountable for her quiet time with the Lord, her relationship with God will grow. Weekly mentoring and discipleship with adult women will enhance her relationship needs with significant adults. When a small group of girls meet weekly to study the Bible, pray for one another, talk through their problems, and just have fun, their need for healthy peer relationships is met. Positive peer pressure will result.

Mentoring can be defined as "coming alongside a young woman to model, teach, and train her through your life's experiences."

Discipleship can be defined as leading and training a young woman to be a follower of Jesus Christ.

Mentoring groups are wise because of legal issues.

Churches are being sued at an increasing rate, especially in the areas of children's and youth ministry. Mentoring groups provide protection for the girls and the adults. One woman learned the value of mentoring groups and having at least two leaders in the group when she was leading a group of girls to discover how they can overcome temptation. She said, "When you girls make wrong choices and give in to temptation, I take that as a personal responsibility."

A couple of girls who had been partying were not there that night. Some of the girls present told those girls that their leader had talked about them behind their backs and said their partying was a bad reflection on her. Needless to say, those girls were devastated to think that their discipleship leader would discuss their behavior with the other girls in the group! Of course, their leader was innocent but the accusation seemed real. The only thing that saved the leader's reputation was that she had two other adults in the group to verify her innocence. Of course, this was not something for which the leader could be sued, but it certainly could have destroyed trust with the girls.

Not only can trust be destroyed, but many serious legal issues may arise as well. Church leaders and volunteers are only one accusation away from ruin. The accusation does not have to be true. This method provides accountability for both the girls and the adults involved: if you need to conduct a private conversation, meet in a semi-private place. A restaurant or an area of a room where other people are in view will work. Although some consider this extreme, I recommend never meeting with one girl alone in a home—either the woman's or the girl's. Many lives and reputations have been ruined because of an unhealthy emotional or physical attachment. Many teenage girls are emotionally unstable because of their home situations, abuse, and neglect. Our society fosters deviant sexual identity among teens today. Magazines, television programs, movies, and books encourage teenage girls in lesbian feelings and behavior. Because of rape, molestation, and incest, many girls have an intense hated for men. When nurtured and cared for by another female, the teen may mistake their care for romantic love. Relationships with teenage girls must be kept in the proper realm. Boundaries must be set and never crossed.

Mentoring groups are more comfortable socially for the girls.

Some teenage girls feel that adults do not like them and don't want to be with them. To them, sitting down one-on-one with an adult may seem threatening or uncomfortable. A group setting alleviates that uncomfortable feeling of not really knowing what to say to an adult or vice versa. Girls feel safer with their peers present. Women who work with teenage girls must remember that they are the adults in the relationship. They should have appropriate mentor/mentee relationships, not peer friendships.

Structure and Organization

Mentoring groups will vary from church to church. They are usually more effective with two women meeting with four to ten girls. Each woman should have no fewer than two girls and no more than five to mentor. More can be overwhelming; fewer can be uncomfortable.

The mentoring group can meet whenever it is convenient. If your church has more than one group, the person in charge should set the guidelines for each group. Some groups meet early in the morning before school, some on Sunday nights, and others at various times during the week. If you have a large group of girls and several mentoring groups, picking a specific time for all groups to meet makes organization and accountability easier.

Meeting places vary from restaurants, homes, church classrooms, teen centers, or coffee shops. Restaurants offer more distractions unless you are able to use a private meeting room. Meeting at the church may be more feasible in Metro areas because of travel distance and time. Meeting in a home provides a comfortable, relaxed atmosphere where girls will see mentors with their families.

Responsibilities of the Mentor

Women who want to become mentors must be willing to accept the responsibilities involved. Commitment is key in mentoring teenage girls. Stable relationships are few and far between. Parents often are not dependable, and life situations can quickly change. One day a girl may have a family, and the next day mom or dad has moved out. Many teenagers cannot bear another disappointment or, in their eyes, rejection. Therefore, counting the cost before deciding to mentor is wise and will prevent the disappointment of a failed mentoring relationship that was not well thought out.

Answering the following questions will help women make the right decision regarding commitment:
- Do I have the time to spend each week with teenage girls?
- Will this commitment leave adequate time for my family and commitments?
- Am I willing to love the girls unconditionally?
- Do I need to give up other commitments to build these relationships?

Mentors should understand that they'll be expected to meet at least once a week for mentoring and discipleship. Using a discipleship curriculum ensure accountability in the topics being taught. Many good resources are available. The staff person over the mentoring program should assist in choosing curriculum and in training the mentors how to use it.

Mentors must also commit to keeping in touch with their girls during the week. They should make phone calls, write notes, send e-mails, and chat on instant messenger. However, they must remember that private topics should be discussed in a situation where others may not overhear.

Mentors should ask for prayer requests weekly and pray for the girls daily. Sticky notes and index cards are wonderful tools on which the girls may write their prayer requests. These should be kept in a convenient place so the mentor can pray for the girls often, but they must not be left where others can see confidential information. Small prayer notebooks are also a good idea for each girl to keep. They can write each other's requests down and pray for each other throughout the week. Girls love meeting someone in their mentoring group at school and being told they were prayed for that morning!

Encouraging dependence on God by holding teens accountable for their daily quiet time is one of a mentor's primary responsibilities. Initially, this may involve teaching them how to have a quiet time. Many devotional books are available for teens. LifeWay publishes EC (Essential Connection), a daily quiet time devotional magazine for youth. You may order these through www.lifeway.com or through your local church. But mentors must hold girls accountable for other areas of their lives as well. Most teenage girls need accountability in their relationship with Jesus, their behavior, and their emotions. The following questions are guidelines in holding girls accountable:

- What did you learn from God's Word this week?
- How did you guard your heart and emotions this week?
- Did you engage in inappropriate behavior this week? If so, what steps will you take to change this behavior?
- How did you develop your godly character this week?
- Did you lie about any of the above?

Mentors must remember to keep a sense of humor in working with the girls. Mentoring teens is serious business, but there is a balance of teaching and fun. Encourage mentors to let their girls know they are "real people."

Responsibilities of the Girls

Leading a girl to decide whether she can commit to a mentoring group is important. Helping her to count the cost before she signs the commitment card will prevent problems after the mentoring relationship begins. Mentoring relationships require willingness from both mentors and mentees.

Asking girls to sign a commitment card before joining a mentoring group is a good idea. The following statements should be included:

- I commit to attend all mentoring/discipleship meetings faithfully.
- I commit to complete all discipleship assignments.
- I commit to keep all personal information shared in mentoring/discipleship group confidential. (I understand that any information shared regarding present abuse, suicide intent, or intent to harm another person is the legal responsibility of the adult in charge to report to the appropriate person.)
- I commit to keep myself pure in thought, word, and deed.
- I commit to faithfully pray for other members of this group.
- I commit to develop my relationship with Jesus Christ by having a regular quiet time, reading my Bible daily, praying, and attending church.

Each girl and mentor should sign this commitment card at the beginning of every semester. By signing the commitment card and following through, mentors teach by example.

Lifestyle Mentoring

Mentoring does not always have to be done in formal groups. Often we expect teenage girls to come to us, but most won't. Sometimes we have to go to their turf. Women should always have their spiritual antennae up for girls who need a motherly touch. Often God brings girls across our paths and a natural bonding takes place. When a mentor has a relationship with a girl, it may mean the world to the teen if she goes to her ball game or piano recital or simply invites her to meet for a burger. Hanging out as "one of the girls" and knowing one's place in a teen girl's life are different. Being appropriately involved can build the foundational relationship that guides her to be exactly what God wants her to be.

Mentors may see many problems in the lives of teenage girls. For this reason, it is very easy to slip into a counselor role instead of a mentoring role. But if one is not a professionally trained counselor, this is very dangerous. Wrong advice may endanger the life of the teen or another person. One well-meaning pastor counseled a teenager who was contemplating suicide. The teen seemed to "feel better" when leaving his office, so the pastor did not inform the parents or get professional help for the teen. Later that night, the teen wrote a suicide note mentioning the pastor's name and killed herself. In a situation like this, legal action against the pastor and church is possible.

Know when to refer a girl to a professional counselor. When a mentor runs into problems out of her league, she should call the pastor or staff person in charge of GEM for advice. A staff person should be informed when serious problems occur with the girls in a mentor's group. That person should be aware of the laws in your state and keep a list of resources such as Christian counseling centers and Christian counselors who work with teen girls. Another excellent resource in working with teens who have emotional or mental problems is Josh McDowell's book, *Handbook on Counseling Youth*. Helping girls work through common problems is part of mentoring, but counseling for problems such as suicidal tendencies, drug abuse, eating disorders, or other serious emotional and psychiatric problems is unwise. Most church staff are able to refer teenagers to Christian counseling when necessary.

Confidentiality is important when working with teens. One of the most common statements from teenage girls to the women who mentor them is, "I will tell you something if you promise not to tell anyone." This statement should send up a red flag immediately. This is a promise a mentor cannot legally make. She will be wise to promptly answer, "I can't make that promise, so, if you tell me something I can't retell, then you probably don't need to tell me." Then she should add, "I can promise you, in the event I do need to tell someone for your protection, I will only tell the person or persons who need to know."

Confidentiality must be discussed with mentors in training. Discussing confidential matters with friends, family, or other youth workers is unethical and inappropriate. Only in the event where the safety of the girl or someone else is at stake, should a mentor tell what she knows to the appropriate person.

Develop a church-wide policy on reporting methods and policies and to train in advance persons working with children and teens. Most states have laws pertaining to reporting abuse, intent to harm oneself, and intent to harm another. Adult aware of certain situations carry the legal responsibility to report to the Department of Social Services when a minor's safety is at risk. Wise church leaders learn the laws of the state from their church attorney or local Department of Social Services. They then develop a Procedures Policy so all leadership will know the church's process in reporting. Having a procedure in place when those situations arise will ensure the safety and well being of everyone involved.

Mentors should be made aware that prayer times among peers can easily digress into gossip sessions. For this reason, prayer requests should be kept to the personal issues of those present and not the personal issues of those who are not there. Once the precedent is set and modeled by the adult, girls will follow suit. Mentors should learn not to talk about others or to listen to gossip from others. When a person begins to tell a woman something about another and the Holy Spirit convicts her that it is gossip, it is OK to respectfully say, "I'm sorry, but I don't feel comfortable talking about this. Can we talk about something else, please?" In doing so, she'll find her reputation will precede her, and people will not attempt to gossip in her presence. Leading by example is important. Gossip—in any form—should not be tolerated.

RESULTS OF MENTORING/DISCIPLESHIP

How can a person measure the success of mentoring? By whether or not the girls are able to recite their lessons back each week? Does it mean a mentoring group is a failure when a girl admits she has not had her quiet time in three weeks? The answer to the last two questions is no.

Mentoring/Discipleship is a process, not a program. This process will go on even after the girls graduate from high school and college. Mentors may see indicators along the way that their efforts are encouraging their girls on to maturity, but to say whether they are successful in mentoring is difficult. However, when you see a process of maturity in a girl's life as she begins to reach out to others and mentor them as well, that is a strong indicator that the mentoring relationship was successful.

SPECIAL EVENTS FOR TEENAGE GIRLS

Special events for teen girls offer another opportunity to help young women become healthy spiritually, physically, mentally, emotionally, and relationally. At different intervals during the year, it is important to bring teenage girls together for special events geared toward their unique needs. Girls only retreats, mother/daughter events, father/daughter events, sleepovers, and makeovers are all big hits with preteens and teenagers. Mentoring trips and mission activities are a vital part in growing young girls to be godly women. Special events designed to help girls grasp what it means to be attractive from the inside out are important because outer beauty enhances inner beauty and boosts a girl's esteem. When a girl is balanced in all five areas of her life, she'll find it easier to accomplish God's complete plan for her.

Purpose of Special Events

Special events should be planned with a specific purpose and should always fall in line with the mission statement for a church's GEM. That is not to say a girl's ministry leader cannot have an event purely for the purpose of girls getting together for fellowship. Fellowship is vital in the relational area of a girl's life! If a mission statement is to enrich the lives of teenage girls spiritually, mentally, emotionally, physically, and relationally, then the options are endless.

You might want to consider retreats, conferences, sleepovers, mother/daughter events, father/daughter events, shopping trips, etiquette luncheons, fashion shows, makeover events, girls' night out events, and weekly or monthly guided "girl talk." Events should be geared toward specific topics of interest to teenage girls within the church. They can be chosen and planned toward the needs of specific girls, in respect to the entire church ministry calendar, and for a specific purpose. The budget will also determine the number of special girls' events a church will be able to plan during the year. Many events can be done with little cost to the church or the participant.

For instance, if a group plans a shopping trip, the purpose may be to guide girls in choosing clothing that is attractive and inexpensive rather than seductive and cheap. Pairing a younger girl with a "cool" college girl or young adult woman to shop provides a great mentoring activity. Leaders may take the event one step further as a competition to see which team can come up with the most attractive outfit for the least amount of money. Having a fashion show afterwards to model the clothing with judges is a fun mentoring special event!

Likely many talented women in each church would love to share their talents with teenage girls. For example, when starting the Girls' Enrichment Ministry at our church, we asked women to let us know what talents they possess that could be used to teach teenage girls during the "girl talk" events. Ladies who wanted to teach etiquette, basic modeling, writing, scrap booking, personality training, setting standards for dating, and nutrition and exercise stepped forward. We even had a female gynecologist who wanted to share with preteen girls and their mothers her expertise in the area of sexual purity, coping with adolescent issues, and abstinence. Many women in our church were excited to know God could use their talents to teach teen girls more about His plan for them.

Planning Special Events

Leaders should consider many options when planning special events. The following questions will help to plan a well thought out event.

Why? When planning a special event, GEM leaders should ask, "What do I want to accomplish with the girls?" Then they can decide what kind of event would best accomplish the goal. For example, if a leader wants to foster relationships between mothers and their daughters, she should choose among a mother/daughter retreat, a conference, a shopping trip, or a banquet. The decision would be based on the youth ministry, church calendar, budget, and the girls and mothers in the church. To what event would they best respond? What other events are planned during this time? Would they respond to an event at the church or an overnight trip? Could they pay for an overnight retreat or would they rather have a potluck banquet at the church?

When? Leaders should always ask, "When is the best time to plan this event?" Determine the time that allows for maximum participation. Coordinating with the church calendar, the youth ministry calendar, school events, and community events will determine an event's attendance. For example, I once planned a community-wide girls' conference without checking the school calendar. The small town's high school had a very large band, and the state band competition was the same day. Not only did the band members and their parents attend the competition, but many others in the town showed their support as well. Needless to say, attendance at the girls' event was low.

Where? The location of an event plays a large part in determining its success. One church planned an overnight conference for teenage girls at a nice hotel, but they did not consider their budget. The girls had elegant rooms in upscale suites, but the budget did not allow enough money for adequate food during the conference. Not surprisingly, the girls' focus was on being hungry; some even pooled their money and called out for pizza in the middle of the night! A girls' conference planned at the church would have allowed girls to decorate Sunday school classes like girls' bedrooms and could have been more effective— their focus would have been on the important things instead of their tummies!

Homes, too, are wonderful places for special events in small groups. Sleepovers promote relationship building and guided girl talk, providing a great atmosphere for mentoring girls in a home setting. Many retreat and conference centers are cost effective as well if you really need to get away for the event.

Who? The next question leaders must ask is, "Who is the target audience?" Will the event be for outreach and include girls from the community and other churches, or is it to promote unity and growth for the girls in the church family? Is the target group middle school, high school, college, or all of these groups? Should mothers and dads be involved or just the girls?

Leaders in larger churches may choose to divide groups by age simply for logistics, but smaller churches groups may meet together. Whether meeting by age groups or with all girls together, it is important to consider age appropriate topics and activities.

Adequate adult supervision and helpers are vital to an event's success. One girls' ministry coordinator planned a large event for mothers and daughters in her church. She tried to do everything on her own and refused help. The event turned out to be a disaster. She was on stage trying to MC the event even though she was very shy and serious. She failed to recognize the presence of the pastor's wife and youth pastor's wife. She prayed, played the guitar, and led the praise and worship music. She did ask someone else to speak but failed to communicate a time limit. By the end of the evening, many of the girls and moms were restlessly looking at their watches. She even failed to ask for reservations and more than a hundred people came than she had planned for, leading her to run out of food, tables, and emotional energy by the evening's end. The woman learned a great lesson, but it cost her position as the girls' ministry coordinator at her church.

Leaders should learn to delegate, follow-up, and cover all of their bases in event planning. Involve as many people as you can in the event. For every person involved, an average of five more will come because of that one's involvement.

Prayer, preparation, and planning are vital for any event. But when the event begins, leaders must let go and let God be in control. The mark of a good coordinator is never losing her cool, even when things don't go the way she planned! Sometimes God tests our dependence and trust in Him by altering our plans.

I planned a mother/daughter conference one weekend at our church and invited an all-girl singing group from Tennessee. One of the biggest ice storms in the history of Atlanta hit that weekend. When I heard the weather forecast, I started a phone tree and called all the participants, asking them to bring sleeping bags and extra clothes. The storm held off until midnight on Friday. The girls and their moms slept in the church, and we had a wonderful conference despite the inclement weather. However, the singing group was snowbound and never made it to the conference. At the last minute, I invited four guys from the youth group to come and impersonate the female singing group. The guys were a big success and went home immediately after their début—and before the ice storm hit! We used a CD for our praise and worship music. The girls loved the revised program, and the weekend turned out to be a great spiritual awakening for those involved.

What? The program is a key part of any event. Choosing the right speaker, musician, small group leaders, topics, breakout sessions, ice breakers, skits, video clips, and testimonies is critical to running a smooth event. Keeping the purpose and target group in mind will determine the kind of music and the speaker's age and focus. Music sets the mood of the conference's large group sessions. It can motivate and help the girls have fun and then—at the right time —bring them into the presence of the Lord for worship. GEM leaders should keep a file of speakers and musicians who are appropriate for each group of girls. Women in your church may also be good resources for breakout sessions.

What about publicity and registration? You can plan an incredible event, but if the girls don't know about it, they won't come. It sounds silly to plan an event and not publicize it, but you would be surprised how often it happens. A simple announcement in the church bulletin on Sunday probably will not catch teenage girls' attention. Thinking of an idea on Monday and trying to pull off the event on Saturday is difficult unless you have only three or four girls.

Planning ahead and building momentum for the event will determine how many girls attend. Deciding whether the event is for in- or outreach will determine where and how you advertise. One church planned and advertised a girls' event with a huge banner hung at the town's busiest intersection. Churches from all over the city brought girls to the event simply because they knew about it. Advertising in the newspaper, on the radio, and through Christian clubs at school are good ways to let others know what is going on, but the very best way to get girls to come is a personal invitation from friends. Choose key students who are respected and ask them to commit to the event and to spread the word. Girls love to know their friends are coming and usually ask, "Who will be there?"

Ask girls to register and pay up front to help you know how many participants to expect. Set a deadline for registering. Canceling an event when people don't register before the deadline will set a precedent; girls will soon learn they have to sign up before the deadline. People need boundaries, and they will push them to see if they break. It is also a wise use of church money. If you spend money and plan an event and the girls do not show up, you have used God's money unwisely. Selling non-refundable tickets is a sure way to cover your expenses and boost attendance.

How about the budget? Leaders should use the church's money wisely. Setting a budget and closely sticking to it will show integrity. Deciding how much money to budget will determine the number of participants and how much each will need to pay. Budgeting is a great help in planning a successful event.

Follow-up: Often times a coordinator forgets about an event when it ends, but follow-up is crucial to the success of future events. The planning team should discuss the event's successes and inadequacies. Girls should be asked to evaluate the event and give their comments and suggestions. These suggestions can be hurtful if viewed as criticism. Negative comments should not ruin the team's enthusiasm for ministry. Instead, they should ask, "Is this comment true, and if so, what can we do to improve the next event?" The leader should send thank-you notes to the planning team, speakers, musicians, and others involved in the event. People need and want to be sincerely thanked. A simple comment, phone call, or e-mail is better than nothing, but a note received in the mail is a treasure to many who have given time to serve with you.

One-on-one counseling may be required for follow up on decisions made during the event. Girls who accept Jesus Christ as personal Savior or who recommit themselves to Christ need encouragement. The prayer coordinator should make sure the prayer team prays for requests expressed in these follow-ups, and the girls need confirmation that someone is praying for their needs.

Planning special events requires much prayer, sufficient time, and a team of people. But all the preparation in the world is futile if God does not show up. Prayers will beckon Him to be there from the beginning to the end.

Generally, people love to be involved in girls' ministry, but they need to know their responsibilities and to be equipped for their roles. Many want to be involved but need an invitation. Each coordinator must recruit the people necessary for the GEM team's success.

SPECIAL EVENTS PLANNING TEAM

One of the biggest mistakes leaders make in girls' ministry is trying to do everything on their own. God has gifted every Christian for service, and we should work with those around us to enhance and accomplish ministry. Comprising a team of women to help coordinate events is essential in girls' ministry. These are suggestions of positions lay people can easily fill:

Event Coordinator—Oversees event, coordinators, and many times will be in charge of the program

Prayer Coordinator—Organizes prayer for the event, speakers, musicians, and specific prayer requests before, during, and after the event. Contacts girls after the event, letting them know someone is praying for their requests. This position is key to the success of the girls' program.

Program Coordinator—Secures speaker, musicians, sets schedule for large group and workshops, determines theme, and works with financial coordinator and event coordinator to stay within budget.

Hospitality Coordinator—Coordinates greeters, food, give-aways, packets, pictures, invitation counselors

Publicity Coordinator—Coordinates publicity, media, mail-outs, flyers, and works with financial coordinator and event coordinator to stay within budget

Financial Coordinator—Works with church staff to set budget; works with each committee to stay within their budget; takes care of registration money, making sure it is turned in to the appropriate person at the church. Requests checks from financial office for speakers, musicians, and other needs.

Registration Coordinator—Works with appropriate staff to design registration forms, in charge of collecting registration forms, and keeps event coordinator informed of attendance. Sets up registration table at the event.

Decorations Coordinator—Coordinates all decorations for the event and works with the financial coordinator to stay within budget

SUPPORT GROUPS FOR TEENAGE GIRLS

Support groups are a necessary part of Girls' Enrichment Ministry. Because girls tend to be more verbally expressive in their problem solving, they thrive in small group settings. While mentoring/discipleship groups meet the needs of most teenage girls, some girls have special needs such as eating disorders, pregnancy, motherhood, addictions, sexual orientation problems, family problems, self-mutilation, illnesses, disabilities, and grief.

Some special needs require professional counseling or the counselor's permission before the girl is allowed to enter a support group. But after the girl has gone through counseling, a church support group may provide her accountability and continued guidance. She also needs to know she is not alone. Others have had similar problems, and many have already made it through their crises.

Support groups may be led by professionals trained in a specific area or by laypersons who are sufficiently trained. Support groups should have beginning and ending dates and a specific agenda each week. Sharing problems, guidance in solving problems, accountability, and prayer should always be included.

BEGINNING SUPPORT GROUPS IN YOUR CHURCH

Support groups are formed because of common needs. Many times a girl may feel as if she is alone in her problems. She may feel she are the only person who has been raped or molested. Or she may feel she is the only person who is a teenage mother.

Once the girls discover others have experienced similar hurts or problems, they feel a common bond. Through guided discussion, prayer, and the truth of God's Word, they can make it through their situation and learn to use it to help others. You will need to follow several steps in beginning support groups for teenage girls in your church.

Step 1: Discover the Needs

First, a leader must survey the needs of girls in the church and community to decide if a special group needs to be formed. She may even use support groups as an outreach to the community. The best way to start is to invite the girls to a preliminary meeting, asking them to fill our a needs survey.

Step 2: Choose and Equip Leadership

Once the need is established, a leader should look for qualified group leaders. These may include qualified professionals in the church who would be willing to volunteer their time to lead a support group. And the church may have women who have successfully worked through some of the personal issues to be dealt with in the group. For example, a young woman who has been a single teenage mother and is now a mature growing Christian can be a wonderful support group leader to others in a similar situation. These women can become good support group leaders once they have gone through appropriate small group facilitation training.

The same principles apply to leaders of support groups that apply to women who mentor teenage girls. Women who lead support groups should be mature, growing Christians who are not out of control in the Titus 2 areas of their lives.

Step 3: Require Group Commitment

The girls involved in support groups should be asked to sign a group commitment card. Confidentiality is vitally important in support group situations. Honesty and admission of one's wrongdoing are necessary in a support group to accomplish the desired goal of working through problems. If group members are not comfortable admitting they have done something wrong for fear it will be told to others, then the group will not be successful. Support group members should hold each other accountable for their thoughts and actions during the week. They should be encouraged to talk about their feelings, actions, and struggles. Praying for each other, writing notes, e-mailing or calling each other during the week for support and encouragement should be promoted.

Support groups should be based on the truth of God's Word. Fostering dependence on God and His Word to work out the problems of life is the best thing a group leader can do. Studying what God's Word says about a certain situation can bring girls into a new lifestyle. They will begin to see God work in their lives and will become dependent on Him for their security and help in times of trouble.

CONCLUSION

Today's church must have intentional, organized plans to reach and enrich the lives of postmodern teenage girls. Many churches are beginning to see the need and answer the call. Each leader must ask, "Am I willing to step up and organize a plan in our church to minister to their needs? Am I willing to put my hand on a girl's shoulder and point her to the One who will love and take care of her unconditionally for eternity?" By answering "yes" to these questions, a woman may eventually encourage hundreds of girls to give their lives to Christ.

---

[1] *Newsweek*, 1975, Adapted from Jimmie Davis, *Girls Enrichment Ministry: Raising a New Generation of Women*, (Spartanburg, S.C.: Girls to Women Resources), 1.
[2] Ibid.

SPECIAL EVENTS: PROGRAMS OR PEOPLE?

JAYE MARTIN

*W*hy did you have your last women's special event? Was it because you have always had it? Was it because you heard that First Church had a similar event that was successful? Did you find a great logo and plan something to go with it?

Every special event should be planned to meet needs of women. Often, it is easier to copy an event we have heard about than it is to determine the needs of our ladies and program to meet those needs. Lots of programs and flashy brochures can be impressive, but are lives being changed because of them?

NEEDS OF WOMEN

Let's begin our discussion of special events by looking at some of the needs of today's women.

Balance

Anytime you offer options to help a woman with one or more of her responsibilities, she will juggle her busy schedule to be there. For instance, give her tips on how to manage her time wisely, to simplify her life, to establish a quiet time, to study the Bible and apply it to her crazy schedule, how to be a better wife or a great mom. Help her find some answers to bring balance to her life. She'll be grateful for the help.

Stress Relief

No matter what season of life a woman is in, she is often stressed. I used to think it was just in large cities. However, after talking to women in small towns and large cities, I have discovered that most women are under stress. Oh, there may be a different degree of it, but it is still there! Offer women an opportunity to get away from the daily grind, and they will come. Give women some ways to handle stress, and they will be there. Help them discover a new perspective on life, and they will be grateful.

Purpose

Far too many women don't know their purpose in life. Creative events can help them find their true purpose! God has a plan for each woman and it is our job as women's leaders to help them know God, grow in their walk with Him, and share their walk with others. Women need to understand that they are uniquely gifted for service; and that until they are bearing fruit, they will not find meaning in their lives. Help women discover their spiritual gifts as well as their talents. Then give them places to use those gifts and talents to further the kingdom of God. When you do, you will find you have women who are fulfilled, joyful, and ready to serve.

Relationships

Significant relationships can be difficult to come by in today's society. Before television and portable stereos, folks used to sit around and chat. And when women would talk, things had a way of working themselves out. Aunt Polly would give her perspective; Granny would tell how it was in her day; and before the evening was over, wisdom had been shared and relationships had been strengthened. Women need each other. They like to share and need to know there are women out there who care about them and the things going on in their lives. Provide ways for your women to get to know each other by taking time to sit and chat. They will build mentoring relationships that will change their lives.

Once you determine that you are going to meet the needs of women, pray and ask God to show you which needs to address and when.

SCRIPTURAL BASIS FOR PLANNING SPECIAL EVENTS

Planning special events is something Jesus addressed in Scripture. In the Book of Luke Jesus tells the parable of someone planning a great banquet. In this passage, Luke gives readers two basic principles about planning: preparing and inviting (14:16-23).

Preparing

Preparation is key to planning special events.

Verse 16 says, "Jesus replied: 'A certain man was preparing a great banquet …' " Preparation is crucial to the success of any event. Anyone who has ever planned a banquet knows how much work goes into it! Much has to take place before the banquet or event happens. In planning events for our women, we want to ask God for direction on what to do and when. When God gives us direction, we must follow through on what He tells us. Preparation is key to planning special events.

Inviting

The other truth we see in Luke 14:16 is the importance of inviting: " 'and [he] invited many guests.' " Why prepare a banquet if we are not going to invite anyone? First, we can assume a group has already been invited because Jesus tells us the man "sent his servant to tell those who had been invited: 'Come, for everything is now ready' " (v. 17). This group makes a lot of excuses why they cannot come. One had bought a field and had to go and look at it. Another had just bought five yoke of oxen and was on his way to try them out. Still another had recently married and couldn't come. The servant came back and reported this to his master. The master then ordered his servant to go out quickly into the streets and the alleys and invite everyone he could find. After the servant did this, there was still room. The master then told him to go further down the roads and the country lanes and invite others to come in so that the house would be full.

Notice how much more information Jesus gives us on inviting than on preparing. We usually spend more time on preparation than we spend on who is coming to our events. That may be because we usually expect to have the same crowd each time. "After all," we reason, "these events are for those actively involved in women's ministry. Maybe one or two others from the church will come." Yet Jesus shows us the importance of reaching out to those who might not be included. In fact, it seems Jesus would have personal invitations sent to them.

Although it is perfectly fine to mail brochures and make phone calls announcing events, it is most important that we personally invite inactive women to come. This includes personal invitations to the woman who works at the school, the neighbor two doors down, and the lady who does our hair. Jesus tells us people will make lots of silly excuses, but we should not let it stop us. He tells us to keep on inviting until we get others to come. Maybe the clerk at the grocery store would like to be included. And the new mother down the street may need a friend. Then there is the lady whose husband just died who would probably be glad to get out of the house. These and many others need our invitation.

We live in a world where women have too many responsibilities, are under too much stress, feel they have no purpose, and have few relationships. All these women and many more are just waiting for someone to care, waiting for someone to stop and notice they exist. Through events, we can reach out to women and show them a new world where Christ can provide them a new perspective, allow them to meet new friends, and give them meaning to life.

We usually spend more time on preparation than we spend on who is coming to our events.

Purpose of Events

A special event is different from ongoing small groups. A special event is a one-time gathering that focuses on a particular issue or theme. Usually we do extra things to make it special, but the purpose of providing special events is still to reach women for Christ. Specifically, the purpose of an events ministry is to:
• reach women for Christ;
• mature women in the faith;
• involve women in service through spiritual gifts and talents;
• support and undergird the church.
Having a purpose gives direction and makes planning easier. In order to reach women, there must be something significant that they want to experience at the event. Then, not only do we reach them, but we disciple them so that they grow closer to Christ and His ways. As women come to Christ and grow in their relationships with Him, they will want to serve. Planning special events

through women's ministry will help them learn to use their gifts and talents for the Lord. This supports the church as well as the women. After all, Christ commands us to "go and make disciples."

What this acrostic means is that special events might need to be thought of a little differently. Here is what needs to happen to R-E-A-C-H women:

Rethink everything!
Encourage nonchurched women to attend.
Announce! Announce! Announce!
Challenge members.
Honor the Holy Spirit's leadership—pray and expect God to move!

Rethink Everything!

Begin by rethinking everything you do! First, think like a woman who is without Christ. Why would she want to come to a special event? We've already looked at some things we know are important in women's lives; they can become ways to bring them to a meaningful relationship with Christ. Helping women prioritize their lives; helping them handle stress; giving women a sense of purpose; and helping them build lasting, meaningful relationships with family members and others are just a few of the things women desire.

PERCEIVED NEEDS VERSUS REAL NEEDS

What do women think they need? Perceived needs include more money, material possessions, a husband (or a new one if they are married), children (or better behaved ones if they have them), fun, and fellowship. Basically, women want quick fixes for their stressed, lonely, and hurting lives. They want help.

Let's think about what they *really* need. We know the answer: they need Jesus. Jesus is the master at meeting needs. He gives help for today and hope for tomorrow. But if women don't understand they need Christ, how can we reach them? We begin by rethinking some things. These include event titles, greeters, groups, and invitations.

TITLES

We have to be careful when we name our events. Titles like "Only Jesus," "Missions Alive," and "He Lifted Me" aren't attractive to many women, especially those who are non-Christians or unchurched. We must rethink our titles. For instance, instead of "A Study of First Corinthians 13," we could try "True Love," "A Love That Never Ends," or even "The Love of Your Life." Themes and titles should appeal to our non-Christian neighbors and not exclude.

GREETERS

Every time you have a special event, smiling greeters or hostesses should make women feel welcomed. Be careful not to embarrass guests by putting them on display or by giving them a name tag when no one else is wearing one. Instead, let them know you care. For example, introduce a visitor to someone who will sit with her and introduce her to others.

GROUPS

We all know how difficult it is to walk into a group where everyone knows everyone and we don't. Sometimes new groups need to be started so that women will feel good about being involved. As you plan a special event, make sure everyone will feel comfortable walking into the event or group. Avoid cliqués. Make each lady feel welcome and her attendance appreciated.

INVITATIONS

Choose a good way to ask women to respond to Christ without making them walk to the front of a banquet hall or assembly room. Make it comfortable for them to respond. Give them the opportunity to hear someone explain the difference Jesus has made in her life. Unchurched women may not be familiar with our traditional "come to the front" invitations.

Response cards (see sample on p. 201) provide a wealth of information for follow up. Ask women to let you know what they thought about your event and include please-respond statements such as:

- I would like to be on the mailing list for your women's events.
- I would like to know more about what this church can do for me.
- I have some spiritual questions. Please have someone call me.
- I would like to talk to someone about knowing Christ personally.
- Today, for the first time, I asked Jesus to be my Lord and Savior.
- Today I recommitted my life to Christ.
- Today I committed to a special ministry of _____ for Christ.

Once women respond, it is easy to follow up after the event. Another good idea is to have them bring the card to a prayer room or give it to a hostess. This way they can be counseled before they leave.

Encourage Nonchurched Women to Attend

We have already looked at some of the needs of women in the world, but we can do things to encourage nonchurched ladies to come to our special events.

PRICE BREAKS

Most women love a good deal. After you figure the cost per person for your event, let members pay a little more and guests pay a little less. For instance, if the event will cost $25 per person, why not let the members pay $30 each and guests pay $20? Even better, offer free entry to visiting guests when you can.

NO LATE FEES

If there is to be a late registration fee, do not require your guests to pay it. Many guests will sign up at the last minute. You want them to attend, not to resent having to pay a penalty for registering late.

Be careful not to embarrass guests by putting them on display or by giving them a name tag when no one else is wearing one.

Go to "Away" Locations

As nice as it is to use church facilities, it is also good to get away from the church. These can be retreat or conference centers, office buildings, or even public parks. They don't have to cost a lot of money and they provide a neutral, nonthreatening setting for visitors.

Giveaways and Door Prizes

Publicize giveaways and door prizes. One of the best things about having guests register for door prizes is that it provides a name, address, phone number, and the name of the friend they came with. Use the back of the event ticket for the information. Draw the tickets for door prizes and and use the information for easy follow-up to the event.

Special Emphasis

Other ways to encourage nonchurched women to come are to have special theme days such as friend days, neighbor days, teacher-appreciation days, family days, work-associate days, brown-bag lunch, or picnic days. These special events may attract someone who hasn't been before. Recognize those who are new and give them extra privileges such as getting their food first.

Announce! Announce! Announce!

Publicity

After we have completed our rethinking process and thought of ways to encourage nonchurched women to attend, we are ready to publicize our special event.

There are numerous ways to let women know you are having a special event. See "Publicity and Promotion," (p. 216) for ideas. But don't stop with these. Let this list serve as a starting place and be creative!

No matter what types of announcements you choose to make, the best form of publicity is person-to-person. Most people come by personal invitation. Church statistics tell us that 95 percent of the people who attend a church for the first time do so because someone invited them. This will also hold true for your women's events.

So, regardless of the type of advertising you choose, be sure that it only supplements the person-to-person invitations that you and your members make to women you contact. "Inviter evangelism" is easy to do for most everyone. We saw this in the passage in Luke about the Great Banquet. Jesus wants us to invite everyone to come so that His house will be full! So, how do we do this? Read on ...

Challenge Members

Most of us tend to stay in our comfort zones. As always, people need to be challenged to reach out to others. Challenge members to get out of their comfort zones and invite unchurched women to attend the event. Providing incentives can help members do what they already know they need to be doing. Let the following suggestions help you with ideas to get the members motivated to invite others to your events.

BRING A FRIEND

Have a "bring a friend" event. You can even go so far as to have an event where no one can come unless they bring a friend (someone not from your church). Believe it or not, this provides great incentive and gets everyone active.

RESERVE SEATS FOR MEMBERS WITH GUESTS

Create a reserved section for those members who bring a friend and for other guests who come alone. Let everyone know in advance that those who go the extra mile will be rewarded with great seats.

HAVE A RECEPTION

Just prior to the event, have a special reception for members with visitors. Have church staff members and women's leaders there to greet and mingle. You might even provide members with guests a different nametag or something else to identify them during the main event. The reception is also helpful to let guests know your church is there to minister to them.

MAKE SPECIAL INTRODUCTIONS

As long as you are careful not to embarrass anyone, you can do some meaningful recognitions during the event. Having members and guests stand is good.

TAKE PHOTOGRAPHS

Allow a time for photographs to be taken with special friends. This is great because the member can tell the guest in advance they want to have photos made together. This especially works well with family members.

PROVIDE EVANGELISM TRAINING

Provide women training in lifestyle witnessing, friendship evangelism, and building relationships. (See resource section at the back of this book for materials.) Help the ladies learn to give their testimonies and share their faith. When the event comes, they will be ready to those who respond.

Honor the Holy Spirit's Leadership...Pray! and Expect God to Move!

Do you expect God to move at your special events? If not, you probably will not notice when He does. We demonstrate our anticipation of God's movement by doing some things in advance.

TRAIN LEADERS TO PRAY

Throughout the planning process, prayer needs to be a major part in all you do. Do not assume your leaders know how to pray for an event. Teach them how to pray and what to pray for. Teach them to look for God's movement and direction.

- *Pray Individually.* Pray for every person who will help you plan, and pray for your attitude and the attitudes of others. Pray for members to bring their friends and that those friends will come to know God personally.
- *Pray Together.* Not only is it important to pray alone, it is important to pray together as a group of leaders. You must be the role model. Let the leaders

hear you pray for God to move. Share what God has already begun to do. Share needs and struggles of those in the group. Pray together before you plan anything. God will bless.

TRAIN LEADERS TO DISCIPLE/MENTOR OTHER WOMEN

As you plan your special event, the mentoring process is going on. Women observe Christlike character as they notice how their leader responds or reacts to details. They will likely observe the spirit in which changes are made and the flexibility of leaders. Therefore, it is beneficial to provide times for your team to plan together.

TRAIN LEADERS TO WITNESS

We have already looked at the importance of teaching women to share Christ with others. Your events will take on new meaning when your leaders experience the joy of sharing their faith.

LISTEN TO GOD

Expecting God to move, praying privately, and praying together are all important, but so is listening to God. If you do not listen, you will miss what He is trying to tell you. It may be about the event's location or speaker; it may even be about a detail such as name tags. Listen to what God tells you. Prayer is two-way communication. Spend time listening to God, and then act on what He tells you to do. Be led by the Holy Spirit.

MOVING TOWARD THE EVENT

Let's consider other details that move us closer to the event.

Determine the Need

Ask yourself the following questions: For whom am I planning this event? What are the needs of the group? How much will the group be able to afford? Will our budget be able to underwrite the expenses? What is the best day of the week? What time of the day? What is the purpose of the event? What is the best location for it?

These questions need to be answered before speakers are booked or dates set. A special event for a group of young, single mothers will look different from an event for young, single adults. Make sure you are realistic about how much women can afford to pay. If you book an expensive speaker and an expensive hotel, your costs will increase. No matter how great your event is, many will not be able to come unless scholarships are provided.

Figure the Budget

Estimating the budget is really easier than you might think. Here are a few things you need to consider.

1. How much will the facility charge? If you book the event at your church, you have just saved money (in most cases). If you use another facility, you'll need to ask for an estimate on all charges that might come up: things such as

easels, overhead projectors, microphones, and skirted tables. These can run the bill up quickly.

2. How much will the food (meals, snacks, water stations) cost? Be sure to include the gratuity charges. Most hotels charge a set percentage for their staff, changing the cost significantly. Remember to absorb expenses for non-paying speakers and guests in participant fees.

3. How much will the brochures or flyers cost? What will it cost to mail them? What other printing needs to be done (prayer cards, evaluation cards, programs, notepads, bookmarks, handouts, tickets, maps)? Printing charges vary depending on the type of paper, number of colors of ink, amount of material printed, whether it goes to the printer copy-ready, and more. If all your printing can be done at the same time, it usually saves money. A printer can help estimate these costs.

4. How much will you be able to spend on decorations? You will probably need some type of centerpiece for the tables, a backdrop for the stage, and various decorations on registration tables and display areas.

5. What are the fees or honorariums for the speaker(s) and worship leader(s)? What other reimbursements will people require (travel, accommodations, meals, miscellaneous expenses)?

6. How many women are you expecting? The more you have, the less it will cost each person because they will share in the cost of the event. How much do the ladies expect to pay? Start by estimating what you feel each will be able to pay. Then, to estimate the budget, add all your expenses. Divide that by the number of "paying customers" you anticipate. This gives you the price each person will have to pay. You may come up with an amount double what you think the group will be able to afford. In that case, it is already time to cut back, and you have hardly begun! Here are a few places to consider cutting expenses.

- *Location or extras* Bring your own sound crew and equipment such as easels and overhead projectors. If this doesn't help, find a less costly location. Ask others for ideas.

- *Menu* See what the facility managers can do for you. Cut snacks down to water stations or ask participants to bring in canned soft drinks or homemade cookies.

- *Printing* Print the brochures in one color on colored paper. Instead of mailing them, depend on the ladies to help you get the word out. Cut all last-minute handouts or limit the number of pages; cut the printed program—either do without it or scale down. You will be surprised how much you can save.

- *Decorations* Use decorations that another ministry has already used or plan to sell what you buy new to minimize the costs. Working with other ministries to share resources can be beneficial to both. Remember that the goal is reaching women and to keep other expenses (such as for decorations) in their proper perspective.

- *Speaker fees* The truth of the matter is that women are more likely to come to an event because they are involved in the planning than because they want to hear a big-name speaker. Be sure it is God calling you to invite a particular speaker.

Developing a realistic budget is important in planning a special event.

199

How are you doing? Are you closer to where you need to be financially? Total your cut-back expenses and divide by the number of women you think will pay. Take this amount and add 10 to 20 percent: that will give you a per person estimate. Also, figure what would happen if you did not have as many sign up as you thought. Will the percentage you added cover it? Will there be any church budget money used to get the price down? Keep figuring until you have a workable budget. Keep your leadership and the church staff informed about your expected expenses and income. If you bring them along with you, they will be more likely to be there for you if you need help later. (See Sample Conference/Retreat Budget, p. 212.)

Enlist the Speakers

Before you enlist a speaker, be sure you (not someone else) have heard her. Listen to tapes, ask for references, and call to get a feel for who the speaker is. Ask for strengths and weaknesses. Speakers are best found by networking with other women's ministries. Call and ask other ministry leaders for recommendations of persons with whom they have been pleased to work.

When enlisting a speaker, some basic things need to be covered. Use this as a checklist. It is also a good idea to put the agreement in writing. Yours will not be the only event the potential speaker is praying about and considering.

- Purpose—communicate the event's purpose clearly to the speaker.
- Topic—Tell her what you want her to speak about.
- Schedule—How many times will she speak? How long will she speak each time? Exactly where in the program will she will speak? Whom will she follow on the program?
- Location—Will the event be held in a church or retreat center? Where will she be spending the night (if applicable)? Most speakers prefer to room alone to have time to prepare for their presentations.
- Participants—Who will attend? What are their ages and needs? How many women do you expect?
- Payment—Does she expect to be paid fees or an honorarium? Let her know which of her expenses you will cover. Prepare the check before the event and present it to her at the event's closing.
- Prayer—Ask her how you can best pray for her.
- Photo and biography—If you plan to use her biography and photograph, let her know when you will need it. Make sure to return it to her at the event or shortly thereafter.
- Contact—Make sure she has the name and number of the person she can contact if she has any needs or questions.

AT THE EVENT

You are finally here! Relax! Keep smiling! Be flexible and calm. Have a great time and keep praying!

God has been with you, and He will continue to be. Don't let the program or event get in the way of the people to whom you are ministering. If you have followed the Holy Spirit's leading, chances are you will have a special event that will help women with their priorities, pull them away from their hectic schedules, give them a purpose, and help them develop significant relationships. Give God the glory!

AFTER THE EVENT

Immediately begin planning for your next event. Compile information from the Response Card and Event Evaluation you asked women to complete at the event (samples provided on the following pages). Follow up on decisions made at the event. Use the other information to begin praying over your next special event. Ask God to direct you and the other leaders in your church so you can continue to meet women's needs through your events.

RESPONSE CARD

○ I would like to be on the mailing list for your women's events.
○ I would like to know more about what this church can do for me.
○ I have some spiritual questions. Please have someone call me.
○ I would like to talk to someone about knowing Christ personally.
○ Today, for the first time, I asked Jesus to be my Lord and Savior.
○ Today I recommitted my life to Christ.
○ Today I committed to a special ministry of _____ for Christ.

Comments about this event: _____

_____

_____

Prayer Request: _____

Name: _____

Address: _____

City/State/Zip: _____

Phone Number: _____

EVENT PLAN SHEET
This plan sheet is designed to assist you in planning a special event for your women's ministry.

	NOTES	COMPLETION DATE	PERSON RESPONSIBLE

O Purpose

_____ _____ _____
_____
_____
_____

O Title/Theme

_____ _____ _____
_____
_____
_____

O Budget

_____ _____ _____
_____
_____
_____

O Location

_____ _____ _____
_____
_____
_____

O Speaker(s)/Musician(s)

_____ _____ _____
_____
_____
_____

O Promotion

_____   _____   _____
_____
_____
_____

O Menu

_____   _____   _____
_____
_____
_____

O Decorations

_____   _____   _____
_____
_____
_____

O Printing

_____   _____   _____
_____
_____
_____

O Honorariums/Expenses of guests

_____   _____   _____
_____
_____
_____

O Evaluation

_____   _____   _____
_____
_____
_____

EVENT EVALUATION

1. HOW DID YOU HEAR ABOUT THE EVENT?
   - ○ Brochure
   - ○ Radio
   - ○ Friend
   - ○ Conference Leader
   - ○ Newsletter
   - ○ Newspaper
   - ○ Web site
   - ○ E-mail
   - ○ Other: _____

2. WHAT IS YOUR OVERALL IMPRESSION OF THE EVENT?
   - ○ What I expected
   - ○ Better than I expected
   - ○ Less than I expected

3. WHAT WAS YOUR FAVORITE OR MOST HELPFUL PART OF THE EVENT? WHY?

   _____

   _____

4. WHAT WAS YOUR LEAST FAVORITE OR HELPFUL PART OF THE EVENT? WHY?

   _____

   _____

5. HOW CAN WE PROVIDE A BETTER EVENT?

   _____

   _____

6. DO YOU HAVE SUGGESTIONS FOR ADDITIONAL TOPICS?

   _____

   _____

7. OTHER COMMENTS:

   _____

8. OPTIONAL:
   Name:_____

   Address: _____

   City/State/ZIP: _____

   Phone: _____ E-mail _____

CONFERENCES AND RETREATS

MERCI DIXON

*P*lanning your first women's conference or retreat is similar to planning for your first child. You anticipate wondrous things, yet you are apprehensive. You are filled with excitement, yet you are uneasy. You look forward to a great day, but you have mixed emotions. And when the day arrives, you are filled with all the hope of the psalmist when he declared to God, "My hope is in you" (Ps. 39:7).

For the past 10 years our church has conducted two very special annual events just for women. One is a spring women's conference, and the other is a fall women's retreat. We define these two events separately, even though many church leaders use the terms interchangeably.

A women's conference is a one-, two-, or three-day meeting held at the church for the purpose of ministering to women. There they will listen to godly speakers, grow in relationship to Christ, and will worship through Christian music, eating, and sharing together.

A women's retreat is an overnight weekend event held in a retreat center or camp. Its purpose is spiritual growth and bonding. The weekend includes skits, music, speakers, small-group prayer times, sleeping (or not sleeping!), and eating together.

The purpose of this chapter is to help you develop effective conferences and retreats, and I will provide a blueprint to keep you on target. No two conferences or retreats will be the same, but with each event there are essentials that cannot be overlooked. These necessary ingredients include prayer, planning, publicity, priority, and purpose. We will look at each of these individually.

Even though much of this material is directed toward the women's ministry coordinator, it also applies to committees and leaders.

Please don't attempt anything for the Lord without first seeking His direction. Before you contact the first speaker or contract for a retreat center, you need to pray for God's guidance. Jesus said it best: "Ask and it will be given to you; seek, and you will find; knock and the door will be opened to you" (Matt. 7:7). God has something special just for the ladies who will attend. Even when you get ideas from other places, don't rely on them to make your conference success-ful—rely on God to do what He wants to do in your midst.

Don't attempt anything for the Lord without first seeking His direction.

PLANNING

The following timeframe guides will help you plan your conference or retreat. Personalize them for your event, but do not shortcut your planning.

One to Two Years Before the Conference or Retreat

○ Set the tentative date for the conference or retreat. Be sure you have the event set for a time when there are no conflicts on your church's calendar. It would be wise to check school and community calendars and sporting events. This is especially important in retreat planning. Since a retreat takes women away overnight, the fewer the conflicts, the better the attendance.

○ Determine your budget. This includes expenses and income. What will the event cost? How much will the church underwrite? How much will the par-ticipants have to pay? (See Sample Conference/Retreat Budget on p. 212.)

○ Contact the first keynote speaker. If the date works for her, contact other speakers. To avoid conflict, do not contact all of the speakers at the same time. Using two or three keynote speakers has worked better for us because different personalities minister to differing needs. Adjust the date if speakers are not available to be with you on your first choice of dates. Ask them if they require an honorarium. Even if the speaker does not have a set amount, be as generous with her as your budget will allow.

○ In the case of planning a retreat, lock in on a location and reserve it. Popu-lar facilities fill up fast.

Four to Six Months Before the Conference or Retreat

○ Decide on a theme based on Scripture. From the theme, develop message titles, seminar topics (optional), decorations, and publicity plans.

○ After you have decided on 12 to 15 seminar (small group) topics, pray about who God wants you to lead them. After you have seminar leaders in mind, give the list to your pastor, other staff member, or fellow committee member to pray about. Once you have both prayed and are assured that the leaders are right for your event, contact each one on the same day. Contacting all of your seminar leaders on the same day discourages suggestions about who could lead. Too much input can be confusing.

○ Write your keynote speakers and let them know how plans are progressing. Give them all the information you can. Ask what you can do for them as they prepare to come.

○ Decide whether to offer scholarships. If the decision is yes, secure funding and decide how to offer them to women who need them.

Two to Three Months Before the Conference or Retreat

○ Send out registration brochures, e-mail blitz.

○ Begin working with your committees. The following committee structure has been helpful to us in planning our conferences and retreats. Retreat committees will not be as structured or detailed as conference committees. A retreat should be much more relaxed and will not require as many planning groups. Even so, to ensure a good response, get as many women as possible involved in planning. Use the following as guides for leader placement:

• Program chairwoman—This is usually the women's ministry director/coordinator. She coordinates the event and is in charge of the program, speakers, music, and all other chairwomen. She sets up meetings with committees as needed and monitors spending to maintain budget guidelines.

• Decorations committee—The ladies are responsible for putting up and removing all decorations (or selling them after the event). This includes decorating for the meals, setting up displays during the conference or retreat, decorating the bathrooms, and any other extra decorations that add a special "woman's touch" in other parts of the facility. This is important to women who tend to look at details. It will convey you are glad they came!

• Prayer committee—These ladies are responsible for contacting women who would be willing to pray daily for the needs of the speakers, the committee chairwomen, the weather, those attending, and the facilities. This committee might also want to prepare a prayer guide. Nothing is too trivial to pray over either before or during the event!

• Food committee—These individuals are responsible for planning an attractive menu for one or two meals, depending on the length of your conference. For sure, meals are a critical element on a retreat. This committee is also responsible for refreshment centers set up with light snacks such as water, coffee, soft drinks, and mints.

• Lodging committee—These ladies are responsible for making arrangements for lodging. For a conference, this might just be for out-of-town leaders. For a retreat, this committee's responsibilities include setting up lodging for leaders and participants.

• Secretary/registration committee—These individuals are responsible for participant registration, childcare registration (if offered), correspondence to registrants, all monies received, and for keeping up with requests for lodging. You may wish to budget money to pay this person if you do not have a support staff in your church.

• Childcare committee—As registrants request childcare (optional), this committee will make the necessary preparations. Childcare registration should be closed two weeks before the event to allow for adequate preparation.

• Publicity committee—These people are responsible for all publicity except registration brochures. Publicity can be through local newspapers, the state denominational paper, on Christian radio stations, or on television. See "Publicity and Promotion," page 216, for ideas.

• Booklet committee—These ladies are responsible for preparing the program booklets. These booklets contains the schedule, speaker's outlines, Scripture references, information about the speakers, and provide room to take notes.

To ensure a good response, get as many women as possible involved in planning.

- Packet committee—These individuals are responsible for the free packet given to each guest. They may contain things such as pens, program booklets, tissues, mints, and key chains. Check with local businesses for giveaways and door prizes. Include a list of donors in the packet. This committee will need to order packets at least three months before the event.
- Transportation committee—plans transportation for event speakers and participants as needed.
- Book store committee—These ladies set up and run the book store and receive suggestions from speakers about resources to make available. Ask the speaker (if she brings and sells her own books) or book store provider for a percentage of sales (10 percent is a good standard).
- Counseling committee—This group prepares or obtains decision cards, tracts, church information, and other follow-up materials. They train women to counsel.
- Audiovisual committee—Members obtain audiovisual equipment as needed.
- Greeters—These friendly ladies are responsible for greeting women and directing them to registration, the book store, childcare, and seminar rooms.
- Follow-up committee—These people call or send letters to attendees—especially those from outside the church. They contact women who made decisions at the event.

○ Request facilities (rooms), food, publicity and printing, audiovisual equipment, and childcare as needed (see form on p. 213).

Two Months Before the Conference or Retreat

○ Contact speakers and seminar leaders, giving them a deadline for providing their outlines for the program booklet. Also encouragement them and direction about the philosophy of the conference and what is expected of them.

○ Make all motel and airline reservations for guest leaders.

○ Work individually with each chairwoman about her responsibilities. Even though group meetings may seem better, you can save time by working individually. This also facilitates the decision-making process.

○ Finalize the schedule and confirm that all details are being handled.

One Month Before the Conference or Retreat

○ Contact musicians: soloists, instrumentalists, and music leaders. Give them a copy of the program and verify their responsibilities. Thank them for agreeing to participate.

○ Make plans for a pre-event reception/prayer time. This reception or prayer time is normally held the afternoon or evening before the conference or retreat. It includes speakers, chairwomen, workers, and musicians. The reception can be in one of your women's homes or at the church. This is a special time of dedication and prayer for the event.

○ Invite all seminar leaders, keynote speakers, committee chairwomen, workers, and musicians to come to the reception.

○ Plan for a meal after the conference or retreat. The purpose of this meal is to feed out-of-town guests before they leave and to have something special for your workers before they clean up the facilities.

○ Send a second mail out and e-mail blitz (optional) to advertise the conference or retreat. Remind ladies to send in their registration forms.

○ If you don't have all the speaker's and leader's outlines, call and request them. The booklets need to be printed and reproduced so they can be assembled at least two weeks before the conference or retreat. If you do your own printing, be sure to order plenty of supplies to complete the booklet. Include paper, binders, and cover pages.

○ During the last two weeks before the conference or retreat, plan three or four workdays for your ladies. Put these dates on your church calendar. Clear the dates with your booklet, packet, and decoration committees—they will need the most help. Publish a sign-up sheet for the workdays and circulate it around the church.

Two Weeks Before the Conference or Retreat

○ Finalize plans with your committee chairwomen, making sure details are covered and they have plenty of volunteer help.

○ Confirm reservations for speakers and leaders.

○ Contact women in your church to act as hostesses and to introduce the program speakers.

○ Complete and assemble the program booklets.

○ Stuff the packets and store them until the event.

○ Write guest speakers and leaders, telling them how many are registered for the event and their individual seminars. Send them each a copy of the program booklet.

○ Complete program plans.

○ Consider postponing extra women's programs the week before the event.

○ Give the financial secretary or church treasurer an itemized list of honorariums, including speakers, singers, musicians, sound personnel, and the conference secretary.

The Day of the Conference or Beginning of the Retreat

Try to relax and enjoy the day. It's in God's hands. He gets all of the credit and the glory!

After the Conference or Retreat

○ Send thank you notes to all the people who helped with the event, including door prize and gift bag donors and the church staff (secretary, maintenance, hostess, and so forth).

PUBLICITY

While prayer and planning are two of the most essential ingredients to a successful conference or retreat, you cannot overlook publicity. You must get the word out!

One of the most effective ways to publicize is through personal invitation. After you have developed your theme and enlisted your speakers, you will want to produce an appealing brochure to send to as many women as possible.

Your target audience might include:
- Women in the church
- Women on mailing lists and e-mail lists from outside the church (from previous conferences, meetings, retreats, or other churches' mailing lists)
- Women in churches in your state (obtain this information from your state denominational offices)

Another way to publicize the event is to send correspondence to all the churches in your area, asking them to publicize the event. You will need to follow up the correspondence with phone calls, making sure someone has agreed to help you. If a church has an active women's ministry, they may be less likely to participate because of their own activities. Nevertheless, encourage their support. Return their kindness by supporting ministry efforts of other churches whenever possible.

You can advertise in your local newspapers, your state denominational paper, on Christian radio, and on television. All of these options need to include the essentials: the what, where, when, why of your event. Don't forget to tell them how they can get more information.

Develop an active file for free advertising: community calendars, listener-supported radio stations, public service announcements. Utilize women in your church who are experienced in public relations. If no one is, don't let that stop you from contacting media outlets in your community.

Don't wait too late to advertise! A month before the conference is not sufficient time!

Don't advertise too early! Four months before the conference gives them plenty of time to put the brochure aside and forget (unless you are going to follow up later).

See "Publicity and Promotion," page 216, for more information on publicity.

PRIORITY

Maintain an appropriate focus on your conference or retreat.

Maintaining an appropriate focus on your conference or retreat is important. It is easy to get sidetracked. Here are a few suggestions that will help you keep your priorities in order.

Focus on God's Goodness.

Count your blessings and consider the women who are going to benefit from the event! Talk about it often; pray about it always; keep the goal in front of your leaders at all times. Plan a day for prayer and fasting.

Support Committees

Support the committee chairwomen and let them do their jobs. If their ways are not exactly the way you would do things, that's OK.

Keep Your Head!

When 20 to 30 women work on a project, disagreements occur. Everyone looks to gauge the leader's response to conflict. Remember that you set the tone.

Set Goals

Set a number goal of women to attend. Stick to that goal, and close registration when you reach it. This is an unpopular thing to do, and no one likes the responsibility, but you do a disservice to those who have registered early when you crowd in more people than you can accommodate.

Be a Servant

As the sponsor of a conference or retreat, your role is that of a servant (or servants). When Simon criticized the woman for weeping and washing Jesus' feet with her tears, Jesus told him, " 'I came into your house. You did not give me any water for my feet. ... You did not give me a kiss. ... You did not put oil on my head' " (Luke 7:44-46). When women attend your event, take the posture of a servant, not of Simon the Pharisee. Make them welcome. Put their comfort above your own.

Purpose

Why is it so important to mention the purpose of a conference or retreat? Isn't it enough to get through the event with no major catastrophes and to stay within the budget?

The most important purpose for having a conference or retreat for women is to bring honor and glory to the Lord! In fact, that's the whole point.

What brings honor and glory to the Lord?
- Changed lives and restored homes.
- A time of spiritual restoration for women.
- Seed planting resulting in salvation.
- God receiving all the credit.

When women attend your event, take the posture of a servant.

SAMPLE CONFERENCE/RETREAT BUDGET

Conference/Retreat Expenses

ARRANGEMENTS

Facilities	$250.00	
Food (includes food for workers during planning)	2550.00	
Total		$2800.00

HOSPITALITY

Hospitality (Reception)	$350.00	
Packets (printed bags, tissues, lotion, novelty items)	1200.00	
Cookbooks	800.00	
Photo expense (photographing conference/scrapbook)	100.00	
Plastic name tag covers	200.00	
Miscellaneous expense	150.00	
Total		$2800.00

PROGRAM

Honorarium (instrumentalists, soloists)	$800.00	
Honorarium (keynote speaker, seminar leaders)	3000.00	
Transportation and lodging for guest leaders	1900.00	
Total		$5700.00

PUBLIC RELATIONS

Newspaper advertisement	$400.00	
Radio advertisement	400.00	
Statewide mail out (postage)	500.00	
Printed materials (brochures and program)	800.00	
Postage (newsletters, registration information)	200.00	
Miscellaneous publicity	200.00	
Total		$2500.00

DECORATIONS

General decorations	$ 1200.00	
Sanctuary decorations	250.00	
Displays and bulletin boards	150.00	
Miscellaneous decorating expense	150.00	
Total		$1750.00

CHILDCARE

	$1000.00	
Total		$1000.00

MISCELLANEOUS

Receptionist during event	$ 150.00	
Maintenance/moving during event	300.00	
Total		$ 450.00
TOTAL EXPENSES		$17,000.00

Conference/Retreat Income

750 Ladies @ $20.00	$15,000.00
50 Ladies @ no expense (speakers, music, scholarships, no shows)	
Women's Ministry Budget	$ 2,000.00
TOTAL INCOME	$17,000.00

WOMEN'S MINISTRY REQUEST FORM

Date Requested: _____

Event: _____   Date of Event: _____

Leader: _____   Leader Phone: _____

CALENDAR REQUEST
○ date _____
○ time _____
○ room(s) _____
○ number attending _____

WORK REQUEST
○ set-up _____
○ piano _____
○ other _____

MEDIA
○ taping needed _____
○ sound system _____
○ other _____

AUDIOVISUAL
○ overhead _____
○ CD player _____
○ VCR/DVD _____
○ data projector _____
○ other _____

RECORDS
○ addressed envelopes _____
○ labels _____
○ mailing list _____
○ other _____

PRINTING
○ how many? _____
○ type of paper _____
○ color(s) of ink _____
○ date needed _____
○ information sheet and sample(s)
  attached _____

FOOD
○ paper goods _____
○ drinks _____
○ food _____
○ time(s) needed _____

BULLETIN/WORSHIP GUIDE
○ date to appear _____
○ information attached _____

NEWSLETTER (E-NEWSLETTER)
○ date to appear _____
○ information attached _____

MONTHLY CALENDAR
○ month to appear _____
○ information attached _____

SUPPLIES (HOW MANY?)
○ Bibles _____
○ childcare cards _____
○ note card _____
○ postcards _____
○ event evaluations _____
○ stationery _____
○ visitor cards _____
○ decision cards _____

CONFERENCE/RETREAT PLAN SHEET

Determine Purpose:

Decide what needs expressed by the women in your church and community you will be able to meet through this conference/retreat. State the purpose in two to three sentences.

_____

_____

_____

Timetable

ONE TO TWO YEARS AHEAD	**PERSON RESPONSIBLE**
○ Set date.	_____
○ Determine budget.	_____
○ Contact keynote speakers and musicians.	_____
○ Reserve location.	_____

FOUR TO SIX MONTHS AHEAD
○ Decide on a theme based on Scripture _____
   (to support the purpose you stated above).
○ Choose seminar topics and leaders. _____
○ Write keynote speakers. _____
○ Decide if and how to handle scholarships. _____

TWO TO THREE MONTHS AHEAD
○ Mail registration brochures/e-mail blitz. _____
○ Begin meeting with committees. _____
○ Request facilities, rooms, food, audiovisual _____
   equipment, childcare, publicity,
   and printing needs.
○ Order packets and materials. _____

TWO MONTHS AHEAD
○ Contact speakers and request outlines. _____
○ Make lodging and transportation _____
   arrangements for speakers.
○ Continue working with committee _____
   chairwomen.
○ Finalize schedule. _____

ONE MONTH AHEAD

○ Contact musicians and speakers and
   provide copy of program.   _____
○ Plan pre-event reception and prayer time. _____
○ Send reception invitation to seminar   _____
   leaders, speakers, musicians,
   committee chairwomen, and workers.
○ Plan post-conference/retreat meal   _____
   for workers.
○ Mail second brochure/e-mail blitz.   _____

TWO WEEKS AHEAD

○ Finalize all details for volunteer workers. _____
○ Confirm reservations for speakers, leaders, _____
   and musicians.
○ Complete and assemble program booklet _____
○ Prepare registration packets.   _____
○ Write guest speakers and leaders;   _____
   include program booklet.
○ Complete program plans.   _____
○ Request checks for honorariums.   _____

DAY OF CONFERENCE/RETREAT

○ Relax and enjoy the day!

AFTER CONFERENCE/RETREAT

○ Send thank you notes to all who helped, _____
   including door prize and gift bag donors
   and church staff.
○ Compile evaluations and begin planning _____
   the next event.

PUBLICITY AND PROMOTION

GERRY SISK

henever and wherever someone imparts hope, joy, peace, and passion, the news will travel. It's as true today as it was two thousand years ago—excitement comes when Jesus is in the house. When a ministry changes lives and homes, it also changes churches. When a women's ministry offers a program built on the Titus 2 mandate for women, God's Word will be honored.

The greatest challenges facing women's ministry are (1) creating an interest in the ministry, (2) communicating the opportunity to be a part of the ministry, and (3) conveying the ministry's heartbeat while competing for time within the busy pace of life.

Certainly, the term *marketing* creates an ambivalent response within the church family. However, it cannot be disputed that God has left the church the responsibility to go and tell others the great things the Lord has done. To be a good steward of that message, it is necessary to utilize every available tool in conveying the opportunity to be a part of a Bible-based, life-changing women's ministry. This chapter serves as a beginning point in developing an effective publicity and promotion plan.

QUESTIONNAIRES

If a women's ministry is just beginning, one way to get women to accept ownership of it is through mailing a questionnaire to every adult woman in the church. Most people love to be asked for their personal opinions. They'd also appreciate a letter from the leadership of the women's ministry, or, in some cases, from the pastor, explaining the heartbeat of the ministry, its goals, and its scriptural basis and purpose. This approach can be invaluable in earning support for the ministry.

The design of the questionnaire should be adapted to the personality and needs of the local church body. Such issues as ideal times, frequency, and themes for a ministry can be addressed through the questionnaire. It can also ask for comments and questions. A self-addressed, stamped envelope or panel on the flyer will guarantee the best response. If budget does not allow postage-paid return mail, ask women to return the questionnaires to a designated location at the church. After the questionnaires are returned, compile the information and assimilate the best ideas into your women's ministry plan. (See Questionnaire, p. 66.)

MAILINGS

To effectively use the mail to promote women's ministry, develop a computer database. If a computer is not available, maintain a written record of church members, visitors, and prospects. Include names of people who have requested information on special events and programs.

Let's look at several options. Information in all mailed correspondence should be complete and consistent.

Mailings can be effective in promoting women's ministry.

Flyers

Different programs and events can be publicized by utilizing various types of mailings. A flyer is usually printed on only one side and in one color. It is most effective when presented on colored paper selected for its appropriateness for women, the event, the purpose of the event, and other details such as season of the year. Check flyers for accuracy regarding details, spelling, and grammar.

When printing flyers, it is usually cost effective to print enough to mail and distribute within the church. Design flyers attractive enough to reproduce on card stock to be placed on doors and walls (place in grippers, if available). Place them in strategic locations and distribute them through church groups after securing permission from appropriate leadership. Minimize cost by printing flyers as self-mailers. Include the return address of the church and an address panel on the back if you are requesting a response. This will eliminate the need for a return envelope.

Postcards

To further minimize cost, limited amounts of information can be conveyed by postcard. Cards 5½" by 4¼" are effective. They are large enough to be noticed but small enough to place on the refrigerator or desk as a reminder.

Brochures

For annual conferences or special seminars, a trifold brochure is effective. A conference normally requires more information than can be conveyed in a flyer. Seminar topics, dates, speakers, length and description of workshops, registration deadlines, child care, and food information should be included. A well-done brochure does not have to be expensive; use colored paper to draw attention if you are limited to black ink. Multiple ink colors and attractive clip art can enhance the message if they don't clutter the presentation. Most important, however, are the accuracy and clarity of the text. The reader depends upon the credibility of the information published. Accuracy and careful, thorough planning go hand-in-hand.

Include your brochures in church guest and new member packets or with packets used in outreach efforts.

Church Newsletters

If a church produces a biweekly or monthly newsletter, announcements regarding the women's ministry should be routinely submitted. The format, details, location within the publication, and style of the announcements should be varied to avoid visual repetition. Information should be kept brief and to the point, while always answering the basic who, what, when, where, why, and how questions. Occasionally include a personal testimony of how God used the ministry to change a life, but always obtain permission before publishing a personal testimony. When printing capabilities allow, a personal photograph adds to the impact of the testimony.

Women's Ministry Newsletters

Other modes of promotion within the church and the ministry itself include weekly, monthly, or quarterly women's ministry newsletters. Newsletters can be mailed to women who are members of the church, as well as those who may have visited the church or have participated in a women's event. Newsletters can include details on special events, opportunities to serve, and encouragement to take part in the ministry.

Area-wide Mailings

When addressing universal needs, an occasional area-wide mailing may be effective. Lists of residents can be purchased from direct mail services. When purchasing a list of names and addresses, it is possible to set the criteria, such as age of addressees, number and age of children, number of female adults in the home, and mile radius from the church. These mass mail outs can be expensive, but they are well worth the investment when the ministry event targets a specific need.

E-Mail

Use electronic mail as an inexpensive and effective way of pomoting your women's ministry. Keep updated e-mail addresses in your women's ministry database.

POSTERS

Posters serve as eye-catching ways to publicize. Use colorful, sturdy materials so the posters will be noticeable and durable. Posters and brochures can be placed in area grocery stores, pharmacies, retail stores, and other businesses—with permission, of course. Be sure to remove them when the event is over.

BOOK MARKERS AND BUSINESS CARDS

Bible or book markers made of card stock may be inserted in the order of service on Sunday. They may include a verse around which an event is planned or the verse upon which the women's ministry is built. Inclusion of clip art and attractive paper and ink colors make the book marker a constant reminder of what God is doing.

Small business cards with information about the women's ministry are easy for members to carry and hand to women they meet during the week. Include dates for major events and a phone number to call for more information.

MINISTRY CALENDAR

Another useful tool for women's ministry is a ministry calendar. Often the calendar can be incorporated into a monthly or quarterly newsletter or flyer. It should be small enough to display on a refrigerator or desk. Keep the calendar's text readable. If you choose to use them, distribute them early.

WEEKLY BULLETIN/WORSHIP GUIDE

To reach the church family, utilize free space in the order of worship or weekly bulletin. Information should be submitted in a timely manner, honoring print deadlines and media format. Attractive clip art is helpful in catching visual attention. Questions the reader or listener might have should be addressed. When publicizing only basic information, list a telephone number or voice mail information line to address additional questions. If the information published regards a weekly event, the format and presentation of the event should be changed often. Otherwise, the reader becomes so accustomed to the visual that effectiveness is minimized. Variety in presentation lends itself to impact.

OTHER CHURCH PUBLICATIONS

Explore all publications distributed within the church. Some churches publish a weekly information sheet, midweek communication handout, or special event list. Women's ministry information should be included, with permission, in every available publication. Use of every outlet lends itself to effective communication at a minimum cost to the ministry and the church. As previously mentioned, publication deadlines and formats differ from church to church. Be aware of those and work closely with the people producing print material.

WORD-OF-MOUTH

The potential for written tools for publication and promotion may vary with the size, location, and personality of the local church. However, the most effective publicity tool is present in every church—word-of-mouth! The leadership of any women's ministry must be able to clearly convey accurate dates, times, and purposes of meetings through announcements within the ministry. At every Bible study or special event, the next three months' events should be shared. Issues such as child care, cost, and dress should be resolved prior to communicating the event. Overcommunication of basic information is impossible. It is neither necessary nor desirable to deal with details orally; however, the who, what, when, where, why, and how should always be clearly defined prior to

The most effective publicity tool is present in every church—word-of-mouth!

announcing or publishing information. Women should be encouraged to invite other ladies within the church, neighborhood, work environment, or family.

Invitations can be designed to be handed out as women share information about the ministry with others. Generic invitation cards can be printed and used for various events if they are designed for specifics to be filled in by hand.

Phone blitzes can be fun for members and also help get the word out to lots of people within a short amount of time. Some church offices have several lines so many calls can be made at the same time.

ANNOUNCEMENTS

Announcements through Bible study classes and from the pulpit are helpful. To use those avenues, however, it is imperative to operate through the correct channels of authority. When asking others to make announcements, provide the information in writing so there are no misunderstood or incorrect details. Keep copies of all information shared. Oral communication alone is insufficient.

TESTIMONIES

The first responsibility regarding publicity and promotion of a women's ministry is to help the women in the church know how the ministry impacts lives for Christ. With this awareness, the next responsibility involves reaching the community for Christ. Each community is unique in its composition and personality. However, every community needs Jesus. Many avenues are available to personally share God's Good News with the community.

Personal testimonies are equally as effective as leadership announcements. Prior to an annual event, testimonies of lay women whose lives have been changed by prior conferences or sessions are very effective. These lay leaders can share in Sunday School classes, Bible study groups, or other areas of ministry within the church. As women hear how others have found peace and power for daily living, the visibility and the viability of the ministry increase.

If your church uses video screens, have a video made featuring some of the women involved in women's ministry. With your church leadership's permission, show this before, during, or after morning and evening worship services.

Many avenues are available to personally share God's Good News with the community.

CHURCH MARQUEE

The church marquee is an effective tool for promotion. Whenever women's ministry begins a new session, holds a special event, or wishes to offer an invitation to a function, the church marquee is a 24-hour bulletin board. The message should be brief—mentioning dates, times, special guests, and a telephone number. It should also be changed often to avoid becoming ineffective. If a telephone number is listed for information, that number should be answered by someone who can give additional details regarding the event. If possible, the phone system should include a recording that states the office hours should the person calling not directly reach a staff member, employee, or volunteer.

In addition to using the marquee for local notification, your community may have area newspapers, radio, and television stations which publicize community information and press releases for free. Contact each outlet for the name of the person in charge of public service announcements. Deadlines for receipt of the material to be promoted vary with individual outlets; requirements range from 15 to 30 days prior to the event. Most outlets require press releases and announcements be generated on official church letterhead, listing the name and phone number of a contact person in case additional information is necessary.

Public service announcements are just that—a service; there is no guarantee they will be printed or announced. However, most local outlets are exceptionally gracious in working with churches to get information into the community.

When composing a public service announcement, brevity is important. Material should be clear the unchurched as well as by those who attend church regularly. Dates, times, purpose, cost, child care, and meal information are important details. If the guest speaker or vocalist has local or national recognition, his or her name should be included. List a contact person and number.

Public service announcements are an untapped resource in reaching the community with program information.

ADVERTISING

Radio stations, newspapers, magazines, and television/cable stations sometimes offer paid advertising packages. Some offer lower prices for increased advertising in any combination of ministries. Most provide specialists who take basic information and create a graphic layout for the ministry. Proofs are available prior to printing and/or broadcasting. They should be viewed and carefully examined for content accuracy and visual design. When running advertisements in the newspaper or on the radio, factors such as publication date as related to event date, high listener times on the radio, and frequency of the advertisement should be considered. The community is most interested in events and programs which address universal needs such as parenting and marriage.

DENOMINATIONAL ASSOCIATIONS

Another wonderful outlet for sharing news of women's ministry events and programs is through the publications of denominational associations. Local associations are eager to share news of the church and its ministry to disciple women. Deadlines and format for submittal may vary from association to association and should be requested well in advance of the event to be publicized.

When a women's ministry begins with the purpose of fulfilling the Titus 2 mandate to teach and counsel women, lives are changed, hearts are encouraged, and homes are strengthened. Though women are busy with jobs, homes, and other responsibilities, a vibrant ministry which offers lifestyle application of God's Word is exciting! Women want to know and will make sure others know that God's Word and God's people make a difference in a demanding, sometimes overwhelming, society. As cold water is to a thirsty soul, so is good news. And it travels fast!

TAPPING RESOURCES FOR WOMEN'S MINISTRY

aving an understanding of the resources available for your women's ministry will be invaluable as you begin and develop your ministry with women. This brief chapter is devoted to making you aware of the types of resources that will serve you well. Resources include printed material, video and audio resources, and maybe the most valuable of all–human resources. The lists provided are by no means complete. You are encouraged to build on the material in this chapter and develop a personal resource list that will serve you and your women's ministry. Your resource list will grow as your ministry grows.

---

1. Resources

The resources in this section are available from LifeWay Church Resources Customer Service, One LifeWay Plaza, Nashville, TN 37234-0113; FAX (615) 251-5933; phone toll-free 1-800-458-2772; online at *www.lifeway.com*; or from the LifeWay Christian Store serving you. Listings include a product number for easy reference when ordering.

Find more great women's ministry helps on LifeWay's Web site at *www.lifeway.com/women*. You can also sign up to receive practical tips, event and resource information, and more with our free monthly e-newsletter, "eSolutions for Women's Ministry," at *www.lifeway.com/newsletters*.

WOMEN
Journey (monthly devotional magazine)
Attending the Bride of Christ Martha Lawley (6 sessions) 1415820910
Believing God: Experiencing a Fresh Explosion of Faith, Beth Moore (10 sessions)
    Workbook #0633096679   Leader Guide #0633096644
    Leader Kit #0633096652   Internet Study #063308882X
    Audio CDs 0633193763
Beloved Disciple, Beth Moore (11 sessions)
    Workbook #0633018511   Leader Guide #0633018538
    Leader Kit #063301852X   Audio CDs #0633018546

Breaking Free: Making Liberty in Christ a Reality in Life, Beth Moore (11 sessions)
    Workbook #0767391128   Leader Guide #0767391136
    Leader Kit #0767391756   Audio CDs #1415828210

Conversation Peace: The Power of Transformed Speech, Mary Kassian (7 sessions)
    Workbook #0633007617   Leader Kit #0633007625

Enjoy: A Thirst-Quenching Look at Philippians, Tianne Moon
    Workbook #0633198412   Leader Kit #0633198420

Fingerprints of God, Jennifer Rothschild
    Workbook #1415820880   Leader Kit #1415820902

The Frazzled Female: Finding Peace in the Midst of Daily Life, Cindi Wood
    (6 sessions) #0633095265

Get a Life! Debunking Six Myths in the Quest for Contentment
    Vicki Courtney (6 Sessions) #0633088900

God's Story: Finding Meaning for Your Life Through Knowing God
    Anne Graham Lotz (5 sessions)
    Workbook #0633007501   Leader Kit #0633035262

He Speaks to Me: Preparing to Hear from God, Priscilla Shirer
    Workbook #1415820937   Leader Kit #1415820945

A Heart Like His: Seeking the Heart of God Through a Study of David,
    Beth Moore (11 sessions)   Audio CDs #1415829144
    Workbook #0767325966   Leader Kit #0767326539

In My Father's House: Women Relating to God As Father,
    Mary Kassian (6 sessions) #0767335732

Jesus, the One and Only, Beth Moore (11 sessions)
    Workbook #076733275X   Leader Guide #0767332768
    Leader Kit #0633003301   Audio CDs #1415825785

Life Lessons from Women in the Bible, Rhonda Kelley (6 sessions) #0767335740

Living Beyond Yourself: Exploring the Fruit of the Spirit,
    Beth Moore (10 sessions) (also Internet study)
    Workbook #0633193801   Leader Guide #063319378X
    Leader Kit #0633193798   Audio CDs #0633193755

Living Your Life as a Beautiful Offering: A Bible Study based on the Sermon on the Mount, Angela Thomas
    Workbook #1415820899   Leader Kit #1415820929

The Patriarchs: Encountering the God of Abraham, Isaac, and Jacob
    Beth Moore (11 sessions)
    Workbook #0633099066   Leader Guide #063319753X
    Leader Kit #0633197637   Audio CDs #0633197548

To Live Is Christ: The Life and Ministry of Paul, Beth Moore (11 sessions)
    Workbook #0767334124   Leader Guide #0767334116
    Leader Kit #0767334027   Audio CDs #1415825793

Vertically Inclined: Climbing Higher with God, Mary Kassian (7 sessions)
    Workbook #0633095257   Leader Kit #0633096687

The Virtuous Woman: Shattering the Superwoman Myth,
    Vicki Courtney (6 sessions) #0633007609

The Vision of His Glory: Finding Hope Through the Revelation of Jesus Christ,
    Anne Graham Lotz   Workbook #0767391160
    Leader Guide #0767391179   Leader Kit #0767391764

Walking by Faith: Lessons Learned in the Dark, Jennifer Rothschild (6 sessions)
    Workbook #0633099325   Leader Kit #0633091456

What Every Mom Needs: Balancing Your Life,
    Elisa Morgan and Carol Kuykendall (9 sessions) #0767393732

When Godly People Do Ungodly Things, Beth Moore (7 sessions)
    Workbook #0633090352   Leader Guide #063309014X
    Leader Kit #0633090360   Audio CDs #0633090298

A Woman's Heart: God's Dwelling Place, Beth Moore (11 sessions)
> Workbook #0805498362   Leader Guide #0767334019
> Leader Kit #0805498265   Audio CDs #1415822255

Women Making a Difference in Marriage: Building Love, Joy, and Commitment
> Lana Packer (8 sessions) #0767393775

LEADERSHIP

Experiencing God: Knowing and Doing the Will of God,
Henry Blackaby and Claude V. King (13 sessions)
> Workbook #0805499547   Leader Guide #0805499512

Heart Friends: Beginning and Maintaining a Small Accountability Group (4 weeks)
> Shirley Moses and Margaret Kennedy, Workbook #1415828180

Jesus on Leadership: Developing Servant Leaders, C. Gene Wilkes (6 sessions)
> Workbook #0805493506   Leader Kit #0805493514
> Leader Guide #0767329481

Transformed Lives: Taking Women's Ministry to the Next Level,
  compiled by Chris Adams, #0767331168

*Woman to Woman Mentoring: How to Start, Grow, and Maintain
  a Mentoring Ministry,* Janet Thompson
> Leader Kit #0633003018   Training Leader's Guide #0633035327
> Mentor Handbook #0633002879 Mentee Handbook #0633002887
> Ministry Coordinator's Guide #0633029505

Women Reaching Women in Crisis, various authors
  available online at www.lifeway.com/WomeninCrisis

PRAYER

Disciple's Prayer Life, T.W. Hunt and Catherine Walker
  (13 sessions) #0767334949

In God's Presence, T.W. Hunt and Claude V. King (6 sessions) #0805499008

Living Free: Learning to Pray God's Word, Beth Moore (6 sessions) 063301978X

Whispers of Hope, Beth Moore #0767392787

SPIRITUAL GIFTS

Spiritual Gifts: A Practical Guide to How God Works Through You, David Francis
(6 sessions) #0633099368

Jesus on Leadership: Developing Servant Leaders, C. Gene Wilkes (6 sessions)
> Workbook #0805493506   Leader Kit #0805493514
> Leader Guide #0767329481

COUNSELING

DecisionTime: Commitment Counseling, Leonard Sanderson and
  Arthur H. Criscoe (6 sessions) #0767391799

WiseCounsel: Skills for Lay Counseling, John W. Drakeford and
  Claude V. King (13 sessions)
> Workbook #0767326156   Leader Guide #0767326768

Women Reaching Women in Crisis, various authors
  available online at www.lifeway.com/WomeninCrisis

WITNESSING

Evangelism Through the Sunday School: A Journey of FAITH,
  Bobby Welch #0767334965

Learning to Share My Faith, Chuck Kelley (6 sessions) #0805498648

Share Jesus Without Fear, William Fay and Ralph Hodge (4 sessions)
> Workbook #0767330595   Leader Guide #0767330587
> Leader Kit #0767330579

Evangelism
HeartCall, Jaye Martin
available online at
http://www.namb.net/site/c.9qKILUOzEpH/b.238503/k.DE2A/Products.htm

2. Events

For events information, call Events Registration 800-254-2022.
- Living Proof LIVE Events (Beth Moore)
- Senior Adult Events
- Toward a Growing Marriage Seminars
- Festivals of Marriage
- Other Mom and Women's Events

Women's Ministry Leadership Training and Enrichment go to *www.LifeWay.com/women*

3. Baptist State Conventions

Many Baptist state conventions have a person assigned to women's ministry. Call your state convention office and record this person's name, address, and telephone number for later use. Make sure your name is included on the state mailing list so you can receive information on training events. An updated list is available at *www.lifeway.com/women.*

4. Missions Organizations

North American Mission Board
4200 North Point Parkway
Alpharetta, Georgia 30202-4174
(707) 410-6000

International Mission Board
Box 6767
Richmond, Virginia 23230
(804) 358-0504

Woman's Missionary Union
P. O. Box 830010
Birmingham, Alabama 35283-0010
(205) 991-8100

5. Other Organizations

MOPS International, Inc.
(Mothers of Preschoolers)
1311 South Clarkson St.
Denver, Colorado 80210
(303) 733-5353
FAX (303) 733-5770

Moms in Touch International
(Organization of mothers who intercede for their children and pray that schools may be guided by biblical values and high moral standards.)
P.O. Box 1120
Poway, CA 72074-1120
(619) 486-4065

WomensMinistry.NET
4319 S. National, Suite 303
Springfield, MO 65810
(417) 888.2067
FAX (417).888.2095
Web: WomensMinistry.net

Leadership Network
2501 Cedar Springs LB-5
Dallas, Texas 75201
(800) 765-5323
FAX (214) 969-9392

Christian Schools & Home Schooling
One LifeWay Plaza
Nashville, TN 37234-0182
(615) 251-5749

Samples of
Organizational Models

Women's Ministry as Umbrella

Women On Mission and Women's Ministry Blended

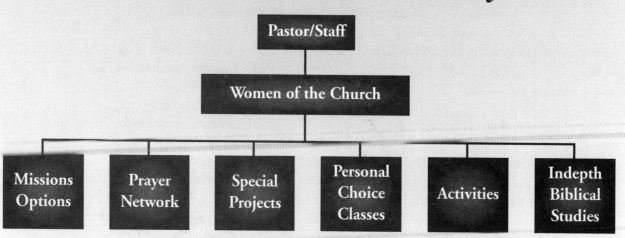

Women On Mission and Women's Ministry Side by Side

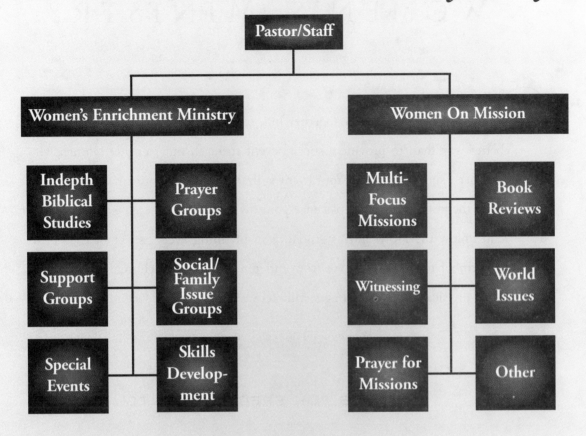

Women On Mission as Umbrella

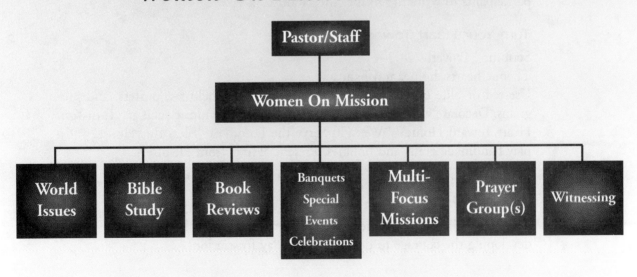

IDEAS, IDEAS, IDEAS! FOR YOUR WOMEN'S MINISTRY

CHRIS ADAMS

Christians love to get together in a safe and fun environment. And what better way than to provide a special event to reach out to other women who also need such a ministry! Your event is limited only by your imagination. Use these themes for a starting place for your own ideas. Bathe each event in prayer, and follow the Holy Spirit's guidance in planning every aspect of the event. Remember to involve women from different areas of the church so that ladies of all physical and spiritual ages will feel welcome and needed.

THEMES FOR SPECIAL EVENTS

Taster's Choice or Taste and Tell
Scripture: Proverbs 31:14-15
Theme: tasting bee and recipe swap
Ask participants to prepare and bring a favorite recipe. Provide recipe cards for participants to write the recipes they want to keep.

Turn Your Heart Toward Home
Scripture: Proverbs 24:3-4
Theme: hearts, home, and hands
Use red or blue ink on brown paper invitations, brochures, posters, and programs. Decorate with vignettes of home settings; play music such as "Turn Your Heart Toward Home," "We Will Serve the Lord," or "Bless this House." Display handmade crafts and hobbies. Present "Hints from Heloise."

Living in the Land of OZ
Scripture: 2 Corinthians 5:13; 1 Timothy 1:5; John 16:33
Theme: dealing with the "real world" needs of a sound mind and pure heart; developing the courage to deal with everyday frustrations.

Decorate with OZ character dolls, a paper yellow brick road, hot air balloons, and stuffed "Toto" dogs.

Gifts That Keep Giving

Scripture: 1 Peter 4:10
Theme: spiritual gifts and sharing the gift of Jesus
Decorate with packages with bows and gift bags with tissue. Provide a gift-wrap and bow-tying demonstration.

Joyful Hearts

Scripture: Proverbs 17:22
Theme: joy
Decorate with hearts.
Provide seminars that deal with joy and heart issues.

The Time of Your Life/In His Time

Scripture: Psalm 31:15
Theme: dealing with the different times or phases of a woman's life
Decorate with clocks and other time pieces
Provide seminars that discuss the beauty and challenges of each life stage.

Tea for Two/High Tea

Scripture: Romans 12:13
Theme: friendship among women
Share the history of English tea; serve tea and scones; and use a different tea service at each table.

Victorian Tea Party

Scripture: Psalm 119:27
Theme: childhood wonders
Read and role play "The Mad Tea Party" from *Alice's Adventures in Wonderland.* Have hostesses set their own tables of eight with their china, crystal, silver, centerpiece, and place mats.

Bride of Christ

Scripture: Revelation 19:7
Theme: Believers are both attendants to and part of the bride of Christ.
Present a bridal fashion show. Share funny or memorable events from weddings. Display wedding pictures, and serve cake and punch for the wedding reception.

God's Woman in a Topsy Turvy World

Scripture: Luke 10:38-42 or Psalm 27
Theme: women's roles
Use hats as decorations (centerpieces with hat boxes and scarves, hat racks around room; have a hat contest). Discuss the many hats a woman wears in her daily roles. Have leaders of each ministry for women decorate hats to help illustrate what others can do through women's ministry.

Communication Skills for the Business Woman

Scripture: Psalm 17:30; 39:1

Theme: communication

Teach communication basics for office/marketplace and personal relationships. Include the art of negotiation, how to listen, and how to be heard. Decorate with telephones, computers, fax machines, speaker stands, pens and stationery.

Here's Your Life

Scripture: Proverbs 31:10-31

Theme: women blessed by God

Host an event in honor of your staff wives; have each of their husbands record a sweet story (not embarrassing) or other special message about his wife to play during a time of introduction. Have staff guys serve the meal and a humorous emcee (maybe a staff member) to talk to each wife at her table, using a mic so all can hear. Give each wife a special gift from the women of the church.

Discovering God's Best for You

Scripture: Isaiah 48:17

Theme: choosing God's best

Hold seminars that deal with choosing the "best" instead of just "better" in issues of family, ministry, relationships, and work.

Set Apart

Scripture: Psalm 4:3

Theme: the fragrance of Christ: holy living in an unholy world

Decorations: urns or vases, perfume bottles

State of the Heart/Get to the Heart of the Matter

Scripture: Ephesians 3:16-20

Theme: being grounded in God's word

Decorations: hearts

One Mind, One Heart

Scripture: Mark 12:30

Theme: how to put Christ first

Decorations: hearts and crosses

Angels Watching Over Me

Scripture: Hebrews 1:14

Theme: "real" angels according to Scripture

Decorations: angel figurines and pictures

Birthday Party

Scripture: First Peter 1:3-9

Theme: celebration of new beginnings

Set up 12 tables decorated for each month of the year. Have women sit at their birthday month table. Provide previews of upcoming events by month.

A Glimpse of Heaven

Scripture: Philippians 3:20
Theme: our citizenship in heaven
Decorate with images of heaven. Use Scripture to clear up common misconceptions about heaven.

Lord, Change Me/Journey Toward Change

Scripture: 2 Corinthians 3:18; Romans 12:2
Theme: God's transforming power
Use mirrors and butterflies to decorate. Offer studies dealing with God's transforming power in our lives, the need to change ourselves, and the affect our changing has on others.

A Breath of Fresh Air

Scripture: John 20:22, Job 33:4
Theme: God's Spirit
Decorate with balloons, clouds, and kites. Offer seminars whose titles deal with wind, air, and the Holy Spirit

Walk in the Light

Scripture: 1 John 1:7; Matthew 5:14-16; Ephesians 4:11-13
Theme: walking in God's presence and allowing His light to shine in a dark world
Decorations: lights, lamps, candles

Grandma's Attic or Precious Memories

Scripture: Deuteronomy 11:18-19; Psalm 145:10-13
Theme: mother/daughter sharing memories
Decorations: quilts, lockets, lace, antiques
Favors: lace hankies

Come, Celebrate Jesus

Scripture: Psalm 100:4
Theme: personal testimonies of the power of Christ in the lives of your women
Decorations: party decorations

Praise God for the Ants

Scripture: 1 Thessalonians 5:16-18
Theme: how to go on with God in spite of the "ants" (things that attack us or cause frustration) in our lives
Decorate the room in a picnic setting. Provide picnic foods such as watermelon and chicken served in buckets.

Women So Precious to God

Scripture: 1 Peter 3:3-6
Theme: being beautiful (clean) from the inside out
Decorations: soap/cleaning products, favors in detergent scoops

Flowering Friendships

Scripture: Titus 2:3-5; John 15:13
Theme: growing relationships among women
Decorations: flowers

Can You Dig It? (Godliness From the Ground Up)

Scripture: Colossians 1:10
Theme: growing in knowledge of God and bearing fruit
Encourage a visit to the 'Garden of Weed'n'. Allow the Gardener to water dry ground, nourish tender shoots, gently pull weeds, and arrange a brilliant bouquet.

Fearfully and Wonderfully Made

Scripture: Psalm 139:14
Theme: caring for our bodies
Provide a health symposium with doctors and nurses. Include a fitness exhibit; take blood pressures and measure body fat. Offer heart-healthy, low-calorie snacks and bottled water.

To God Be the Glory, Great Things He Has Done

Scripture: Psalm 100:4
Theme: thankfulness for God's faithfulness
Decorate the room with palm trees, tiki lanterns or lights, and leis. Coordinate members' testimonies of God's work in their lives. Have them share their spiritual "survivor" stories.

Christmas Memories

Scripture: Luke 2:19
Theme: Christmas memories
Ask each lady to share a Christmas memory that highlights Christ in "Christ"mas. Decorate with nativity scenes; provide hot cider and gingerbread.

Christmas Tour of Homes

Scripture: Luke 2:19
Theme: spiritual family traditions
Hostess decorates each room and shares one spiritual tradition.

In the Good Old Summertime

Scripture: Isaiah 40:31
Theme: renewed strength; refreshment
Music: "beach" songs
Decorations: beach chairs, umbrellas, sunshine

Our Patchwork Lives

Scripture: Psalm 145:10-13; Ephesians 3:16-20
Theme: God's unfailing love
Decorate with quilts. Make the room look like a porch or sewing room. Play "Old Time Religion" music. Ask members to share stories of God's work in their lives.

Hawaiian Luau

Scripture: Proverbs 17:22
Theme: choose a fun and uplifting topic
Decorate with bright colors and shells. Act out silly commercials from "Getchagoin' Travel and Rental" and "Aloha Beach Shack."

Victorian Christmas

Scripture: Isaiah 9:6-7
Theme: Special Christmas memories
Decoration with rich colors. Create a Sweet Shoppe or Toy Store. Or, put up a Victorian Christmas tree and decorate the room like a parlor. Provide Victorian fan ornaments. Share special Christmas memories.

Love in Bloom

Scripture: 1 Corinthians 13
Theme: wedding with emphasis on true Christian love
Decorations: wedding bells, wedding shower, wedding store
Favors: net bags filled with pastel candies
Ministry: Participants bring a shower gift for a needy person

Treasures of the Heart

Scripture: Ephesians 3:16-20
Theme: How you allow God to reign in your heart
Decorations: treasure chests, jewels, and hearts

Designer Genes

Scripture: Ephesians 4:11-13
Theme: study of personalities, spiritual gifts, uniqueness of women and how they work together in the body of Christ

Your Home a Lighthouse

Scripture: Matthew 5:14-16; Ephesians 5:8-9; Hebrews 13:2
Theme: Christian hospitality or being a light in a dark world
Decorations: lighthouses and lamps

The Perfect Outfit: Christ's Designer Label

Scripture: Colossians 3:12-14
Theme: How God's people are to clothe themselves
Decorate with patchwork squares labeled patience, kindness, love, humility, forgiveness, gentleness, compassion.

Dolls From Around the World

Scripture: Mark 16:15
Theme: God's love around the world
Decorate with international dolls. Use the gathering as an opportunity to introduce missionaries your church supports around the world.

Going for the Gold

Scripture: Hebrews 12:1-2; 1 Corinthians 9:24-27
Theme: Running the race with endurance
Decorations: Hula hoops for Olympic rings, gold medal ribbons

Putting It Together

Scripture: Colossians 3:17
Theme: putting the pieces of a woman's life together
Decorations: use puzzle pieces for name tags

Name Above All Names

Scripture: Various names of God found throughout Scripture
Theme: one God by many names
Decorate tables to depict names of God: For example, "Light of the World" with varying sizes and shapes of candles; "Living Water" with a fountain; "The Great Physician" with a doctor's bag and instruments.

Family Reunion

Scripture: Psalm 78:1-7
Theme: family spiritual heritage
Decorations: things found at family reunions—old pictures, heirloom quilts, softball equipment, and so forth

Going for the Gold

Scripture: 1 Corinthians 9:24-25
Theme: Winning … In Personal Bible Study, Over Your Past, As a Mom, As a Lifestyle, in Hospitality

Sail into Spring

Scripture: John 20:22, Job 33:4
Theme: for spring event use as re-introducing the "new" in women's ministry to your church
Decorations: Kites

Mothers and Others

Scripture: Hebrews 11
Theme: leaving a legacy of faith; investing in other women
Plan an event for mothers and daughters, but include anyone by using the title "Mothers and Others."

With All My Heart

Scripture: Jeremiah 19:13
Theme: with all my heart
Sessions: A Heart for Budgeting, The Seeking Heart, Pulling at Our Heart Strings, A Matter of the Heart, Grace for the Wounded Heart

New Mothers

ministers to new mothers in the community; provides gift basket with gospel tracts, baby items, packets of verses about mothers and children

Phone Friends

women answer calls from latch-key children after school. Clear this with your church staff before offering this service.

Welcoming Newcomers

visits prospects, takes packet of information about women's ministry and other activities, answers questions about the church

Correspondence Committee

writes letters of welcome to newcomers, condolence to the bereaved, and congratulations to new mothers in the community

Tutorial Program

provides role models as well as tutoring for children

Abortion Recovery

ministers to those who have abortions

Clothes Closet

provides clothing for needy (used or new donated by stores)

Support Group Ministry

covers topics such as eating disorders, codependency, substance addictions, physical or sexual abuse, (this is discipleship, not therapy); cancer and other terminal illnesses, divorce recovery, families dealing with homosexual family members, and the adult children of alcoholics

Crisis Pregnancy Center

provides abortion alternative through emotional, practical, and spiritual encouragement

Soup Kitchen

provides meals to the homeless

Nursing Home Ministries

provides treats or tray favors for holidays; sends "thinking of you" cards; leads or provides music periodically; celebrates birthdays with gift bags or cakes; provides manicures or hairstyle "make-overs"; reads or visits

Jail/Prison Ministry

provides Bible studies and discipleship groups for inmates

Volunteer Christian Builders

use vacations or retirement to help build churches across the United States

Caring Hands

makes comfort dolls for patients or children's hospital, lap robes for nursing home residents, other items for mission projects

Single Mom's Expo

offers day of fellowship and seminars to meet unique needs of single moms at a reasonable cost; provides child care; includes topics such as financial planning, *Love Languages of Children* (Gary Chapman/LifeWay), spiritual growth, dressing on a dime, home decorating, and parenting.

Senior Adult Outreach

provides community outreach to retirement-age women; health lectures and luncheons; centerpieces with health care and first aid items tucked among flowers; door prizes for tickets to movies, concerts, lunches awarded in pairs so seniors can go with a new friend

INREACH MINISTRIES

New Member Shepherding

Committee members each take one Sunday a quarter to make contact with all women who join that day. They commit to have five touches: personal visits, phone calls, written correspondence, or a ride to women's activities) with each one before taking another new member (see more in *Transformed Lives: Taking Women's Ministry to the Next Level*).

Adopt a Grandparent

Members get to know an elderly person who does not have family nearby, invite them to participate in children's and families activities, and celebrate birthdays and holidays with them.

Widow Support Group

Women attend a monthly Saturday morning gathering that has a theme, devotional, food and fellowship. While they are at the gathering, men from the church provide a practical ministry such as changing oil and filters in their cars.

Woman to Woman

mentoring ministry between the generations (see *Woman to Woman Mentoring: How to Start, Maintain and Grow a Mentoring Ministry* by Janet Thompson)

Bereavement Meals

provides meals for families who have lost loved ones, even if they are not members of the church

Farm Fellowship (Rural Bible Study)

Women meet once a week on a farm for fellowship and Bible study. Volunteers care for children; mothers bring lunch for children and potluck for themselves.

Summer Fun and Fellowship

for moms and kids in the parks—teenagers care for children while mothers study; each mother brings a picnic lunch to eat with children afterward

Summer Smorgasbord

Scale down your summer program for women, but don't stop it. Offer a variety of speakers using your own women and staff to share testimony, teaching, or music.

"PieceMakers" Quilting Ministry

teach the younger generation of women the lost art of quilting, while sharing life and faith stories all at the same time.

Women's Encouragement (Lay Counseling) Ministry

Match women in crisis with a woman who has "been there and made it" for encouragement and prayer support. Be sure to train your women in basic lay counseling skills so they will know what to do in case referrals are necessary (see *Transformed Lives: Taking Women's Ministry to the Next Level,* compiled by Chris Adams and *Women Reaching Women in Crisis,* online resource from LifeWay.

Kaleidoscope of Ministries

Plan an evening to exhibit all the ministries and mission opportunities members of your church can take part in.

Breast Cancer Packet

Put together a packet of helpful information in an attractive gift packet for women in your church diagnosed with breast cancer; include a letter of encouragement from the women's ministry director, testimonies from breast cancer survivors, helpful tips for chemotherapy and radiation treatments, medical information on breast cancer, a *Journey* magazine, contact information for the women's ministry director or someone she can call if necessary, and a Scripture bookmark.

For Women in the Workplace/Marketplace:

Evening or noon Bible study—make sure you start and end promptly so women can return to work on time if you have a group during the work day
Weekend retreats—focus on workplace issues
Saturday get together—7-8am for early risers; return to family before they are out of bed!
Internet devotionals
Drive-time devotions
Train women how to begin workplace Bible studies at their places of business

CHRISTIAN GROWTH STUDY PLAN

In the **Christian Growth Study Plan (formerly Church Study Course),** this book *Women Reaching Women* is a resource for course credit in 3 Leadership and Skill Development plans. To receive credit, read the book, complete the learning activities, show your work to your pastor, a staff member or church leader, then complete the following information. This page may be duplicated. Send the completed page to:

**Christian Growth Study Plan
One LifeWay Plaza
Nashville, TN 37234-0117
FAX: (615)251-5067
Email: *cgspnet@lifeway.com***

For information about the Christian Growth Study Plan, refer to the Christian Growth Study Plan Catalog. It is located online at *www.lifeway.com/cgsp*. If you do not have access to the Internet, contact the Christian Growth Study Plan office (1.800.968.5519) for the specific plan you need for your ministry.

Please check the appropriate box indicating the plan you want to apply this credit. You may check more than one.

❑ Women's Enrichment Ministry (LS-0034)
❑ Church Leadership (LS-0083)
❑ Evangelism (LS-0143)

PARTICIPANT INFORMATION

Social Security Number (USA ONLY-optional)	Personal CGSP Number*	Date of Birth (MONTH, DAY, YEAR)
– –	– –	– –

Name (First, Middle, Last)	Home Phone
	– –

Address (Street, Route, or P.O. Box)	City, State, or Province	Zip/Postal Code

Email Address for CGSP use

Please check appropriate box: ❑ Resource purchased by church ❑ Resource purchased by self ❑ Other

CHURCH INFORMATION

Church Name

Address (Street, Route, or P.O. Box)	City, State, or Province	Zip/Postal Code

CHANGE REQUEST ONLY

☐ Former Name

☐ Former Address	City, State, or Province	Zip/Postal Code

☐ Former Church	City, State, or Province	Zip/Postal Code

Signature of Pastor, Conference Leader, or Other Church Leader	Date

*New participants are requested but not required to give SS# and date of birth. Existing participants, please give CGSP# when using SS# for the first time. Thereafter, only one ID# is required. **Mail to:** Christian Growth Study Plan, One LifeWay Plaza, Nashville, TN 37234-0117. Fax: (615)251-5067.

Revised 4-05